Alan J. Pakula: Interviews

Conversations with Filmmakers Series
Gerald Peary, General Editor

ALAN J.
PAKULA
I N T E R V I E W S

Edited by Tom Ryan

The University Press of Mississippi is the scholarly publishing agency of
the Mississippi Institutions of Higher Learning: Alcorn State University,
Delta State University, Jackson State University, Mississippi State University,
Mississippi University for Women, Mississippi Valley State University,
University of Mississippi, and University of Southern Mississippi.

www.upress.state.ms.us

The University Press of Mississippi is a member
of the Association of University Presses.

Library of Congress Cataloging-in-Publication Data

Names: Ryan, Tom (Film writer), editor.
Title: Alan J. Pakula : interviews / Tom Ryan.
Other titles: Conversations with filmmakers series.
Description: Jackson : University Press of Mississippi, 2024. | Series: Conversations
    with filmmakers series | Includes bibliographical references and index.
Identifiers: LCCN 2024012661 (print) | LCCN 2024012662 (ebook) |
    ISBN 9781496852892 (hardback) | ISBN 9781496852885 (trade paperback) |
    ISBN 9781496852878 (epub) | ISBN 9781496852861 (epub) |
    ISBN 9781496852854 (pdf) | ISBN 9781496852847 (pdf)
Subjects: LCSH: Pakula, Alan J., 1928–1998—Interviews. | Motion picture producers
    and directors—United States—Interviews. | Motion pictures—Production and
    direction—United States.
Classification: LCC PN1998.A3 P345 2024 (print) | LCC PN1998.A3 (ebook) |
    DDC 791.4302/33092—dc23/eng/20240514
LC record available at https://lccn.loc.gov/2024012661
LC ebook record available at https://lccn.loc.gov/2024012662

British Library Cataloging-in-Publication Data available

Contents

Foreword by Don McAlpine   vii

Introduction   xi

Chronology   xxxix

Filmography   xliii

Unlikely Elements: Alan J. Pakula in an Interview with Gordon Gow   3
  Gordon Gow / 1972

Klute Review   11
  Tom Milne / 1971

"Not a Garbo or a Gilbert in the Bunch": Alan Pakula Talks to Tom Milne   15
  Tom Milne / 1972

The Parallax View: An Interview with Alan Pakula   29
  Andrew C. Bobrow / 1974

Under the Influence: An Interview with Alan J. Pakula   40
  Steven Soderbergh / 1998

Mr. Pakula Goes to Washington: Alan J. Pakula on *All the President's Men*   51
  Rick Thompson / 1976

Making a Film about Two Reporters   69
  Alan J. Pakula / 1976

World without Shadows   76
  Richard Combs / 1976

The American Film Institute's Dialogue on Film: Alan J. Pakula   79
    American Film / 1979

Lichtenstein, Legends, and Leviathan: Pakula on *Rollover*   94
    Alan J. Pakula / 1982

Pakula's Choices   97
    Jonathan Rosenbaum / 1982

"I Am Very American in Many, Many Ways": An Interview with
Alan J. Pakula   100
    Tom Ryan / 1983

The American Film Institute's Dialogue on Film #2: Alan J. Pakula   111
    American Film / 1985

Family Ties Bind Pakula to His *Morning*   117
    Bruce Weber / 1989

A Walk with Good and Evil: Alan J. Pakula Interviewed   122
    Ana Maria Bahiana / 1990

Disaster? Was There a Disaster?   127
    Ian Fisher / 1997

Additional Resources   131

Index   133

Foreword

Memories of Alan

Mostly I remember Alan as a refined, urbane, gentle person. His bearing was aristocratic, and he lived well, but he never looked down on anybody. And at the same time as he was very much a leader in front of his army, he was always open to constructive suggestions from those of us who were collaborating with him (as I did twice, memorably for me on *Orphans* and also on *See You in the Morning*).

I cannot recall exactly how I got the opportunity to work with him, but I'm very glad that I did. *Orphans* came first. At that point in my career, most of my work came to me via my agent. I probably got a call saying Alan was interested in me shooting his next project. When I joined the circus, I found out that he'd been intrigued with my work on *Tempest*, which I shot for Paul Mazursky. In the hurly-burly of making a film, for some reason this subject is rarely openly discussed. Too many other things to absorb and discover. Especially with Alan.

If I recall correctly—it was a long time ago—we had about eight weeks of preproduction, most of which was involved in working with George Jenkins on the set and on the location of the isolated house in Newark, where the film was set and which we were very fortunate to find. The whole area around it had been demolished for more intensive housing, but the company doing the building had left one standing as a construction office. And, after the building project failed, we were fortunately able to gain access to it.

The house was used as you saw it on the screen. All the interiors, though, were shot in the studio across the river in New York. What we had there was basically the front living room, a central dining room, and the kitchen in the back. Most of the exterior walls could fly, although arranging for this proved to be an unnecessary expense. Alan had decided that the camera should not travel beyond the interior spaces we'd set up on the sound stage. The motivation for shooting the film like this had its origin in the fact that *Orphans* was originally a stage play (by Lyle Kessler), and Alan and I wanted to make every effort to disguise this fact.

Alan's methods in orchestrating everything and the way he was with actors and others involved in the shoot made him a joy to work with. I'll try to give you a sense of how he went about it. His approach was concentrated, disciplined and very organized. Only three actors were initially involved in the stage work: Albert Finney, Matthew Modine, and Kevin Anderson, who wasn't as well known as the others but was a very fine young actor in his own right. And Alan gave everyone plenty of room to move. For the first two hours or so, they would rehearse with him. I remained a nonparticipant, absorbing the process from a distance. The rest of the crew were not on the stage yet.

When it was decided they had sorted out the mechanics of the performance and done the polishing work, the three stand-ins would come in and observe two or three run-throughs. They were amazing in their ability to reproduce the movements and the manners of each actor. Our task was to make it all cinematic, and, because of the nature of the two boys' characters, everything was always on the move.

Then the crew got involved. Probably the most difficult job for us all was getting a whole scene in a single take. And, given that the camera was constantly on the move and most of the walls of the rooms were in frame throughout, the task of finding where to put the lighting was exceedingly complex.

We would all work on these problems for possibly three to four hours, with Alan drawing on the fantastic contributions of the camera operator (Dan Lerner), the gaffer (Russ Engels), and the grip department (George Patsos was the key grip). He made them always feel free to make suggestions. It required a massive amount of energy, but it was exciting to be involved, and a lot of the energy we put in was transferred onto the screen and, I think, achieved Alan's vision.

Only rarely did he use much of the master shot without a cut, but that master was always the glue that held the scene together. There was always coverage and, of course, the inevitable reverse shots. On the surface, the approach we took appears to be a very demanding way to shoot a movie. But, in actual fact, it was surprisingly efficient, and we produced probably more screen time a day than most productions are able to manage. The wonderful part about Alan's system was that, after that morning rehearsal, everything was locked, and there weren't those inevitable time-consuming discussions about what we were doing.

Our collaboration worked very smoothly. I am very proud of the results and have truly enjoyed revisiting this part of my past. Our work on *See You in the Morning* was more routine, but also very satisfying. It was a film that was very close to Alan's heart, and it clearly meant a lot to him.

It's very pleasing to see a book taking Alan's career seriously. He's left us now, but he deserves it. He was a very complex personality, but his calm presence and lovely sense of humor affected both me and the crew in a very positive way. A minor but welcome idiosyncrasy of his was that—on the call of "Wrap" and within the count of ten—he'd assigned the third production assistant the responsibility of bringing him a fresh martini and me a Glenlivet on the rocks. At the end of the day at the edge of the set, you could observe this young man going through several mixes to make sure he got it exactly right. It became quite a ritual and enormously entertained the cast and crew.

Don McAlpine, cinematographer

Introduction

"I consider myself one of the blessed. I do something I'd gladly do for no money. The joy of making films fills my life. Each film is a new life, a new beginning. Filmmaking has been, and still is, my drug of choice. With each film I enter a new world."[1]

On the basis of *Klute* (1971), *The Parallax View* (1974), and *All the President's Men* (1976), Alan J. Pakula (1928–1998) earned a reputation as one of the key American filmmakers of the 1970s. Not only was he—with the assistance of several notable cinematographers (especially Gordon Willis)—one of the era's most fluid stylists, but he also earned acclamation as "an actors' director" from many of those who worked with him—including Liza Minnelli, Jane Fonda, Meryl Streep, Robert Redford, Dustin Hoffman, and Harrison Ford.

He began his career in 1956 as producer for Robert Mulligan. They made seven films together, including *To Kill a Mockingbird* (1962), for which he was Oscar nominated. (The film received eight nominations in total and won three awards.) His directorial debut came with *The Sterile Cuckoo* (1969), for which Liza Minnelli earned an Oscar nomination. It was followed by fifteen further features, including the widely lauded *Sophie's Choice* (1982), for which Meryl Streep won her second Oscar and for which he was Oscar nominated. There was also the romantic comedy, *Starting Over* (1979), and its companion piece, *See You in the Morning* (1989), as well as a further collection of thrillers, including *Presumed Innocent* (1990), *The Pelican Brief* (1993), and *The Devil's Own* (1997).

He died in a car accident on November 19, 1998, on the Long Island Expressway at the age of seventy.

Part One: Beginnings

Before joining forces with Mulligan in 1956, Pakula spent five years at Paramount as an assistant to production head Don Hartman. Although it was very much a desk job, requiring him to read and evaluate scripts, he was where he wanted to be. As a student, he'd briefly toyed with the idea of pursuing a career as a psychiatrist, but he'd come to the conclusion that his future lay elsewhere.

Opportunity knocked in 1956 when the manuscript for *Fear Strikes Out* arrived on his desk. An autobiography written by professional baseballer Jimmy Piersall (with famed sportswriter Al Hirshberg), its tale about the pressures that led to the Boston Red Sox center fielder's psychological breakdown immediately caught the twenty-eight-year-old Pakula's eye. He managed to persuade Paramount to buy the rights, even though, on August 18 of the previous year, CBS had screened a TV adaptation of the same book as an episode in its live-to-air *Climax!* series, with Tab Hunter as Piersall.

However, Paramount was reluctant to allow the inexperienced young man to direct, leading him to seek out Mulligan, a director who was also in his late twenties but whose substantial TV experience stood him in good stead. Their partnership was born with a handshake. And everything appears to have gone smoothly on the production, even if the finished film turned out to be far from satisfying.

Its drama is overplayed and, right from the start, Piersall's father, John (Karl Malden), is identified as the source of his son's problems. Having recognized the boy's raw talent, John relentlessly pushes him to succeed, his never-good-enough approach to rearing stifling the growing youth's personality. Leaving little room for nuance, the film even tosses in a perfunctory pipe-puffing psychiatrist (Adam Williams) who "discovers" what it has made glaringly obvious all along.

In their book, *Psychiatry and the Cinema*, communications academic Krin Gabbard and his psychoanalyst brother, Glen, sensibly situate the psychiatrist's treatment of the young man's breakdown in the context of 1950s depictions of practice. "Psychiatric disorders are," they write, "caused by bad parents, and cure is affected by convincing the blameless offspring that he must forgive his parents."[2] Mulligan and Pakula's thinking on the subject appears to unquestioningly share this view of the problem and the remedy for it.

For his part, Piersall denounced the film for, amongst other things, misrepresenting his relationship with his father. "[It] played my father as a real rotten individual," he told ESPN sports commentator Phillip Lee. "Certainly, that was not what I was thinking about. I told my dad what they were doing, but the money we got in those days was money we never had and he didn't really let it bother him."[3]

It doesn't help the film that Anthony Perkins's performance as Jimmy—he's also played as a youth by Peter J. Votrian—is so overwrought, often reducing his character to a pre-*Psycho* psycho, one produced this time by a disturbed father. To make matters worse, despite the work he's reported to have done on his technique, the actor never moves or throws like a baseballer.

There's no question that Pakula was fully committed to the project. "I felt passionately about that film," he told *New York Times* writer John Culhane. "The central theme was a boy repressing all his ambivalent feelings toward a parent who had taken over his life, a boy who did not have the freedom to finally grow up and become his own man."[4]

But Mulligan, and the film, might have been better served by a more experienced producer, one who could have steered the director away from the sledgehammer treatment of the subject and the overreliance on shot/reverse-shot rhythms to shape the exchanges between the characters. Routine practice for the television of the time, the method denies the actors room to move and drains the life out of their interactions.

Especially by way of comparison with much of Mulligan and Pakula's later work, both together and separately, there's a disappointing lack of delicacy to the filmmaking in *Fear Strikes Out*. And after this inauspicious beginning to their partnership, both went their separate ways for a few years. Pakula turned his attention to producing for the theater, including a play directed by Mulligan.[5] Meanwhile, Mulligan made four theatrical features with other producers—*The Rat Race* and *The Great Impostor* (both 1960), *Come September* (1961), and *The Spiral Road* (1962)—as well as two TV movies and episodes of a handful of TV series.

Part Two: Mulligan without Pakula

From the vantage point of 2024—perhaps from any vantage point—it's impossible to assess what role Pakula played in the development of Mulligan's style as a filmmaker. However, there is an obvious thematic similarity between much of their work together and apart: both were drawn to protagonists who find themselves confronting new experiences, sometimes successfully, sometimes not, and many of their films chart the course of this kind of struggle. The coming-of-age story is one version, but there are many others.

The scenario neatly fits both *Fear Strikes Out* and *To Kill a Mockingbird*, which was made five years later. But it also readily aligns with the films that Mulligan made away from Pakula during the intervening years.[6] For three of these, his producer was veteran Robert Arthur, whose previous credits included a trio of Abbott and Costello pictures (1948–1950), *The Big Heat* (1953), and *A Time to Love and a Time to Die* (1958), on which he had a falling out with director Douglas Sirk.

In both *The Rat Race*[7] and *The Great Impostor*,[8] Tony Curtis plays a character who chooses to go his own way rather than accept the realities of the world around him. In the first, he's Pete Hammond Jr., an innocent from Milwaukee, who arrives in New York City on a Greyhound bus, carrying his musical instruments and planning to take the place by storm. The bus driver (Stanley Greene) even refers to him as "a pilgrim on the way to Mecca."

In the second, a classic "great pretender" tale based on the real-life exploits of Ferdinand Waldo Demara Jr., he's an opportunist who asserts his personal worth and exposes others' small-mindedness by assuming a range of different identities: as a US marine, a Trappist monk, a prison warden, a surgeon, and a teacher.

Both films celebrate the power of the imagination, prioritizing it over the mindset that insists that—in the words of Karl Malden's Father Devlin in *The Great Impostor*—"sooner or later you've got to face facts." The Curtis characters reject those "facts" and, against the odds, refuse to "settle for less."

By immersing themselves in who *they* want to be and how they want the world to be, they not only provide themselves with a protective armor against misfortune but also manage to soften the hard-bitten ways of those around them. In *The Rat Race*, for example, Pete's optimism throughout his collision with NYC leaves world world-weary taxi dancer Peggy (Debbie Reynolds), cynical landlady Soda (Kay Medford) and seen-it-all bartender Mac (Jack Oakie) with a renewed hope for humanity.

Both films point to Mulligan's preoccupation with the interaction between subjective experience and external reality that was to become central to *To Kill a Mockingbird*, although they don't exhibit that film's more fully developed structural and stylistic evocation of the theme. Nor do the other two films the director made during the five years before renewing his partnership with Pakula, although they too deal with characters—both played by Rock Hudson—who find themselves unexpectedly confronted by unfamiliar circumstances.

At first glance, *Come September*[9] is a straightforward reworking of the elements driving other Hudson sex comedies, minus Doris Day. The screenplay is by Stanley Shapiro and Maurice Richlin, who were also responsible for *Pillow Talk* (1959). Alexander Walker notes in his book, *Sex and the Movies*, that it was made at a time "when the Playboy idea was in full seed."[10] And it's not hard to see why Hudson's character might have been conceived as a variation on Hugh Hefner and the film's central location as a surrogate for the Playboy mansion.

Come September is a comedy of manners in which propriety confronts what passes for debauchery in films like this, and the values of one generation clash with those of another. The plot pivots on what ensues after plans go amiss for the holiday that businessman bachelor Robert L. Talbot (Hudson) had planned to take in his Italian villa. He'd anticipated time alone with his one-month-a-year lover, Lisa Fellini (Gina Lollobrigida), but the unexpected arrival of, first, a group of American college girls (including Sandra Dee) and their chaperone (Brenda de Banzie), and then a trio of American students (including Bobby Darin and Joel Grey) turns his world upside down. Benefiting enormously from the censor's prohibitions of the time, the film constantly thwarts the potential lovers' efforts to get together while pondering the place that sex ought to occupy in the lives of its characters.

Seen through the filter of Mulligan's previous films, the material also fits, albeit uncomfortably, with the interests evident in them. Talbot might be a playboy type, but he's also very much an innocent in the situation in which he finds himself. "It's more than a villa," he sighs early on about his magnificent mansion overlooking the ocean. "It's a refuge where a man can look out on the rest of the world." Except that his refuge has been invaded and, once again, Mulligan has on his hands a story about a man trying to make unfamiliar circumstances conform to his wishes.

The same principle is at work in *The Spiral Road*,[11] although it's a very different kind of film. Here Hudson is arrogant Dutchman Anton Drager, a doctor and an avowed atheist assigned to an internship in the unfamiliar terrain of Java during the 1930s (when it was the Dutch East Indies). In the jungles there, he finds himself dealing with situations that lie far outside his previous experiences, learning in the process that the world isn't necessarily ordered in the way he'd thought. A bit like a cross between Joseph Conrad's *Heart of Darkness* and Douglas Sirk's *Magnificent Obsession*, the film was a curious choice for Mulligan and perhaps served as one of the factors that led him back to Pakula—with whom he'd remained on good terms throughout—and to *To Kill a Mockingbird*.

What is clear from their time apart, and from Mulligan's work after their partnership finally ended, is that he was, all along, developing his own distinctive methods of storytelling. And Pakula appears to have been fully sensitive to that, his later work as a director both underlining their mutual interests as storytellers and pointing to the lessons he learned from his time with Mulligan.

Part Three: *To Kill a Mockingbird*

They came back together as a filmmaking team in 1962. Forming Pakula-Mulligan Productions, Inc., they collaborated on Mulligan's next six features. And, as Mulligan told Pakula-biographer Jared Brown, their working relationship continued to be harmonious. "Alan was without question a creative collaborator," he said. "He often initiated projects but we'd move ahead on them only if we agreed."[12] However, while Pakula might have been extensively involved in the preparation of their films, he wasn't a hands-on producer. Despite harboring ambitions to direct one day himself, he was committed to keeping his distance from the creative process once the shoot had begun, even if it pained him to do so.

"I always would go into a depression when those pictures started shooting," he explained years later to Culhane, "because I do know this: once a director's on a set, there can only be one person working with those actors. I don't believe in producers who hang around sets. I would meet with Bob at the end of the day, and we'd see dailies together and we'd discuss the work, but he was absolutely in charge of those actors—and that's the way it should be."[13]

Mulligan confirmed to Brown that Pakula remained true to his word. "Alan was never on set during shooting," he said. "It was his choice and not something I demanded. . . . Once the camera was ready to roll, he'd wish me luck and leave. His visits were always calm and positive."[14] Pakula further discusses their working relationship in Gordon Gow's 1972 interview with him in this book.

Their first film together might have been a disappointment, but it was soon clear that both had learned from the earlier experience, and *To Kill a Mockingbird* (1962) represented a giant step forward for both of them. Not only did its eight Oscar nominations signal that they had officially "arrived" in the film business, but one can also see in it the crystallizing of key aspects of Mulligan's style as a filmmaker.

As was the case with *Fear Strikes Out*, it was Pakula who set everything in motion: proposing the screen adaptation of Harper Lee's book to Mulligan and working extensively on the screenplay with writer Horton Foote (whose involvement had been initiated by Mulligan) and on the casting. Mulligan had wanted to cast Rock Hudson in the lead after working with him on *Come September* and *The Spiral Road*; Pakula insisted on Gregory Peck. Spencer Tracy and James Stewart were also considered.

Set in the fictional small town of Maycomb County in the American South during the depression of the 1930s, *To Kill a Mockingbird* was—as his own work as a director subsequently indicated—clearly the kind of socially conscious subject matter that immediately grabbed Pakula's attention. Not only did it confront the ugly face of racism in the US, but it also probed the ways in which ignorance and impoverishment are powerful forces thwarting the possibilities of community.

It would be a mistake to suggest that these issues weren't important to Mulligan too. His TV work, on productions such as *The Alcoa Hour* (1955–1956), CBS's *Studio One* (1956–1957), *Judgment at Nuremberg* (1957–1960), and *Ah, Wilderness!* (1959), had already established his commitment to weighty subject matter. But *To Kill a Mockingbird* also lent itself to what was emerging as a recurring feature of his work.

As John Belton has observed,[15] one of the most distinctive qualities of Mulligan's approach, with or without Pakula, was his ability to build a subjective mise-en-scène. This is achieved not so much via conventional point-of-view shots as through his framing of the action as a whole, his ability to immerse us in his characters' circumstances as they might experience them, encountering them through what he chooses to show us and how that information is presented to or withheld from us.

In Belton's words, "By looking at the world through his characters' feelings towards it, Mulligan filters objective reality through subjective experience."[16] At the same time, though, he maintains a distance between us and his characters, inviting us to bring our own understandings of the workings of the world to what we're watching. And from its credit sequence onwards, *To Kill a Mockingbird* works exactly like that.

After a survey of the contents of a treasure box that signify the world of a child—crayons, a fob watch, a couple of wooden totem dolls, a key, coins, a kid's necklace, a whistle, a marble—the camera tilts downward from a low-angle shot of tree branches. As the adult Scout (Kim Stanley) reflects in voice-over on this earlier time in her life, its forward movement gently guides us along the unpaved street where young Jean Louise Finch, nicknamed "Scout" (Mary Badham), lives in a cozy weatherboard home with her older brother, Jem (Phillip Alford), and their lawyer father, Atticus (Gregory Peck).

The effect is complicated. At the same time as the sequence suggests that we're moving into a wonderland, the voice-over sets us slightly apart from that, introducing the fact that the following events are being filtered through Scout's memory of them. And, throughout the film, we mainly learn about things that happen offscreen only when she and her brother do.

Furthermore, we're invited to understand much of what they experience firsthand differently from the way that they do. When a mob gathers outside the town jail planning to lynch the African American man their father has been defending (Brock Peters), Atticus stands between them and their goal. The scene is reminiscent of the one set on the front doorstep of the Sangamon County Jail in John Ford's *Young Mr. Lincoln* (1939) where lawyer "Honest" Abe (Henry Fonda) takes a stand against a would-be lynch mob.

As Scout and Jem arrive on the scene, Atticus tells the righteous wretches to go about their business. They refuse. He also tells Jem and Scout to go home. Jem disobeys him, and Scout follows her brother's lead. Then she spies a man she knows as a regular, and amiable, visitor to their home (Crahan Denton). She innocently asks how he is and what he's doing there, inadvertently embarrassing him, and the rest of the mob, into doing as Atticus had urged.

Mulligan used to describe himself simply as a teller of others' stories. "Things have to sift through me," he said. "That's me up there on the screen. The shooting, the editing, the use of music—all that represents my attitude toward the material."[17] His films become subtle and eloquent incursions into their characters' encounters with the world, although his modus operandi isn't always the same. The material dictated how he went about implementing his methods.

Part Four: Pakula-Mulligan Productions, Inc.

Between 1963 and 1968, Pakula and Mulligan made five further films together. The first, *Love with the Proper Stranger* (1963), is something of a companion piece to *The Rat Race*, a romantic comedy set in New York about an unlikely couple (played by Natalie Wood and Steve McQueen) grappling with the vagaries of the place and negotiating the apparent chasm between them. But the contrasting styles that Mulligan brings to the two films suggest that he was determined to avoid repeating himself, an outlook both filmmakers sustained through the rest of their time together.

Working with a screenplay by a mutual friend, Arnold Schulman—whose later credits include *Goodbye, Columbus* (1969), *Funny Lady* (1975), and *A Chorus Line* (1985)—they chose to shoot *Love with the Proper Stranger* in black and white rather than color and mostly on location in the city rather than on studio sets, lending the film a realist edge and underscoring its edgy subject matter.

The central characters' discomfort with each other is evident from the opening sequence, set in a crowded gathering of the Associated Musicians of Greater New York. Rocky Papasano (McQueen) is there looking for work; Angie Rossini (Wood) has been trying to track him down. She emerges from the throng to claim that he's responsible for her pregnancy after a recent one-night stand; he says he doesn't remember her.

The rest of the film deals with the development of their very uneasy relationship. Although they share an Italian American background, they're otherwise worlds apart. He's a mixed-up guy who's been around the block a few times. She's a relatively naïve working girl who lives with her family in a cramped apartment, is employed as a salesclerk on the fifth floor at Macy's, and has dreams of being swept off her feet by a handsome Romeo. In a grueling sequence, Papasano tries to help her get an abortion and, when that fails and he's confronted by her protective brother (Herschel Bernardi), clumsily proposes marriage. "I'm willing to take my medicine," he nobly tells her.

As Belton points out,[18] the settings play a prominent role in the film: the crowded hall at the start, her department-store workplace bustling with shoppers, the eerily empty streets as they try to make contact with the abortionist, the cramped apartments they call home, and the strategically unsettling closing sequence outside Macy's. The lovers finally come together in an embrace as the receding camera loses them in the crowded street, together but without having resolved any of the issues that have kept them at odds with each other throughout the film.

The film might qualify as a romantic comedy, just (a description that, along with its qualification, also applies to Pakula's later ventures into the genre). But, despite its similarities to *The Rat Race*, the depiction of the city suggests that there are no safe places for this would-be couple. It sits at the opposite end of the genre's spectrum from *Come September*, which, like *The Rat Race*, was made without Pakula as producer.

One can only hypothesize that it was Pakula's influence that steered Mulligan in this new direction. But, given Pakula's general avoidance of reassuring endings, it's certainly a possibility. He talks about this tendency in his work in the first of the AFI Dialogue on Film sessions in this book and discusses his concerns about *Love with the Proper Stranger* in the Gow interview.

Their next film together was *Baby the Rain Must Fall* (1964), adapted by Horton Foote from his play, *The Traveling Lady*, which had a brief run on Broadway in 1954. In 1957, Mulligan and Foote had collaborated on an earlier adaptation of it, a one-hour live-to-air episode of Fletcher Markle's long-running *Studio One* anthology series, with a cast led by Kim Stanley, Steven Hill, Robert Loggia (in his TV debut), and Mildred Dunnock. According to Brown,[19] Pakula worked closely with Foote on the shaping of the screenplay for the film version.

The film opens with Georgette Thomas (Lee Remick) and her daughter, Margaret Rose (Kimberly Block) aboard a Greyhound bus heading from Tyler, Texas, to Houston to try to get back together with Henry (Steve McQueen), her estranged musician husband and Margaret Rose's father. He's just been released from prison, where he's served a term for stabbing a man in a bar fight.

Henry is introduced via a slow dissolve that takes us from Georgette inside the bus to a shot of the road along which she's traveling towards him, a progression that quietly suggests that she's being drawn into his world and introduces what is to be a recurring mode of transition from one scene to the next in the film. Again, ever so subtly, the focus of Mulligan's style is his protagonist's emotional journey.

Henry is a troubled soul, and there are echoes of *Fear Strikes Out* in the film's depiction of him as an individual who's been seriously damaged by his upbringing.[20] His nemesis is his former guardian, Miss Kate (Georgia Simmons), an old woman whose melodramatic presence lends the film a Gothic edge. Her hardedged contempt for him, it proposes, is the primary source of his self-destructive ways. "You're no good, Henry," she tells him on her deathbed. "You never have been. You're not worth killin'."

It's soon apparent that, just as Georgette's hope to build a future with Henry is misguided, his dreams of making it in the music business in California are doomed (and not just because McQueen's lip-synching of Billy Strange's pedestrian vocals is so unconvincing). With Remick's performance bringing a persuasive power to Georgette's yearnings, Mulligan situates her struggle to find hope in an oppressively inhospitable setting made up of deserted small-town streets, a gloomy mansion, a cemetery, a seedy bar, a lonely house in the middle of nowhere, and overcast skies.

In such a context, the ending seems inevitable. Haunted by the ghosts of his past, Henry has become a lost cause, a sad case, his final separation from Georgette carrying a sense of history repeating itself. On the other hand, Mulligan invites us to see Georgette and her daughter's situation at the end less as a letdown and more as an escape from bleak circumstances. Framing the sapling that Georgette has been nurturing squarely in the foreground as they leave their home for a new future, the film presents us with an emblem of growth and allows some room for hope. It's an ending that anticipates the one in *Sophie's Choice* as Peter MacNicol's Stingo leaves his Brooklyn traumas behind and moves towards a new life.

The next Pakula-Mulligan film, the ambitiously stylized but seriously flawed *Inside Daisy Clover* (1965), comes to its conclusion at a similar point in its protagonist's life. Dismayed about where her dreams have led her, Daisy (Natalie Wood) has unsuccessfully tried to commit suicide by switching on the gas oven in her beach shack and putting her head inside. Her efforts in vain, she heads out on to the beach with an unexpected bounce in her step, the camera tracking backwards with her movement as the house explodes behind her. "Lady, what happened back there?" a man asks as she passes. "Someone declared war," she proudly replies, on her way to a fresh start.

Adapted from his own novel by Gavin Lambert, the film is a pitch-black fairytale fashioned as a corrective to the feel-good star-is-born fantasy. After she's "discovered" by Raymond Swan, a ruthless Svengali-like studio head (Christopher Plummer), young Daisy's voyage to disillusionment takes her from a poverty-stricken upbringing to the realization that that stardom is a poison for which there is no known antidote. Her adventures and the style that Mulligan brings to them make the film something of a nightmarish variation on *Alice in Wonderland*.

She becomes a musical star (voiced in part by Jackie Ward) and is peddled to the world as "America's Little Valentine." After that, she's betrayed by an actor who'd presented himself as her knight in shining white armor (Robert Redford in his big-screen debut), reminded that "fame has its obligations," and driven to the suicide attempt. Swan's ruthless exploitation of her leads to her breakdown, making her a fellow traveler with Piersall in *Fear Strikes Out* and Henry in *Baby the Rain Must Fall*.

The film wasn't well received—Brown reports that Pakula blamed himself for its perceived flaws[21]—and Mulligan's extravagant, cartoon-like approach largely eliminates any dramatic interest from most of the character interactions. At the start, Wood plays the fifteen-year-old Daisy like a dead-end kid out of an old

Hollywood movie, a gum-chewing adolescent whose dress and demeanor are as arch as her dialogue. The ramshackle setting for the beachside home where she lives with her wacky mother (Ruth Gordon)—another of Mulligan's aberrant parents—is fashioned along the same lines.

The Redford character's knowing description of the situation into which they've both stepped suggests that the film is best appreciated as a fable in which moral lessons are of greater import than rounded characterizations and real-world settings. "We meet in the castle of lost souls in the land of the black Swan, otherwise known as the Prince of Darkness," he tells the starry-eyed Daisy, adopting the vernacular of the fairytale. Which might be a useful lens through which to see the film were its moral lessons more sympathetically and persuasively fleshed out.

The best that can be said for *Inside Daisy Clover* is that it again illustrates Pakula and Mulligan's readiness to take risks. However, they found themselves on much safer ground with *Up the Down Staircase* (1967), which sees Mulligan returning to the gritty realities of New York City, which had been such a potent presence in *Love with the Proper Stranger*. Written by Tad Mosel, *Up the Down Staircase* is based on Bel Kaufman's 1964 bestseller drawn from her experiences as a teacher in the New York high school system. The release date was June 1967, around the same time as *To Sir with Love*, which is set in a high school in London's East End, and a little over a decade after *Blackboard Jungle* (1955), which is also set in New York. Mosel had previously worked with Mulligan on the *Studio One* TV series (on the 1957 episode, "The Five Dollar Bill").

To go "up the down staircase," as the title proposes, is to go against the grain, to do something that might cause confusion but can still get you to where you want to go. It's not exactly how Sylvia Barrett (Sandy Dennis in her film debut) goes about her teaching at Calvin Coolidge High School; her methods are far too conventional for that. But it does point to the frustration she feels with the way her fellow staff members accept the status quo there and with how her students regard the education she's offering them.

As he did for *To Kill a Mockingbird*, Mulligan builds a subjective mise-en-scène, filtering events through his central character's experience of them. Shot and edited in a mostly hand-held, you-are-there documentary style, the opening sequences are built around Sylvia's arrival at the school. As she gets off the morning bus—she's yet another Mulligan character who rides into the story on a bus, although this time it's a crosstown one—she's drawn into the to-and-fro bustle of the students heading for the school. It's her first day, and Mulligan is placing us inside the organized chaos that she's encountering, at the same time informing us via the rundown buildings, vacant lots, and dirty streets all around that we're entering a "problem area."

The same hand-held style follows her entry into the school building. She's lost in the general hubbub—bells ringing, students and teachers pushing their way along the corridors, doors slamming—as she tries to make her way to the staffroom. And it's sustained through her initial encounters with the place: in the assembly hall, where everyone's talking and nobody's listening, and where students and teachers alike rush for the door as the session comes to a close; in the library, where the staff gathers, much is said, and nothing is decided; in the classroom, where disorder is the order of the day.

Gradually, however, as Sylvia becomes more accustomed to her surroundings, the pace of the camera movement and the cutting slows. The organized chaos becomes less disorienting, and she finds that she's able to adjust to what's required of her in the classroom, even managing to configure it to better fit with her personality. Mulligan's compositions regularly frame her alongside or in front of posters of historical figures who are important to her and to the kinds of thinking that she wants to bring into her students' lives: Robert Frost, Emily Dickinson, Archibald MacLeish, William Faulkner, W. B. Yeats.

All the film gives us of life outside the school are the exterior shots during the opening and the surrounding slums that are intermittently glimpsed through the classroom windows. We're shown nothing of her life (or anyone else's) away from the school and its immediate surroundings. We know that she's arrived on that crosstown bus, nothing more.

Up the Down Staircase is about Sylvia's experience of the school. The arrangements she brings to her classroom, what she does in it, and her attempts to improve life at the school generally mold together to become extensions of her personality. Other teachers, students, and a few parents come and go. Some problems are solved, none of them easily. Some aren't. Life goes on.

Like many of Mulligan's other films, with or without Pakula, *Up the Down Staircase* is essentially about an individual's encounter with unfamiliar circumstances and the attempt to find ways of adapting to it. It's what binds Sylvia together with Daisy, Georgette, Scout, and Jem; with Tony Curtis's characters in *The Rat Race* and *The Great Impostor*; and with Rock Hudson's in *Come September* and *The Spiral Road*; as well as with Gregory Peck's retired army scout in Pakula and Mulligan's final film together.

Originally slated for veteran director George Stevens, *The Stalking Moon* (1968) came to Pakula and Mulligan via Gregory Peck. According to Brown,[22] citing Horton Foote, what they first saw was Foote's screenplay, although they eventually turned to Alvin Sargent for a complete rewrite. While the finished film's credits list him as the sole screenwriter, underneath his name, they nominate Wendell Mayes as being responsible for the original adaptation of Theodore V. Olsen's 1965 novel.

A masterly and apparently inadvertent reworking of the elements of writer-director Tom Gries's *Will Penny* (1967), *The Stalking Moon* is a Western made long after the genre's golden era.[23] As always, Pakula and Mulligan were drawn to the challenge the film offered. "I loved it because it's kind of Hitchcock in the West," Mulligan said, "a Western full of terror as opposed to adventure."[24] And Peck brings to it the same air of dignity and decency that he gave to Atticus in *To Kill a Mockingbird*.

Having just retired, his Sam Varner is about to head homewards, leaving behind him the dusty, windswept cavalry camp in the Colorado desert where he'd been stationed and the problems of the world. Guided by him, the unit has been raiding Apache camps, rescuing women and children and providing them with shelter.

The opening image presents him in heavily shadowed profile, carrying a rifle, a man of the West, clambering over rocks, stalking his prey. But he's about to put that kind of action behind him. His destination is his ranch in New Mexico, and his mind has turned to the comforts of being free to do what he wants in his own time.

But then, like Angie in *Love with the Proper Stranger* and Sylvia in *Up the Down Staircase*, Sarah (Eva Marie Saint) and her young half-breed son, known only as "boy" (Noland Clay), emerge from an anonymous crowd, and his plans change. Sarah pleads for his help, and, reluctantly, he agrees to let them join him as he heads homewards. What he doesn't know is that his benevolence will result in the boy's vengeful Apache father, Salvaje (Nathaniel Narciso), following them, a largely unseen threat who represents a particular problem of the world that won't be left behind. What unfolds becomes yet another Mulligan tale about characters' adjustments to the new circumstances in which they find themselves.

For Sarah, it's the companionship of a man who wants nothing from her and the possibility of a return to the kind of life she thought had been forever taken from her. For her son, who knows no English and who doesn't speak in the film, it's the recognition that not all white men are like the racist (Lonny Chapman) who attacks him at the way station during their journey. And for Varner, it's the realization that maybe he doesn't want to live alone after all. His gently clumsy offer of a haven to her—"I've never lived with anyone in my life, but I've agreed with myself that you're welcome to come"—is both funny and deeply moving, as is the quiet comedy of their first meal-time together. As an awkward silence hangs over the dining table, he finally offers, "I got nothin' against talkin'," going on to suggest that the boy might benefit from a lesson in how to use food utensils. To which Sarah responds protectively, "There is already too much for him to learn."

In his fine commentary on the film, Kent Jones astutely observes that "in atmosphere and even in design, *The Stalking Moon* feels close to the films Pakula would make after he and Mulligan brought their partnership to an amicable end."[25] And there's much evidence in the film to support his impression: the evocative use of the wide-screen frame, the brilliant creation of an offscreen menace, the readiness to let scenes unfold in wide shot, the general impulse toward understatement.

But it's also very much a Mulligan film, drawn to the inner lives of its characters, working to provide access to their subjective experiences of the world, attentive to its details, richly measured in its approach, its plot tracing an arc from its protagonists' state of relative innocence to their increased appreciation of the workings of the world and of their place in it.

A widely overlooked gem, it brought the Pakula-Mulligan partnership to an end. "Alan's decision was a reason to celebrate," Mulligan said, "and we did. He was excited about what was coming. I was happy for him and offered whatever help he'd need at any time. Just as he'd done for me for so many years. When the time came, our partnership ended as it had begun—with a handshake."[26] And Pakula assessed the situation with great magnanimity: "I think one of the reasons I didn't direct till later was that it was such a pleasant relationship. I thought we complemented each other. The irony is that if I hadn't worked with a director I respected and admired, I might have done my own work so much more quickly."[27]

Part Five: Pakula without Mulligan

Successful producer-director collaborations in Hollywood are rare. Sometimes they occur despite the differences between those involved, as was the case with Ross Hunter and Douglas Sirk. Sometimes it's because both happen to be on the same wavelength, as were Val Lewton and Jacques Tourneur during their brief but extremely fruitful partnership. Likewise, Christine Vachon and Todd Haynes on more than a dozen projects to date. Pakula and Mulligan also clearly had interests in common, although Pakula's subsequent career strongly suggests that, had he been the director of the films they made together, they might have turned out very differently.

Their association had certainly laid solid foundations for his solo career as a director. As he indicates in several of the interviews in this book, he'd been thinking all along like one, even if he'd remained at a distance from that part of the creative process. But after he came across John Nichols's 1965 novel, *The Sterile Cuckoo*, while browsing in a New York bookshop, all that changed. He took out an option on it and, this time, successfully pitched himself to Paramount as the director.

Once it might have been a property he took to Mulligan, a simple-enough story about the uneasy romance between two college students whose lives are bogged down in their social awkwardness. Like Jimmy in *Fear Strikes Out*, Henry in *Baby the Rain Must Fall*, Daisy in *Inside Daisy Clover*, and many of the protagonists in Pakula's subsequent films—such as *Love and Pain and the Whole Damn Thing* (1972), *Sophie's Choice*, *Dream Lover* (1984), and *Orphans* (1987)—Pookie (Liza Minnelli) appears to have been doomed to carry the oppressive weight of her upbringing into the rest of her life. Her refuge becomes her claim that the world around is made up of "weirdos," with the sole exception of Jerry (Wendell Burton), to whom she attaches herself.

Written by Alvin Sargent, the film (made in 1968) offers a clear illustration of the qualities that Mulligan and Pakula had in common at the same time as it points to their differences. Pakula's intimate portrait of the young couple's adolescent fumblings is presented with an emotional generosity akin to Mulligan's as his characters struggle with their circumstances. And it's filled with the same overarching curiosity about what it is that makes people tick. But the visual style Pakula brings to it is in sharp contrast to Mulligan's inclinations.

Despite the fact that, in the Steven Soderbergh interview in this book, Pakula recalls that it was on *Klute* that he "began to believe in [his] own eye," his first film—in which he's aided by veteran cinematographer Milton Krasner—already suggests a knowing grasp of how he wanted his work to look. And how he wants us to respond to it. Whereas Mulligan frequently tries to immerse us in his characters' experiences, Pakula strives to remain at a compassionate distance from them, to sit back and watch, as it were, rather than to intervene.

From soon after they meet to their separation at the end, whenever they're together, Pookie and Jerry are rarely alone in the wide-screen frame. Pakula is more interested in observing the uneasy ebb and flow of their interactions than in spotlighting dramatic highlights with close-ups or zooms. Their hesitancy around and discomfort with each other can thus be measured in the way they share the same space. Like Mulligan, Pakula wants us to care about his characters' innermost feelings, but he also wants us to be able to see them in a wider context.

He takes a similar approach in *Love and Pain and the Whole Damn Thing*, having Walter (Timothy Bottoms) and Lila (Maggie Smith) conduct their uncomfortable courtship in two shots and long takes as they cross the barren landscape of southern Spain. The cinematographer is different, the much-in-demand English veteran Geoffrey Unsworth instead of Krasner, but the directorial vision that informs the way the film was shaped is virtually identical.

And despite being shot by a range of skilled artists—most prominently Gordon Willis (six times), but also Don McAlpine, Sven Nykvist and Stephen Goldblatt (all twice), and Krasner, Unsworth, Nestor Almendros and Giuseppe Rotunno (once)—his films usually keep their distance. They allow us to engage with their characters but they also work to situate them in their surroundings.

For Pakula, *The Sterile Cuckoo* had seemed a logical choice for his debut, its dramatic framework consistent with much of his previous work with Mulligan and an indication of their mutual interests. In the interview with Gordon Gow, Pakula concedes that his choice of the crime thriller, *Klute*, was unexpected: "I'm still surprised that I did that film," he tells Gow, "because *The Sterile Cuckoo* is more obviously something I would do."

And, over the following decade, he came to see continuities between his films that he'd previously not noticed, some in tune with the recurrent elements of his work with Mulligan, others that see him going his own way. An example of the former is the collision between naivety and knowingness that recurs not only in *The Sterile Cuckoo* and *Klute*, where Donald Sutherland's uptight investigator from small-town Tuscarora—which Jane Fonda's call girl refers to as "Cabbageville"—finds himself far from his comfort zone, but also throughout most of Pakula's sixteen-film career as a director.

An illustration of the latter emerges from one of his anecdotes in the first of the two AFI Dialogues in this book (repeated to Dick Cavett). "I gave a talk at the British Film Institute right after I did *Klute*," he recalls. "The young man who introduced me said, 'Mr. Pakula makes films about the pursuit of happiness as pursued by people who have an inordinately difficult time pursuing it.'" It's an introduction that could have been delivered unchanged had Mulligan been the guest.

An amused Pakula implicitly acknowledges the accuracy of the observation—which is also readily applicable to three other films he went on to make during the 1970s: *Love and Pain and the Whole Damn Thing*, *Comes a Horseman*, and *Starting Over*—but hastens to point out that it doesn't apply to either *The Parallax View* or *All the President's Men*. Still, seen in a particular light—to do with the satisfaction of uncovering the truth that is the pot of gold at the end of the rainbow for those films' protagonists—one could persuasively argue that it does.

However, after he and Mulligan dissolved their partnership, it's instructive to note that when Mulligan went on to make a film about the fractures in American society, it came out as *The Pursuit of Happiness* (1971). An impressively melancholy drama in which "there's a nervous breakdown going on out there," it ends with its disaffected young protagonist (Michael Sarrazin) simply fleeing for somewhere else. When Pakula made a film on the same subject three years later, it was *The Parallax View*, whose would-be hero finds that there's nowhere to run.

And when Mulligan made a film in which an adult writer reflects in voice-over about his "voyage of discovery" as a naïve youth with an older woman far more experienced in the ways of the world, it turned out to be the estimable *Summer of '42* (1971), set on Nantucket Island (and starring Gary Grimes and Jennifer O'Neill, with Mulligan providing the voice-over). When Pakula tackled the same kind of situation a decade later, it was in *Sophie's Choice*, largely set in a boarding house in Brooklyn with the woman a deeply disturbed survivor of the Holocaust (and Josef Sommer providing the voice-over).

In this context, it's also worth returning to the earlier point that Pakula was generally reluctant to allow comfortable closures for his characters. Perhaps the reunited Richard (Kevin Kline) and Priscilla (Mary Elizabeth Mastrantonio) sharing a smile as they move into a large new home at the end of *Consenting Adults* provides an exception. As do Ella (Jane Fonda) and Frank (James Caan) as they set about rebuilding her burned-down home in the estimably bold and affecting long-shot that draws *Comes a Horseman* to a close. Likewise, *See You in the Morning*, which ends hopefully with Nat King Cole's "Our Love Is Here to Stay." And while *All the President's Men* (and our knowledge of what came afterward) does point to justice being done somewhere down the track, the final shots show the accused president being inaugurated, with the journalist heroes still hard at work and the job yet to be finished.

Otherwise, Pakula's endings are either dismayingly bleak or leave their characters poised on the brink of uncertain futures (which, if one is not to be too pessimistic, could alternatively be described as new possibilities). Characters with whom we're invited to empathize die, or are killed, before the closing credits roll on *Love and Pain and the Whole Damn Thing*, *The Parallax View*, *Sophie's Choice*, *Orphans*, and *The Devil's Own*. And while Rusty Sabich (Harrison Ford) and wife Barbara (Bonnie Bedelia) are bound together at the end of *Presumed Innocent*, the US justice system seems irrevocably broken, the murder of a relatively sympathetic character has officially gone unpunished, and everyone has been implicated in it.

On the slightly brighter side, the best that could be said for the characters at the end of more than half his films—*The Sterile Cuckoo*, *Klute*, *Love and Pain and the Whole Damn Thing*, *Starting Over*, *Rollover*, *Sophie's Choice*, *Dream Lover*, *Orphans*, *See You in the Morning*, and *The Pelican Brief*—is that they've arrived at a point in their lives where they're "starting over." In fact, not only does this state of being provide the title for a Pakula film—one which, like its romantic comedy companion piece, *See You in the Morning*, has largely gone unheralded in commentary about the director—but it also arguably points to his underlying view of what might constitute the permanent state of the human condition. "Blundering on" might perhaps serve as a more accurate assessment of it.

The notion that an uncertain future awaits the characters in Pakula's films, whatever their specific situations, is reinforced by the general mistrust of institutions that persists throughout the director's career. The films he is probably best known for—*Klute*, *The Parallax View*, and *All the President's Men*—are often collectively referred to as "the paranoia cycle" and linked to other American films of the 1970s, such as Francis Ford Coppola's *The Conversation* and Roman Polanski's *Chinatown* (both 1974). To those one could reasonably add *Rollover*, *Presumed Innocent*, and *The Pelican Brief*.

In all of them, it's either unseen menaces lurking offscreen that endanger the characters—like echoes of the vengeful Apache in *The Stalking Moon*—or the collapse of a moral order that's supposed to be watching over them. *Sophie's Choice* and *The Devil's Own* both feature characters who have become victims of the history they were born into. And *Consenting Adults'* they-won't-believe-me tale has Kevin Kline's unfaithful husband accused of a murder he didn't commit.

Ethical quandaries lie in wait for them like land mines, and it's not by chance that a recurring motif throughout Pakula's work is that of the idyll interrupted. It's a strategy designed to unsettle audiences, which Pakula talks about in his discussion with Tom Milne in relation to the family gathering in the opening sequence in *Klute*. "I wanted it to look almost posed, like family pictures, romanticized as you like to remember family celebrations. People against that glass wall, against sunlight and all that foliage, like a group of warm plants in the sun; then the darkness, and you go into a world where people are enclosed . . ."

He deploys a similar strategy in *The Parallax View*, with its business-as-usual opening as the media gather in Seattle's Space Needle to hear the polished politician's address before a shot rings out and his blood spatters across a window. The same film also features one of cinema's great shock moments: the abrupt cut, from the please-believe-me pleas of Paula Prentiss's journalist—to a skeptical Frady about there being a conspiracy to eliminate all those who'd witnessed the assassination—to a shot of her lying on a gurney in a morgue, is heart wrenching.

With admirable economy, the elliptical opening of *See You in the Morning* introduces us to two scenes of domestic bliss before a sudden cut to three years later suddenly reveals that it's all fallen apart for both of the families. *The Devil's Own* follows a similar trajectory: it begins with a pastoral sequence of a boy and his family on the Irish coast before two gun-wielding, balaclava-clad men burst in and shatter the mood.

Everything that follows scenes like this in Pakula's films exists in the shadow of what's been lost. Life is fragile; the everyday is an illusion; there is no safe place, and there are no certainties; danger is hovering around the edges just waiting for its moment; the future is fraught; moral compasses no longer keep characters on course.

It needs to be said, however, that, without entirely rejecting the notion of the auteur, Pakula was always notably reluctant to regard himself as one. As he tells Andy Bobrow during their conversation about *The Parallax View* in this book, "The auteur theory is a half-truth." Repeatedly, he would insist that his filmmaking was a collaborative endeavor, reminding interviewers about how much he relied on the artistry of others to achieve his ends.

"I pride myself on having a specific vision of what I want a film to be," he says in the first AFI Dialogue. "But, unlike an author or composer, I am dependent. I am working with a writer, with the actors, with a set designer, with a costume designer, with the cameramen. I am working with endless numbers of people."

Still, there are numerous elements in his films that provide evidence of recurring creative strategies and pointers to the sensibility that informed his use of them, even if he drew on the talents of many others, and even if the material he was working with dictated the particular approach(es) he took.

Among them, as he tells Rick Thompson during their conversation, is the way he would go about locating his characters in particular social circumstances. "I love to use architecture to dramatize a society," he says, pointing to *Klute* and *The Parallax View* (which visually resembles a cross between an Antonioni film and an urban film noir in the way the surroundings envelop the characters). Elsewhere—in his talk to the American Society of Cinematographers and in his conversation with Soderbergh—Pakula acknowledges the importance of cinematographer Gordon Willis to this aspect of his work.

And his point about the importance of architecture to his films is equally applicable to the settings for his stories. In both the Thompson interview and his talk to the American Society of Cinematographers (ASC), he reflects at length on his use of various Washington locations in *All the President's Men*. And the endless landscape with its lonely ranch house in *Comes a Horseman* provides a telling framework for the human drama at its heart.

Critic Jack Hughes describes the New York financial district setting for *Rollover*, shot by Giuseppe Rotunno, as "a world of rich, glistening surfaces, where money and technology merge into a lavish but preoccupied playground."[28] In *Orphans*, shot by Don McAlpine, Pakula's visual strategy turns the claustrophobic interiors of the broken-down old New Jersey home into a kind of fish tank for its characters. As he explains in the press notes for the film, "The house is the core of the film."[29]

Shot by Willis, *Presumed Innocent*'s imposingly solid courtroom, ordered office spaces, and leafy suburbia exist in sharp contrast to the legal and moral chaos that swirls inside them. In much the same way, the plush suburbia with its Victorian era architecture can do little to pacify the inhabitants' simmering dissatisfactions in *Consenting Adults*, shot by Stephen Goldblatt. And everywhere the characters go in *The Pelican Brief*, also shot by Goldblatt, seems to be dangerous: crowds press in on them in the streets, the business districts dwarf them, the Capitol buildings—what Pakula describes to the ASC as "citadels of power"—provide reminders of what is at stake.

Shot by Willis, *The Devil's Own* winds together contrasting settings that are ultimately inseparable. One is a comfortable suburbia where people live peaceful ordinary lives and the only thing families can find to fight about is whose turn it is for the bathroom. The other is the realm of shadow, which the domestic harmony barely notices but that lurks in the basement.

Then there are the issues and character types that Pakula was repeatedly drawn to, both in the films he produced for Mulligan and in the ones he directed. Right from the start, his fascination with the way an individual's upbringing can impinge on what lies ahead is clear to see. Psychological disturbances are frequently traced back to family histories, and psychiatry and psychiatrists play significant roles in the lives of many of his characters.

Jane Fonda's Bree regularly visits a psychiatrist in *Klute*; Walter's treatments are part of the background provided for him in *Love and Pain and the Whole Damn Thing*; an undercover Frady undergoes a test designed to weed out his aptitude as an assassin in *The Parallax View*; Phil (Burt Reynolds) attends a divorced men's workshop in *Starting Over*; Larry (Jeff Bridges) is a psychiatrist in *See You in the Morning*; in the same film, single mother Beth (Alice Krige) also consults one (George Hearn) to talk about her children and her sense of guilt; and so on.

In interviews, like the one I did with him about *Sophie's Choice*, Pakula was also perfectly comfortable putting himself on the couch. And he makes no secret about how both *Starting Over*, which he cowrote with James L. Brooks, and *See You in the Morning*, for which he wrote an original screenplay, served as a kind of therapy, allowing him to reflect through fiction on the breakdown of his first marriage, to actress Hope Lange.

In his interview in this book with famed photographer Bruce Weber, he joined the dots between his experiences and those of *See You in the Morning*'s recently divorced Larry. "Coming out of a bad experience, a relationship that failed, there's a part of you that matures underneath that," he said. "But there's a part of you that goes back to younger kinds of insecurities and vulnerabilities. Rejection can do that to you."

Many of Pakula's collaborators, especially the actors, even likened the way he went about his work to the kind of thing a psychiatrist might do. Donald Sutherland for one: "Alan's interest in psychotherapy was just a device to getting at the most definitive explanation of a character's motives. I would sometimes ask him what he wanted out of a scene, and he was always able to tell me *exactly* what he wanted, and then it was my job to go and get it."[30]

Aligned to the psychiatrists who provide their insights into the conditions afflicting Pakula's characters are the investigators who become central, one way or another, to most of his films, some professionally, some because situations so demand. *Klute*'s title character is doing a favor for the family of a missing man.

In *All the President's Men, The Parallax View,* and *The Pelican Brief,* journalists are on the case (with Julia Roberts's Darby Shaw as an involved bystander in the last). The protagonists of *Presumed Innocent* and *Consenting Adults* have both been implicated in murders and want to extricate themselves. In *Sophie's Choice,* a young writer is trying to make sense of what's going on between his upstairs neighbors. The lost men of *Starting Over, See You in the Morning,* and *Orphans,* as well as Kristy McNichol's Kathy in *Dream Lover,* all want to make sense of what's happening to them. In *The Devil's Own,* Harrison Ford's cop has unknowingly invited danger into his home and needs to find a way to understand it.

Several critics have written insightfully about Pakula's work—among them, Richard T. Jameson,[31] Jean-Pierre Coursodon and Bertrand Tavernier,[32] Neil Sinyard,[33] Hughes and Adrian Martin[34]—but, as the following interviews attest, Pakula was often there ahead of them. He describes himself to Thompson as "an analytic buff," and there are numerous examples in this book of the ways in which he was ready and willing (even eager) to engage in critical dialogue with his interviewers.

In the second AFI Dialogue, Pakula himself points to what the Mulligan-Pakula film, *Fear Strikes Out,* has in common with *Dream Lover.* "I don't know how many pictures later, my most recent film, *Dream Lover,* a psychological thriller with Kristy McNichol, is the story of a girl dominated by her father who attempts to break away and lead her own life, with rather disturbing and perhaps shocking results. That's not all that it's about by any means, but the fact that, after all these years, those same things still haunt me means that you never get away from being who you are."

In an enlightening essay for the *Monthly Film Bulletin,* included in this book, he identified the underlying thread that binds several of his films together. "*Klute* and, perhaps even more so, *The Parallax View* are related in point of view and style to *Rollover,*" he writes. "The Warren Beatty character in *The Parallax View* and the Jane Fonda and Kris Kristofferson characters in *Rollover* share the same sense of hubris: the American belief in the power of the individual." He further elaborated on the point in the interview I did with him in 1983.

And, in the original press notes for *Orphans,* he places his 1987 drama in the context of his career. "I've done several films that have to do with parenting," he says. "I produced *To Kill a Mockingbird,* which had to do with children's first experience of evil, and *Fear Strikes Out* was about a father living through his son, which was very destructive. This film is about the absence of parenting. I'm the stepfather of five children from two marriages, and it's interesting for me to contemplate the way that this character, Harold [Albert Finney], comes into the boys' lives and becomes a kind of parent, though he isn't the boys' father."[35]

He also expounds insightfully in his comments throughout this book about the aesthetic choices that determine the shape of his films: about the visual design of *Klute* (Milne), *The Parallax View* (Bobrow, Soderbergh), *Rollover* (the *Monthly Film Bulletin* essay), and *All the President's Men* (Thompson, Pakula's talk to the ASC); and, in almost all of the interviews and presentations, about the consultative process that enabled him to give his actors and other collaborators room to move and to get what he wanted from them.

Part Six: Pakula's Way

What was Pakula like in person? To what extent can one see him through his work? Collectively, in their comments about him, his collaborators offer a glimpse of the man. Most are both respectful of him and grateful to him for how he encouraged them to contribute to their work together. Meryl Streep is worth quoting at length about her experience on *Sophie's Choice*. "I think he really laid a map of integrity for artists, and that, more than anything, is his legacy for me," she told Susan King of the *Los Angeles Times*:

> He was such a moral filmmaker. It's like an old-fashioned idea, but he was. He was a moral man and he had a backbone. . . . [During rehearsals] he was really asking a million questions. We just sat at the table and picked apart the text, almost like a rabbinical exegesis of texts, inquiring into motivations. . . . We shot the whole movie in the afternoons. I was home in time to cook dinner for my husband and baby. It felt so natural. I felt so free. Believe me, most of the time I'd come home [from filming], and I'm complaining about something. But in this case, I came home and said, "I feel like I can't make a mistake, make a wrong move." He wasn't someone who drew all the limelight to himself. It was all about the work. He was so proud of what he did. It was such a pleasure to work with him.[36]

Jane Fonda was also effusive in her praise. "He's the only director I've worked with three times," she told Culhane. "I hope it won't end there. I told Meryl, 'You have no idea the joy that's in store for you, working with Alan Pakula.'"[37] And Candice Bergen, who took substantial risks in her performance as Burt Reynolds's estranged first wife in *Starting Over*, shares their view: " 'I would never have taken the chances I took with anyone else. The set was just the safest and most secure of havens, where you could take real chances and know that you would not be made to feel ridiculous.'"[38]

Harrison Ford worked with Pakula on *Presumed Innocent* and the director's final film, *The Devil's Own* (Ian Fisher's interview deals in detail with the controversy that swirled around it). "I enjoyed the work . . . because of Alan's affection for actors and his respect for their processes," he writes in the foreword to Brown's Pakula biography. "He understood what the costs were for actors in terms of being vulnerable—not only in portraying vulnerability, but the vulnerability that is at the core of every actor. He respected the spirit and experiences of actors, and found ways to bring those qualities to the screen."[39]

Jeff Bridges too was an admirer: "Alan is such a great leader in the way he makes you feel so comfortable coming to work and really calls upon you to give everything you've got." Also Dustin Hoffman: "I've worked with a variety of directors and they all have their own way of directing," he told Susan King. "There were directors who were certainly as thorough, but usually they have a very set way of working. Alan wasn't married to that. . . . He let you just play around in order to find things that worked for you. [There was] a kind of documentary style to his work. He even said, 'Put the camera there and let the scene show itself. You don't have to cut to a close-up, back and forth'—the kind of thing that a documentary does. And at the same time, I think he was a hidden poet."[40]

Kevin Kline recalled having an especially rewarding time on *Sophie's Choice*— "Alan constantly took great pains to create this kind of bubble around us, to protect us"—although he was unsettled when his director took a different tack with *Consenting Adults*. Brown cites Kline's recall of Pakula's response to his complaint: "This is totally different. This is all about suspense and having a field day with the camera."[41] Which, incidentally, may well be a clue as to what went wrong with the film, arguably the least successful of the director's entire career.

Although he gives a fine performance in *Comes a Horseman*, it's hard to take the late James Caan's bizarre belligerence about Pakula seriously. "The guy cannot direct traffic," he told *Rolling Stone* in 1981. "Making [that film] felt like I was doing time. I can't work with someone just because he's a creative genius. I have to like him personally. I wouldn't work for Antonioni on a bet. I hear he doesn't want anyone too good in his goddamned films because he wants to show everyone just how well he can direct."[42]

Robert Mulligan always spoke highly of his old partner, as did writer Horton Foote. "He was wonderful to work with," Foote told Brown. "He had great respect for the process of writing. And he never tried to tamper with your vision. He simply tried to help you free it."[43]

Whenever Pakula spoke of Gordon Willis, it was always in the spirit of their shared creative endeavor. "I learned a great deal from Gordon, and he helped me to trust my instincts," he said in response to my question to him about their work together, mainly in relation to *Klute*. For his part, in an interview with Steven Soderbergh in *An Amazing Time: A Conversation about "The End of the Road"* (2012), Willis, perhaps revealing more about his own impatience to get the job done than his appreciation of the value of Pakula's way, spoke of his mixed feelings about the amount of time the director would take to plan and set up a scene. "He was not good at making up his mind. But he was a very nice man, intellectual, and very, very appreciative of good stuff on the screen, very appreciative."[44]

And composer Michael Small, who worked for Pakula on nine films, always regarded him as a mentor. "I try to come up with a concept that relates to the whole idea of the picture rather than trying to just underscore dramatically each little moment," he explained to fellow musician Rudy Koppl. "My teacher in this regard is Alan Pakula, because when I did *Klute* his expectation for the score was far beyond anything that I had attempted. He wanted the score to not only be a suspense score, but to underscore the psychology of the main character. Ever since that experience I always look for that extra voice that a score can add to a film."[45]

Then there were his interviewers—journalists, film critics, and others—whose job was to draw him out about his work and, in some cases, himself. Their writing about him provides a word portrait of the way their subject would present himself in such situations. In 1982, Culhane described him as "a boyish-looking 54, tall, gentle-voiced, with a rust-colored beard" and, while forthright in his opinions, "not the usual image of a macho director."[46] In the following year, when Pakula did a promotional tour to coincide with the West Coast premiere of *Sophie's Choice*, veteran San Francisco film critic Judy Stone opened her piece on him by noting that "Alan Pakula hates to give interviews when one of his films is newly released because he feels like 'Willy Loman peddling his wares.'"[47] In 1983, when I spoke to him, I found him thoughtful, engaging, patient, and methodical. When a phone call interrupted our conversation, he paused, dealt with it courteously, and then returned to what he'd been saying, scarcely missing a beat.

In his 1989 interview, included in this book, Weber encountered him as "a dapper man, chatty, soft-spoken but insistently self-scrutinizing, an animated pop psychologist, interested in and amused by the way his mind works and occasionally seeming chagrined by the fact that he thinks about it so much." In 1997, the year before Pakula's death, Ian Fisher observed that "with his white beard and conservative blazers, he looks and speaks like an English professor who happens to have a connection to Hollywood."

What emerges from these observations is that Pakula took his work, his art, seriously; that he took pleasure in the process of creating it, of working with his collaborators to get it right; and that he enjoyed analyzing it and, as the interviews in this book indicate, could do so eloquently and with sharp insight.

However, one further characteristic emerges from his appearance in 1978 on *The Dick Cavett Show*, where the erudite TV talk show host gave his cerebral guest room to display a side of his personality that generally didn't come to the fore in other interviews: his wit and his humor. Indications of the way that Pakula could be funny have filtered through some of the comments from actors who worked with him—they're sprinkled throughout Brown's biography—but they tended to get lost behind his professorial demeanor.

Also lost is the fact that, from the start of his career, to greater or lesser degrees, he was an adventurous soul. Like Mulligan, Pakula hated the idea of repeating himself, even though he was working in an industry where yesterday's commercial success dictates the plan for tomorrow. Asked about why it's so difficult to get a clear idea of what a "Pakula film" might look like or be about, he tells Andy Bobrow: "I don't do different kinds of films just to show people that I can do different kinds of films. . . . Each [one] is a new adventure, and the more I direct, the more I am fascinated by film, the more I try to extend myself to see what I am capable of, and the more different kinds of cinematic vocabulary I would like to master." He told Dick Cavett: "If you start something and say, 'I know how to do this,' the chances are you know how to do it but in a tired way because you're using old nerve endings you've used before. You're imitating yourself, and that's a great danger to me."[48]

The differences between his films might initially be more immediately evident than their similarities. But one thing that they do have in common is the way they represent Pakula's willingness to take risks, even if those risks don't always produce positive results, as *Consenting Adults* indicates. With it, he wanted to make a thriller like Hitchcock used to—and there are echoes of *Vertigo* (1958) in its increasingly strained plot progression—only to discover that he might have been better advised to abandon the idea or to pursue it elsewhere.

But while his adventurous spirit may sometimes have led him into projects he might better have avoided—*Dream Lover* is another example, despite the fine performance he gets from Kristy McNichol—more often than not it served him well. He tells Soderbergh that he's proud of the "commercial risk" that *The Parallax View* represented at the time of its release—by "kill(ing) off the American hero"—and the way the film has stood the test of time is proof that he was right to be. Based on a play by Lyle Kessler, *Orphans* is an audacious adaptation for the screen of a play almost entirely set inside a dilapidated old house, which Pakula makes his own by creatively drawing on the drama's notion of life as theater and eliciting compelling performances from a strong cast led by Albert Finney.

For the group of his films that can loosely be described as romantic comedies, he eschewed the notion of the made-for-each-other couple. For him it was more interesting to have an audience wondering how on earth he's going to get these two characters together than to have it simply waiting for the inevitable to happen. So he came up with unlikely lovers, odd couples if you like, like Walter and Lila in *Love and Pain and the Whole Damn Thing*—which Pakula described as "a love story of the absurd, a kind of sexual Laurel and Hardy"[49]—and like either of the partners Burt Reynolds's character pairs up with in *Starting Over*. With the former film as exhibit number one, Pakula's interest lay in dealing with relationships that show how easily things can go wrong and suggesting that happily-ever-after endings are illusory.

The following interviews provide a broad overview of Pakula's career: his work as Mulligan's producer, the bulk of films he made as director, and his approach to the art of filmmaking. That some of his work receives only scant attention in the interview section—*Starting Over, Dream Lover, Orphans, The Pelican Brief*—reflects the fact that general critical interest in his work has tended to focus on the films he made up to and including *Sophie's Choice*. Hopefully, what this book has to offer will inspire the kind of interest that will remedy that oversight.

My thanks to all those whose work has played a significant part in the shaping of the book—

The contributors, the value of whose work speaks for itself;

Don McAlpine, for sharing his memories;

Kyrene Carter, for her impeccable technical assistance;

Emily Bandy and her team at the University Press of Mississippi;

Olympia Szilagyi, chief librarian at the Australian Film Institute Research Collection, for her enthusiastic and energetic assistance and support (this book wouldn't have happened without your diligence);

Emily Wittenburg and Ben Proctor at the American Film Institute;

Jovita Dominguez and Morgan Rumpf at the Directors' Guild of America;

Saul Molina and David Williams at the American Society of Cinematographers;

Dana M. Lamporello of the McCormick Library of Special Collections and University Archives, Northwestern University in Illinois;

Madame Jacqueline Lesage for her attentive translation back into English of Jonathan Rosenbaum's Pakula interview, originally translated from English to French by Odile Finkielsztajn.

For general support and assistance in acquiring copyright release for the book's publication, my thanks to Rick Thompson (whose superb interview with Pakula was the initial inspiration for this book), Charles Barr, Kieron Corless, Peter Tonguette, Geoff Gardner, D. K. (Douglas) Holm, Adrian Martin, Fred Schepisi, and Asha Holmes.

And most of all to the late Alan J. Pakula, a fine filmmaker and a most gracious and eloquent interviewee.

Finally, to my late parents, Thomas Michael Ryan and Eileen Margaret Ryan (née Porter), for their inspiration and love; to my wife and soulmate, Debi Enker, for her patience and irreplaceable editorial advice; and, for getting me going on this project in the first place, to our wonderful daughter, novelist, and (in collaboration with partner Hector Mackenzie) filmmaker of the future, Madeleine Ryan.

TR

Notes

1. Alan J. Pakula, Address to the Class of 1997 at Vassar College's 130th commencement, May 25, 1997.

2. Krin Gabbard and Glen O. Gabbard, *Psychiatry and the Cinema* (Chicago: University of Chicago Press, 1987), 42.

3. Phillip Lee, "Classic Catches Up with Jimmy Piersall." ESPN Classic, November 19, 2003. (http://www.espn.com/classic/s/Where_now_piersall_jimmy.html).

4. John Culhane, "Pakula's Approach," *New York Times Magazine*, November 21, 1982.

5. Jared Brown, *Alan J. Pakula—His Films and His Life* (New York: Back Stage Books, 2005), 33–40.

6. While the Pakula name doesn't appear in the credits for these films, *The Rat Race* does feature a store-keeper named Mrs. Pakula, from whom the youthful Fred (Fred Crawford) buys twenty-two boxes of candy.

7. *The Rat Race*: adapted by Garson Kanin from his 1950 play; shot by Robert Burks; produced by William Perlberg and George Seaton.

8. *The Great Impostor*: adapted by Liam O'Brien from Robert Crichton's 1959 novel; shot by Robert Burks; produced by Robert Arthur.

9. *Come September*: written by Stanley Shapiro and Maurice Richlin; shot by William Daniels; produced by Robert Arthur.

10. Alexander Walker, *Sex in the Movies* (London: Pelican, 1968), 243.

11. *The Spiral Road*: adapted by John Lee Mahin and Neil Paterson from Jan de Hartog's 1947 novel; shot by Russell Harlan; produced by Robert Arthur.

12. Brown, 57.

13. Culhane.

14. Brown, 29.

15. John Belton, *Cinema Stylists* (Metuchen, NJ, and London: Scarecrow, 1983), 88–98.

16. Belton, 89.

17. Belton, http://www.thefilmjournal.com/issue11/adrobertmulligan.html; also in Jean-Pierre Coursodon, with Pierre Sauvage, *American Directors, Vol. II* (New York: McGraw-Hill, 1983).

18. Belton, *Cinema Stylists*, 102–3.

19. Brown, 66.

20. There are also noteworthy similarities between *Baby the Rain Must Fall* and *Tender Mercies* (1983), which Foote wrote and Australian filmmaker Bruce Beresford directed. Also set in Texas, *Tender Mercies* features Robert Duvall as an alcoholic musician struggling to make a fresh start with the help of a widow (Tess Harper) and her young son (Allan Hubbard).

21. Brown, 71.

22. Brown, 75–76.

23. Notwithstanding the fact that the following year saw the release of *The Wild Bunch* and *True Grit* (for which John Wayne won a long overdue Oscar).

24. Ralph Appelbaum, "Time for Thought: Robert Mulligan," *Films and Filming*, January 1975, 24.

25. Kent Jones, "*The Stalking Moon*: Safe at Home," *Film Comment*, March–April 2009, 51 (or https://www.filmcomment.com/article/the-stalking-moon-review/).

26. Brown, 27.

27. Culhane.

28. Jack Hughes, "This Is Not a Game—Alan J. Pakula's *Rollover*," *Cineaction* 66, Spring 2005, 45.

29. *Orphans* Media Information Kit, Village Roadshow Corporation, 15.

30. Brown, 111.

31. Richard T. Jameson, "The Pakula Parallax," *Film Comment*, September/October 1976, 8–12.

32. Jean-Pierre Coursodon and Bertrand Tavernier, *50 ans de cinema américain*, Omnibus, 1995, 742–48.

33. Neil Sinyard, "Pakula's Choice: Some Thoughts on Alan J. Pakula," *Cinema Papers* (Melbourne), July 1984, 144–48.

34. Adrian Martin, *The Sterile Cuckoo* (https://filmcritic.com.au/reviews/s/sterile_cuckoo.html).

35. *Orphans* Media Information Kit, 8.

36. Susan King, "Remembering Alan J. Pakula," *Los Angeles Times*, November 15, 2019 (https://www.latimes.com/entertainment-arts/movies/story/2019-11-15/meryl-streep-dustin-hoffman-remember-all-the-presidents-men-director-alan-pakula).

37. Culhane.

38. Culhane.

39. Brown, 5–6.

40. King.

41. Brown, 259, 327.

42. Jean Vallely, *Rolling Stone* (https://www.rollingstone.com/tv-movies/tv-movie-features/lost-james-caan-interview-thief-sonny-godfather-1379823/).

43. Brown, 43.

44. Steven Soderbergh, "An Amazing Time: A Conversation about 'The End of the Road' shot by Willis," *American Cinematographer*, September 1978.

45. Tim Greiving, "Michael Small, Film Music's Prince of Paranoia," *The Criterion Collection*, March 10, 2021 (https://www.michaelsmallmusic.com/the-man).

46. Culhane.

47. Judy Stone, "Meryl Streep: Definitely the Director's Choice," *San Francisco Chronicle*, December 19, 1982.

48. *The Dick Cavett Show*, aired on November 13, 1978 (see https://www.youtube.com/watch?v=PibY4pWkJOo).

49. Hugh Hebert, "Front Office, Back Street, High Rise," *The Guardian*, January 21, 1972.

Chronology

1928   Born Alan Jay Pakula on April 7, in the Bronx, New York City, to Jeanette (née Goldstein) and Paul Pakula. She was New York–born to Russian Jewish parents; he was a Polish Jewish émigré who came to the United States soon after the turn of the century at the age of six.

1932   Moves with his parents from the Bronx to Long Beach.

1941   Now thirteen years old, Pakula celebrates his bar mitzvah.

1942   Moves back to Manhattan. His parents enroll him at the Bronx High School of Science, for gifted students.

1944   For his last year of high school, he enrolls at the Hill School, Pennsylvania.

1945   Enrolls at Yale University. Before classes begin, he takes on a summer job as an office boy at the Leland Hayward Theatrical Agency.

1948   Graduates with a Bachelor of Arts degree in drama studies, receiving top marks for his senior thesis, "The Psychology of the Drama."

1949   His parents' hope has long been for him to join the family printing business, the Bryant Press, and eventually (in partnership with his cousin) take it over. Begins work as an assistant in the cartoon department at Warner Bros.

1950   Takes up a job offer as an apprentice to writer-producer Don Hartman at Metro-Goldwyn-Mayer after Hartman sees his stage production of Jean Anouilh's *Antigone* at Hollywood's Circle Theatre.

1951   After Hartman is appointed head of production at Paramount, he takes Pakula there with him as his assistant. Pakula begins writing an eventually unproduced play for his then-actor friend, Alvin Sargent.

1956   Takes on the role of producer on *Fear Strikes Out*, the first of what is to become a seven-film partnership with director Robert Mulligan. The film begins shooting in July.

1957   *Fear Strikes Out* opens in March.

1958   Pakula sets in motion a series of New York theater productions. The first is Speed Lamkins's *Comes a Day*, directed by Mulligan, co-produced by Cheryl Crawford, and starring Judith Anderson and George C. Scott.

1962   Forms Pakula-Mulligan Productions with Mulligan on the basis of "a handshake deal." Shooting begins on their second collaboration, *To Kill a Mockingbird*, in February. The film is released in December.

1963   For their work on it, Gregory Peck wins the Oscar for Best Actor, and Horton Foote also wins for Best Screenplay Based on Material from Another Medium, Pakula accepting the award on his behalf. The film had earned a nomination for Best Picture, along with Mulligan for Best Director; Mary Badham for Best Actress in a Supporting Role; Russell Harlan for Best Cinematography, Black-and-White; Alexander Golitzen, Henry Bumstead and Oliver Emert for Best Art Direction-Set Decoration Black-and-White; and Elmer Bernstein for Best Music, Score—Substantially Original. Pakula-Mulligan Productions' *Love with the Proper Stranger* begins shooting in March and is released in December. Arnold Schulman is Oscar nominated for his screenplay for the film. Marries actress Hope Elise Ross Lange on October 19, becoming stepfather to her children, Christopher and Patricia Murray. Nine days later, shooting begins on *Baby the Rain Must Fall*, Mulligan and Pakula's fourth film together. Pakula and Lange establish a home in Brentwood, California.

1965   *Baby the Rain Must Fall* is released in January. In April, filming begins on their next collaboration, *Inside Daisy Clover*, which is released in December.

1966   In July, shooting begins on their *Up the Down Staircase*.

1967   *Up the Down Staircase* is released in June.

1968   Shooting begins in January on what turns out to be the final Mulligan-Pakula collaboration, *The Stalking Moon*, written by Alvin Sargent. Filming begins in September on Pakula's directorial debut, *The Sterile Cuckoo*, with him also as producer and Sargent as writer. *The Stalking Moon* is released in December.

1969   *The Sterile Cuckoo* is released in October. Liza Minnelli is nominated for a Best Actress Oscar, along with composers Fred Karlin and Dory Previn for Best Music, Original Song ("Come Saturday Morning" by The Sandpipers).

1970   Filming begins in July on *Klute*, with Pakula again as producer and director.

1971   *Klute* is released in June. Writers Andy Lewis and David E. Lewis are nominated for Oscars. Pakula is divorced from Hope Lange in July. Shooting on *Love and Pain and the Whole Damn Thing*, Pakula's third feature as producer-director, begins in November.

1972   Jane Fonda wins Best Actress Oscar for *Klute*.

1973   Marries author Hannah Cohn Boorstin (née Hannah Cohn, subsequently Hannah Pakula) on February 17, becoming stepfather to her three children, Louis, Robert, and Anna. The Hollywood Screenwriters' strike begins in March, lasting for three and a half months. The Watergate hearings begin on May 17. Filming of *The Parallax View* begins on April 2, with Pakula as producer, director, and uncredited cowriter. (Robert Towne was also rumored to be doing rewrites during the shoot, although he denied this.) *Love and Pain and the Whole Damn Thing* is released later the same month.

1974   *The Parallax View* is released in June.

1975   Shooting begins on *All the President's Men* in Hollywood in May, directed by Pakula.

1976   The film is released in May. It's nominated for an Oscar, along with Pakula (for Best Director), Jane Alexander (Best Supporting Actress), and Robert L. Wolfe (editing). Pakula and Hannah move to New York City.

1977   Jason Robards wins the Best Supporting Actor Oscar for his work on *All the President's Men*, along with William Goldman (screenplay), George Jenkins and George Gaines (Best Art Direction/Set Decoration), Arthur Piantadosi, Les Fresholtz, Dick Alexander and James E. Webb (sound). In June, filming begins in Colorado on *Comes a Horseman*.

1978   Pakula serves as president of the Official Competition Jury at the 31st Cannes International Film Festival in May. *Comes a Horseman* is released in October. Richard Farnsworth is nominated for an Oscar for Best Supporting Actor. Filming on *Starting Over* begins in Manhattan in November.

1979   *Starting Over* is released in October. Jill Clayburgh is nominated for an Oscar for Best Actress and Candice Bergen as Best Supporting Actress.

1981   Shooting begins on *Rollover* in January. It's released in December.

1982   In March, filming begins on *Sophie's Choice*, written and directed by Pakula. It's released in December. Pakula is nominated for an Oscar (for the Best Adapted Screenplay), along with Meryl Streep (for Best Actress), Nestor Almendros (cinematography), Albert Wolsky (costume design), and Marvin Hamlisch (music).

1983   Streep wins the Best Actress Oscar for *Sophie's Choice*.

1984   Shooting begins on *Dream Lover* in April.

1986   *Dream Lover* opens in February. Filming on *Orphans* begins in New York in September.

1987   *Orphans* is released in September.

1988   Filming begins on *See You in the Morning* in February.

1989   *See You in the Morning* is released in April. *Presumed Innocent* begins shooting in July.

1990   *Presumed Innocent* is released in July.

1992   Shooting begins on *Consenting Adults* in Atlanta in January. It opens in October.

1993   Shooting begins on *The Pelican Brief* in May. It's released in December.

1995   *To Kill a Mockingbird* is selected for preservation in the US National Film Registry by the Library of Congress as being "culturally, historically, or aesthetically significant."

1996   Shooting begins on *The Devil's Own* in New Jersey in February.

1997   *The Devil's Own* opens in March.

1998   Dies on November 19 at the age of seventy after a car accident on the Long Island Expressway, near the Melville exit. He is taken to the North Shore University Hospital in Nassau County where he is pronounced dead at 12:22 p.m. At the time, he had been working on an adaptation of Doris Kearns Goodwin's Pulitzer Prize–winning *No Ordinary Time: Franklin and Eleanor Roosevelt—The Home Front in World War II*, published in 1995. Goodwin said of Pakula, "He loved this project—this era, the people, the drama—as do I" (https://www .shelf-awareness.com/issue.html?issue=2322#m25413). He was also reported to have been set to direct a comedy he'd written entitled *A Tale of Two Strippers*, with Josh Duhamel and Ashton Kutcher, about two male exotic dancers in Las Vegas who find themselves trying to evade a hit man after they stumble across an arranged murder.

2008   On December 20, Pakula-collaborator Robert Mulligan dies of heart disease at the age of eighty-three.

2010   Like *To Kill a Mockingbird* fifteen years earlier, *All the President's Men* is selected for preservation in the US National Film Registry by the Library of Congress on the grounds of being "culturally, historically, or aesthetically significant."

Filmography

FEAR STRIKES OUT (1956)
Director: Robert Mulligan
Producer: **Alan Pakula**
Writers: Ted Nerkman and Raphael Blau (based on *Fear Strikes Out: The Jim Piersall Story*, by James A. Piersall and Albert S. Hirshberg)
Photography: Haskell Boggs
Editor: Aaron Stell
Music: Elmer Bernstein
Cast: Anthony Perkins (Jim Piersall), Karl Malden (John Piersall), Norma Moore (Mary Piersall), Adam Williams (Dr. Brown), Peter J. Votrian (Jim Piersall as a boy), Perry Wilson (Mrs. John Piersall), Art Gilmore, Edd Byrnes, Brian G. Hutton (uncredited)
Distributor: Paramount
100 minutes

TO KILL A MOCKINGBIRD (1962)
Director: Robert Mulligan
Producer: **Alan J. Pakula**
Writer: Horton Foote (based on the novel by Harper Lee)
Photography: Russell Harlan
Editor: Aaron Stell
Music: Elmer Bernstein
Cast: Gregory Peck (Atticus Finch), Mary Badham (Scout Finch), Phillip Alford (Jem Finch), Ruth White (Mrs. Dubose), Brock Peters (Tom Robinson), Paul Fix (Judge Taylor), Robert Duvall (Boo Radley), Kim Stanley (narrator, voice of adult Scout)
Distributor: Universal
129 minutes

LOVE WITH THE PROPER STRANGER (1963)
Director: Robert Mulligan
Producer: **Alan J. Pakula**

Writer: Arnold Schulman
Photography: Milton Krasner
Editor: Aaron Stell
Music: Elmer Bernstein
Cast: Natalie Wood (Angie Rossini), Steve McQueen (Rocky Papasano), Edie Adams (Barbie), Herschel Bernardi (Dominick Rossini), Harvey Lembeck (Julio Rossini), Mams Rossini (Penny Santon), Tom Bosley (Anthony Columbo)
Distributor: Paramount
102 minutes

BABY THE RAIN MUST FALL (1964)
Director: Robert Mulligan
Producer: **Alan J. Pakula**
Writer: Horton Foote (based on his play *The Traveling Lady*)
Photography: Ernest Laszlo
Editor: Aaron Stell
Music: Elmer Bernstein
Cast: Lee Remick (Georgette Thomas), Steve McQueen (Henry Thomas), Don Murray (Slim), Kimberly Block (Margaret Rose Thomas), Paul Fix (Judge Ewing), Ruth White (Miss Clara), Charles Watts (Mr. Tillman), Carol Veazie (Mrs. Tillman), Georgia Simmons (Miss Kate Dawson)
Distributor: Columbia
100 minutes

INSIDE DAISY CLOVER (1965)
Director: Robert Mulligan (with musical numbers staged by Herbert Ross)
Producer: **Alan J. Pakula**
Writer: Gavin Lambert (based on his novel)
Photography: Charles Lang
Editor: Aaron Stell
Music: Andre Previn
Cast: Natalie Wood (Daisy Clover), Robert Redford (Wade Lewis), Christopher Plummer (Raymond Swan), Ruth Gordon (Lucile Clover), Roddy McDowall (Walter Baines), Katharine Bard (Melora Swan)
Distributor: Warner Bros.
128 minutes

UP THE DOWN STAIRCASE (1967)
Director: Robert Mulligan
Producer: **Alan J. Pakula**

Writer: Tad Mosel (based on the novel by Bel Kaufman)
Photography: Joseph Coffey
Editor: Folmar Blangsted
Music: Fred Karlin
Cast: Sandy Dennis (Sylvia Barrett), Patrick Bedford (Paul Barringer), Eileen Heckart (Henrietta Pastorfield), Ruth White (Beatrice Schacter), Jean Stapleton (Sadie Finch), Sorrell Booke (Dr. Bester), Roy Poole (Mr. McHabe), Jeff Howard (Joe Ferone), Jose Rodriguez (Jose Rodriguez), Bel Kaufman (uncredited)
Distributor: Warner Bros.
124 minutes

THE STALKING MOON (1968)
Director: Robert Mulligan
Producer: **Alan J. Pakula**
Writer: Alvin Sargent (adaptation by Wendell Mayes; based on the novel by Theodore V. Olsen)
Photography: Charles Lang
Editor: Aaron Stell
Music: Fred Karlin
Cast: Gregory Peck (Sam Varner), Eva Marie Saint (Sarah Carver), Noland Clay (Sarah's son, known only as "boy"), Robert Forster (Nick Tana), Russell Thorsen (Ned)
Distributor: National General Pictures
109 minutes

THE STERILE CUCKOO (1969)
Director: **Alan J. Pakula**
Producer: **Alan J. Pakula**
Writer: Alvin Sargent (based on the novel by John Nichols)
Photography: Milton R. Krasner
Editor: Sam O'Steen, John W. Wheeler
Music: Fred Karlin
Cast: Liza Minnelli (Pookie Adams), Wendell Burton (Jerry Payne), Tom McIntyre (Charlie Schumacher), Austin Green (Pookie's father), Elizabeth Harrower (landlady)
Distributor: Paramount Pictures
107 minutes

KLUTE (1971)
Director: **Alan J. Pakula**
Producer: **Alan J. Pakula**

Writers: Andy Lewis and Dave Lewis
Photography: Gordon Willis
Editor: Carl Lerner
Music: Michael Small
Cast: Jane Fonda (Bree Daniels), Donald Sutherland (John Klute), Charles Cioffi (Peter Cable), Roy Scheider (Frank Ligourin), Dorothy Tristan (Arlyn Page), Betty Murray (Holly Gruneman), Rita Gam (Trina Gruneman), Vivian Nathan (psychiatrist), Morris Strasburg (Mr. Goldfarb)
Distributor: Warner Bros.
114 minutes

LOVE AND PAIN AND THE WHOLE DAMN THING (1972)
Director: **Alan J. Pakula**
Producer: **Alan J. Pakula**
Writer: Alvin Sargent
Photography: Geoffrey Unsworth
Editor: Russell Lloyd
Music: Michael Small
Cast: Maggie Smith (Lila Fisher), Timothy Bottoms (Walter Elbertson), Don Jaime de Mora y Aragon (the duke), Emiliano Redondo (the Spanish gentleman), Charles Baxter (Dr. Elbertson), Margaret Modlin (Mrs. Elbertson)
Distributor: Columbia Pictures
110 minutes

THE PARALLAX VIEW (1974)
Director: **Alan J. Pakula**
Producer: **Alan J. Pakula**
Writers: David Giler and Lorenzo Semple Jr. (based on the novel by Loren Singer)
Photography: Gordon Willis
Editor: John W. Wheeler
Music: Michael Small
Cast: Warren Beatty (Joseph Frady), Paula Prentiss (Lee Carter), Hume Cronyn (Bill Ritels), William Daniels (Austin Tucker), Kenneth Mars (Will Turner), Jim Davis (Senator George Hammond), Walter McGinn (Jack Younger), Anthony Zerbe (psychiatrist)
Distributor: Paramount Pictures
102 minutes

ALL THE PRESIDENT'S MEN (1975)
Director: **Alan J. Pakula**

Producer: Walter Coblenz
Writer: William Goldman (based on the book by Bob Woodward and Carl Bernstein)
Photography: Gordon Willis
Editor: Robert L. Wolfe
Music: David Shire
Cast: Robert Redford (Bob Woodward), Dustin Hoffman (Carl Bernstein), Jason Robards (Ben Bradlee), Jack Warden (Harry M. Rosenfeld), Martin Balsam (Howard Simons), Jane Alexander (the bookkeeper/Judy Hoback Miller), Stephen Collins (Hugh Sloan), Hal Holbrook ("Deep Throat")
Distributor: Warner Bros.
138 minutes

COMES A HORSEMAN (1977)
Director: **Alan J. Pakula**
Producers: Gene Kirkwood, Dan Paulson
Writer: Denis Lynton Clark
Photography: Gordon Willis
Editor: Marion Rothman
Music: Michael Small
Cast: Jane Fonda (Ella Connors), James Caan (Frank "Buck" Athearn), Jason Robards (J. W. "Jacob" Ewing), Richard Farnsworth (Dodger), Jim Davis (Julie Blocker), Mark Harmon (Billy Joe Meynert), James Keach (Emil Kroegh)
Distributor: United Artists
118 minutes

STARTING OVER (1979)
Director: **Alan J. Pakula**
Producers: James L. Brooks, **Alan J. Pakula**
Writer: James L. Brooks (based on the novel by Dan Wakefield)
Photography: Sven Nykvist
Editor: Marion Rothman
Music: Marvin Hamlisch
Cast: Burt Reynolds (Phil Potter), Jill Clayburgh (Marilyn Holmberg), Candice Bergen (Jessica Potter), Charles Durning (Mickey), Frances Sternhagen (Marva), Mary Kay Place (Marie), Austin Pendleton (Paul), Wallace Shawn (workshop member)
Distributor: Paramount Pictures
105 minutes

ROLLOVER (1981)
Director: **Alan J. Pakula**
Producer: Bruce Gilbert
Writer: David Shaber (based on a story by Howard Kohn, David Shaber, David Weir)
Photography: William Garroni, Giuseppe Rotunno
Editor: Evan A. Lottman
Music: Michael Small
Cast: Jane Fonda (Lee Winters), Kris Kristofferson (Hubbell Smith), Hume Cronyn (Maxwell Emery), Josef Sommer (Roy Lefcourt), Bob Gunton (Sal Naftari), Macon McCalman (Jerry Fewster)
Distributor: Warner Bros.
118 minutes

SOPHIE'S CHOICE (1982)
Director: **Alan J. Pakula**
Producers: Keith Barish, **Alan J. Pakula**
Writer: **Alan J. Pakula** (based on the novel by William Styron)
Photography: Nestor Almendros
Editor: Evan Lottman
Music: Marvin Hamlisch
Cast: Meryl Streep (Sophie Zawistowska), Kevin Kline (Nathan Landau), Peter MacNicol (Stingo), Josef Sommer (narrator/voice of older Stingo), Rita Karin (Yetta Zimmerman), Josh Mostel (Morris Fink), Stephen D. Newman (Larry Landau), Gunter Maria Halmer (Rudolph Hoess), Eugene Lipinski (Polish professor)
Distributors: Universal Pictures/Associated Film Distribution
151 minutes

DREAM LOVER (1984)
Director: **Alan J. Pakula**
Producers: Jon Boorstin, **Alan J. Pakula**
Writer: Jon Boorstin
Photography: Sven Nykvist
Editors: Trudy Ship, Angelo Corrao
Music: Michael Small
Cast: Kristy McNichol (Kathy Gardner), Ben Masters (Michael Hansen), Paul Shenar (Ben Gardner), Justin Deas (Kevin McCann), John McMartin (Martin), Gayle Hunnicutt (Claire)
Distributor: MGM/UA Entertainment Co.
104 minutes

ORPHANS (1987)
Director: **Alan J. Pakula**
Producer: **Alan J. Pakula**
Writer: Lyle Kessler (based on his play)
Photography: Donald McAlpine
Editor: Evan Lottman
Music: Michael Small
Cast: Albert Finney (Harold), Matthew Modine (Treat), Kevin Anderson (Philip), John Kellog (Barney)
Distributor: Lorimar Motion Pictures
115 minutes

SEE YOU IN THE MORNING (1988)
Director: **Alan J. Pakula**
Producers: **Alan J. Pakula**, Susan Solt
Writer: **Alan J. Pakula**
Photography: Donald McAlpine
Editor: Evan Lottman
Music: Michael Small
Cast: Jeff Bridges (Larry Livingstone), Alice Krige (Beth Goodwin), Farrah Fawcett (Jo Livingstone), Drew Barrymore (Cathy Goodwin), Lukas Haas (Petey Goodwin), David Dukes (Pete Goodwin), Frances Sternhagen (Neenie), Theodore Bikel (Bronie), Macaulay Culkin (Billy Livingstone)
Distributor: Warner Bros.
119 minutes

PRESUMED INNOCENT (1989)
Director: **Alan J. Pakula**
Producers: Sydney Pollack, Mark Rosenberg
Writers: Frank Pierson and **Alan J. Pakula** (based on the novel by Scott Turow)
Photography: Gordon Willis
Editor: Evan Lottman
Music: John Williams
Cast: Harrison Ford (Rusty Sabich), Brian Dennehy (Raymond Horgan), Raul Julia (Alejandro "Sandy" Stern), Gretta Scacchi (Carolyn Polhemus), Bonnie Bedelia (Barbara Sabich), Paul Winfield (Judge Larren L. Lyttle), John Spencer (Dan Lipranzer), Bradley Whitford (Quentin "Jamie" Kemp), Jeffrey Wright (prosecuting attorney)
Distributor: Warner Bros.
127 minutes

CONSENTING ADULTS (1992)
Director: **Alan J. Pakula**
Producers: **Alan J. Pakula**, David Permut
Writer: Matthew Chapman
Photography: Stephen Goldblatt
Editor: Sam O'Steen
Music: Michael Small
Cast: Kevin Kline (Richard Parker), Mary Elizabeth Mastrantonio (Priscilla Parker), Kevin Spacey (Eddie Otis), Rebecca Miller (Kay Otis), Forest Whittaker (David Duttonville), E. G. Marshall (George Gutton), Kimberly McCullough (Lori Parker)
Distributor: Buena Vista Pictures
95 minutes

THE PELICAN BRIEF (1993)
Director: **Alan J. Pakula**
Producers: Pieter Jan Brugge, **Alan J. Pakula**
Writer: **Alan J. Pakula** (based on the novel by John Grisham)
Photography: Stephen Goldblatt
Editors: Tom Rolf, Trudy Ship
Music: James Horner
Cast: Julia Roberts (Darby Shaw), Denzel Washington (Gray Grantham), Sam Shepard (Thomas Callahan), John Heard (Gavin Verheek), Tony Goldwyn (Fletcher Coal), James B. Sikking (Denton Voyles), Robert Culp (the president), Stanley Tucci (Khamel), Hume Cronyn (Justice Rosenberg), John Lithgow (Smith Keane), William Atherton (Bob Gminski), Cynthia Nixon (Alice Stark)
Distributor: Warner Bros.
141 minutes

THE DEVIL'S OWN (1997)
Director: **Alan J. Pakula**
Producer: Lawrence Gordon, Robert F. Colesberry
Writers: David Aaron Cohen, Vincent Patrick, Kevin Jarre, and (uncredited) Robert Mark Kamen (from a story by Jarre)
Photography: Gordon Willis
Editor: Tom Rolf, Dennis Virkler
Music: James Horner
Cast: Harrison Ford (Tom O'Meara), Brad Pitt (Frankie McGuire), Natascha McElhone (Megan Doherty), Margaret Colin (Sheila O'Meara), Ruben Blades

(Edwin Diaz), Treat Williams (Billy Burke), Julia Stiles (Bridget O'Meara), George Hearn (Peter Fitzsimmons), Mitchell Ryan (Jim Kelly)
Distributor: Columbia Pictures
111 minutes

Appearances

Pakula did an abundance of interviews for bloggers and other commentators, many of them available on-line. He also made numerous TV appearances on talk shows, such as *The Dick Cavett Show* (November 13, 1978, and September 26, 1986/PBS) and *Charlie Rose* (October 14, 1992, and January 5, 1994/PBS), as well as on current affairs programs and in documentaries. The key documentaries are listed below.

KLUTE IN NEW YORK: A BACKGROUND FOR SUSPENSE (1971)
Director: Elliot Geisinger
Writer: Jay Ansen
Producer: Michael Midlin Jr.
Photography: Lou St. Andres
Editor: Ron Morante
With: Jane Fonda, Rita Gam, **Alan J. Pakula**, Donald Sutherland, Gordon Willis
Distributor: Warner Home Video (Featured on the 2002 DVD release for *Klute*)
8 minutes

PRESSURE AND THE PRESS: THE MAKING OF *ALL THE PRESIDENT'S MEN* (1976)
Producers: Bill Cox, Dave Gilbert, Andrew J. Kuehn
With: Bob Woodward, Carl Bernstein, Ben Bradlee, Robert Redford, Dustin Hoffman, **Alan J. Pakula**, Jane Alexander, Hal Holbrook
Distributor: Warner Bros. (This short making-of documentary is included on the two-disc "Special Edition" DVD for *All the President's Men* released in 2006)
10 minutes

DEATH DREAMS OF MORNING (1997)
Director: Charles Kiselyak
Writer: Charles Kiselyak
Producer: Charles Kiselyak
Editor: Simeon Hutner
With: Michael Berenbaum, Silvia Grohs Martin, Marvin Hamlisch, Kevin Kline, Peter MacNicol, **Alan J. Pakula**, Meryl Streep, William Styron

(This making-of documentary is included on the Artisan Entertainment DVD of *Sophie's Choice*)
53 minutes

FEARFUL SYMMETRY (1998)
Director: Charles Kiselyak
Producer: Charles Kiselyak
Photography: Robert Jaye
Editor: Denise Anne Cochran
With: Horton Foote, Robert Mulligan, **Alan J. Pakula**, Gregory Peck, Phillip Alford, Mary Badham, Elmer Bernstein, Brock Peters, Robert Duvall
Distributor: Universal Studios Home Video (This film can be found on the "Special Edition" DVD for *To Kill a Mockingbird*)
90 minutes

ALAN PAKULA: GOING FOR TRUTH (2019)
Director: Matthew Miele
Producers: Anne Chertoff, Matthew Miele, Michael Weismann
Photography: James Mac Edgerton, Justin Bare
Editor: Matthew Miele
Music: Earl Rose
With: **Alan J. Pakula**, James L. Brooks, Annette Insdorf, Kevin Kline, Jane Fonda, Robert Redford, Meryl Streep, James L. Brooks, Harrison Ford, Candice Bergen, Carl Bernstein, Jeff Bridges
Production Company: Qe Deux
98 minutes

CITIZEN JANE, L'AMERIQUE SELON FONDA (2020)
Director: Florence Platarets
Producers: David Coujard, Emilie de Jong, Isabelle Mestre
Editor: Khalid Mamoun
Music: Matteo Locasciulli
With: Jane Fonda, Henry Fonda, Tom Hayden, **Alan J. Pakula**, Sydney Pollack, Donald Sutherland, Ted Turner, Roger Vadim
Distributor: Arte Distribution
53 minutes

Alan J. Pakula: Interviews

Unlikely Elements: Alan J. Pakula in an Interview with Gordon Gow

Gordon Gow / 1972

From *Films and Filming* 19, no. 3, December 1972. Reprinted by permission of Stephen Gow.

Having impressed a number of us with his direction of *The Sterile Cuckoo*, which was known in the UK by the less intriguing title of *Pookie*, Alan J. Pakula proceeded to make a deservedly big splash with *Klute*. In Europe, he has completed his newest directorial work, *The Widower* [eventually released as *Love and Pain and the Whole Damn Thing*], with Maggie Smith and Timothy Bottoms.

And before any of that, of course, he was known with gratitude as the producer of a heap of films, mostly very good, that were directed by Robert Mulligan. With sufficient levity to keep it cool, Pakula concedes that one good reason for him to turn director has been the habit of critics and others to associate a film firmly with the director rather than the producer. At the same time, he obviously got along well with Mulligan, or they would never have worked together over a whole decade, beginning so powerfully with *Fear Strikes Out* in 1957.

"Bob directed the films," Pakula explains, "and I know enough about directing, from my work in the theater, so that I never could believe in two directors on a set. I would work a great deal on the preparation of the film. I'd work very closely with the writer; and often I'd be closely involved in the selection of the material from the start. In the case of *To Kill a Mockingbird*, for example, it was I who brought the material to Bob. And very often, while I was working with the writers on the next script, Bob would be directing another film.

"There'd be the casting, the visual concept of the film, the basic production decisions: I'd be in on all of that very closely, too. The physical style of it concerned me. But once Bob got on the sound stage with the actors, they were his. Very often, I would see the daily rushes before the actors would, or even before Bob would. But I'd say to the actors, 'Don't expect me to comment to you about the film—any criticism of your work should come from the director.' It's like having an analyst or a father—it's very hard to have two. If you divide authority when you're dealing with actors, then you're just creating chaos.

"I would also spend very little time on the set, unlike some producers who like to hover over the director. You see, by the time one gets on the set, a producer has done a very big chunk of his work, and at that point his job really is to give a perspective that the director may not have. The producer then is that much further away from it, so he does have a different perspective.

"I would not like to sit on the set and know everything that Bob did to reach a certain result. I might not even know what he was trying to reach *for* at times. I would see the dailies cold, and then I would talk with him about them, whether my reaction was positive or negative or whatever. Sometimes he would reshoot something as a result of that—and our conversations after dailies would also have an effect upon the shooting to come.

"But we always had those conversations alone together, sometimes at lunch, sometimes at the end of a day. Therefore, the actors didn't hear me. They worked with only one director. But when it came to postproduction and to cutting, I would again quite often work very closely with Bob and the editor. But finally I think that one either directs or one doesn't direct. And I decided I'd become a director.

"There are some producers who do feel that they can half direct. They can sit on the set and kibitz the director and kibitz the actors. I think that's enormously destructive. There aren't really many creative producers who can give their directors the chance to talk to somebody they can relate to, and give them second thoughts that may be valuable. That depends also on having a close relationship with the director. Not necessarily a close social relationship—I don't mean that—but an understanding and a rapport, some sense of the man's talents and some sense of the man himself. And indeed, without being sentimental about it, some liking and respect for the man.

"Bob came to cinema from television. And a lot of people think I was in the television, too—just because he was. But I wasn't. I was in the front office at Paramount Studios, and I was assistant head of production. I'd been there from the age of twenty-two, and by then I was twenty-eight and feeling that I was getting older. And it was at this time that a book came in that I believed in. It was *Fear Strikes Out*. I said I wanted to produce it, and they gave it to me."

The book was the autobiography of Jim Piersall, a baseball player, telling of the drive imposed upon him by his father, the constant injunctions to try harder and harder to become good at the game. This led to a mental breakdown and psychiatric treatment. In the film, son and father were played by Anthony Perkins and Karl Malden. Pakula was fascinated by the story.

"It was dealing with psychosis in terms of the American hero, not in terms of somebody the audience would consider more obvious, like an artist or some creative person, but the great American athletic hero. I thought there would be more chance of audiences relating to this, in a more immediate and specific way.

"I saw Tony Perkins in some dailies from *Friendly Persuasion* [1956], which he was doing with William Wyler at that time. I signed him for the film. And I interviewed several directors, and Mulligan was one of these—a young director. The studio wanted me to use him. We'd never met before, although I'd seen some of his work on television. I met several young theatrical directors in New York and interviewed them, too, and became quite friendly with all of them. And I met Bob briefly. It was a very pleasant meeting, as those half-hour meetings go. I could see he was an intelligent man, and I knew I liked his work.

"And then, after that, several months went by before I made a decision. The screenplay was being written. And I kept watching work that Tony did. He did several television shows. And I was a bit concerned because I felt he'd got mannered—and this was probably the insecurity of a young actor who was just starting out. I got a little nervous. And then I saw Tony in a television play that Bob directed—a live TV show, with Kim Stanley in it too [*Joey* (1956), an episode of *Goodyear Playhouse*]. And Tony was just marvelous: all the mannerisms were gone. It really was a dramatic change, and I thought it must be on account of the director.

"Tony flew back to California the next day, and I called him into my office and asked him how he liked working with Mulligan, and he said it had been an absolutely wonderful experience for him. So I said, 'How would you like him to direct the film?' And he said he'd be all in favor. So I flew to New York the next day, and Bob and I talked some more, and that's how we started working together."

There had been other careers in Pakula's mind from time to time. Once he had thought of becoming a psychiatrist. The dramatic arts, however, took precedence. He was born in New York City and studied for his BA degree at Yale. His father had wanted him to go into the family business, which was a printing and advertising firm, but the theater attracted him, and he majored in drama at Yale as well as studying the liberal arts. For a time, he worked in the cartoon section at Warner Bros. After this, he went to the Circle Theatre in Hollywood, where he directed Jean Anouilh's *Antigone* and his work drew the attention of Don Hartman, who was then at MGM and soon afterward at Paramount. There he served his front office days, and, even when he had begun to produce, he managed to intersperse a few excursions to Broadway to work on various theater productions: *Comes a Day* with Judith Anderson and George C. Scott, *Laurette* with Judy Holliday, *There Must Be a Pony* with Myrna Loy, and *Blood and Thunder* with Mary Martin.

The success of the liaison with Mulligan was richly affirmed by their second film together, *To Kill a Mockingbird*, from the novel by Harper Lee with Gregory Peck in the lead: virtually an antiviolence essay, notable for its avoidance of explicit violence, as well as for being an emotive attack upon racial prejudice. Some thought it oversentimental.

"I've met some people who felt it was corny," says Pakula. "What a number of people resented—and fortunately they were not in the majority—was that it dealt with a childhood that most of us have never had. Whatever the terrors, these were children who belonged somewhere. And in their first confrontation with evil, they had a father figure who represented what most of us would like to have had and probably didn't. The whole small-town upbringing is almost of another time. So for people who have had rather more rootless childhoods, it seemed corny. Yet it was very true to much of the author Harper Lee's own childhood.

"Personally, I had a childhood that was neither abnormally insecure nor exceedingly secure. There were areas of insecurity, but it was a rather solid and middle-class feeling of belonging. I lived in a comparatively small town, but just outside of New York City, so it was quite different from the Alabama setting of *To Kill a Mockingbird*. But of course, I could recognize truth in that story; and there were certain things I could relate to, some on a real level and some on my own fantasy level. I went down, and I met the author's father, who was over eighty then. And the whole sense of place and time and people was very accurate."

The character played by Peck was Atticus Finch, a wise and exceedingly tolerant lawyer in a small town, a widower with children to raise, teaching them the simple truths like the wrongness of killing a mockingbird, which does nobody any harm. But Atticus himself will take up a gun to shoot down a mad dog, and he will incline his children eventually to be neither afraid nor derisive in their attitude to the troubled Boo Radley who lives next door.

Bravely attempting the impossible, Atticus in his legal capacity will defend a black man who has been accused, wrongly, of raping a white girl. This was beautifully filmed. In analyzing why it should have met with occasional resistance, Pakula says, "If you deal with a character and indicate a kind of simplicity and a kind of strength, and a capacity to love without self-dramatization and hysteria, it's questioned—possibly because we live in rather hysterical times, possibly because we live in an enormously doubting time. But there are certain truths. There are certain people who are better adjusted, happier, and more giving and stronger than others. It may be unfashionable to deal with them, but I find it enormously appealing. If you're dealing with parent-and-child relationships, this is a tremendously personal thing, and people are much more likely to accuse you of sentimentalizing there than in other subjects."

Love With the Proper Stranger, which followed, with Natalie Wood and Steve McQueen, was considered fairly advanced in its day—1963—primarily because of its episode with a scruffy abortionist. "I don't think that either Bob or myself saw it as a daring or advanced picture, although it's true that most films at that time didn't mention things like abortion—least of all a film that was essentially a romantic comedy.

"It really was an attempt at a modern version of a 1930s kind of film: a love story of two very unlikely people. The great danger of that film, when we were making it, was that it starts out rather dramatically, and there is comedy along the way. It gets to the abortion—which is a terrifying scene, really almost a horror scene—and then from that goes into almost straight romantic comedy. We were always concerned about the welding of this and the synthesis of it, and indeed whether it would ever work. It seemed to work for a lot of audiences, but we were always concerned about it.

"I have a welding problem right now with *The Widower*. I am attracted to welding unlikely elements together: like doing something that seems rather tragic and then seeing the comedy in it. *The Widower* is a romantic story that could be done rather tragically and rather somberly, but it's done with many farce elements. That's what interests me about the material, and in a sense that was the part of the interest of *Love with the Proper Stranger*.

"I never see these earlier films again. I hate to see them on television. As long as there's something I can do about a film, I love to keep seeing it. But once it's out and finished, that's it for me. There's no more I can do about it. It would merely become an obsession. And I don't believe in living in the past, even if it's only the past of six months ago. When one thing is finished, you go on to the next.

"Of course, I love looking at other people's old pictures. Before I did *Klute*, I ran a lot of old Hitchcock pictures. And I realized when I directed *Klute* that I was going against one of the tenets in the Truffaut-Hitchcock book,[1] which is that you don't try to do a character study in a melodrama. *Klute*, of course, is a violation of that. Hitchcock's interests and mine are in many ways very, very different. His attitude toward actors is nothing like mine. He's a great games player; and I have a hunch that, if he could do something for real, he'd rather fake it to make it look real, because he just loves to be a magician—that's his delight. But you can just run a Hitchcock film silent, and just watch it for visual storytelling.

"The ones I saw before making *Klute* included *Notorious* [1946], in which the Ingrid Bergman character is, in fact, more complex than he usually deals with. I saw *Strangers on a Train* [1951], which one major critic has said is his best American film, but I don't agree with that at all, although a lot of the work in it is marvelous. But the merry-go-round thing at the end just doesn't work for me. I didn't see *Spellbound* [1945] this time around, but I have. Likewise, *Rebecca* [1940], which is damn good, made with such style."

It seems moderately surprising that Pakula should go into this kind of near-classic recall for the preparatory phases of a work as ultracontemporary as *Klute*. It marks a very important place in his career. The association with Mulligan, while somewhat intermittent because Mulligan occasionally worked with other producers, had been solid and in the main rewarding. *Love with the Proper Stranger* had been followed by one of Steve McQueen's best films, *Baby the Rain Must Fall*. Then came *Inside Daisy Clover*, *Up the Down Staircase*, and *The Stalking Moon*.

In branching out into direction with *The Sterile Cuckoo*, Pakula was still roughly within the ambiance of several of the films he had made with Mulligan. The emotive element was recognizably similar, whereas *Klute* would be something rather apart. Nevertheless, *The Sterile Cuckoo* was markedly individual as a director's film.

Liza Minnelli was especially notable as the girl called Pookie, eaten away inside by her insecurity and her ugly-duckling complex, but presenting a prankish demeanor to the world and being extremely persistent about her designs upon the college student played by Wendell Burton. Despite its high rate of charm and its superbly controlled pathos, however, *The Sterile Cuckoo* was not a widespread success outside the USA.

"The critical reaction was, by and large, good but mixed," Pakula says. "From the audience point of view in the States, it was surprisingly successful. It grossed over six million dollars. But with the exception of some countries in South America, and a fairly nice reception in Japan, it really didn't do well over the world. Nothing comparable to what it did in America.

"I don't think the change of title in the UK to *Pookie* was a good idea: I never liked *The Sterile* Cuckoo as a title, but *Pookie* is worse. I don't know that I'd say *Klute* was a better film, but there were certain things about *Klute* that were enormous advances for me as a director, in terms of visual storytelling and use of the camera, and in terms of creating a mood visually. I felt that technically it was a much more skilled film.

"I'm still surprised that I did that film, because *The Sterile Cuckoo* is more obviously something I would do. *Klute* was a bit outside me. It made new demands on me. But *The Sterile Cuckoo* was my first film, and Liza's first starring part, and we were both thrilled to be doing it. It was a joyful experience. So I have great nostalgia for it."

As to the visual storytelling of *Klute*, it came nearest to the classic suspense precepts—and not necessarily only of Hitchcock—when Jane Fonda was at the mercy of the killer in the deserted workshop of the clothing manufacturer. The creepy perambulations of the girl, the glimpse of the murderer through plastic:

these were potent. The climax of the sequence with the body hurtling through a high window and leaving a big hole was possibly near to the Tom-and-Jerry kind of imagery, and Pakula allows that he "was very nervous that it might be," but it worked in the context of a film that blended its assimilated influences quite splendidly with the freshness of its overall approach.

"It's always a question of how far you can go. That scene we've been talking about didn't take place in that setting in the original script. The murderer came to her flat and sat there and confessed everything, and then he took out a gun and shot himself. Well, guns and all that did not seem particularly interesting to me. And the device of using the tape machine was not in the script. And then going out the window . . . well, I didn't want to deal with guns, and I didn't want to deal with knives. And, also, this character is a very enclosed man, and I kept photographing him through windows and in his strange kind of dead office, encased in that glass office up there on top of the world so that the rest of the people are just ants. So when he goes through a window—it's as if he breaks through in a way—and at least that melodramatic end has a kind of catharsis for the character, and some kind of inevitability."

Pakula's aversion to guns and knives is possibly a limitation for a director who might want to broach suspense again, or it could be an asset. "I didn't want guns because I think that filming shoot-'em-ups is very tough to do. It's been done too much. And also, I suppose I'm repulsed by weapons anyway. I mean I've seen the knifing scene in *Psycho* [1960] several times. It's a film I didn't like when I first saw it, although I admired the work. You can't help but admire that. But I still find it a horrifying film, and I'm not even sure it's not an immoral film. And the knifing of Janet Leigh—well, the skill is so great that numerous directors have run that sequence on Moviolas just because it is so brilliantly designed and cut. But, on the other hand, the end that is achieved is an orgiastic murder; and it really becomes almost like a man having an orgasm—murder as a sexual act. Very well done as that, and, for me, horrifying because of that.

"Now, although *Klute* deals with distorted sexual behavior, and even in the case of the heavy it deals with sadistic sexual behavior, I was very frightened of romanticizing—or sentimentalizing—sadism. If you think about it, you see very little violence in *Klute*. You hear murder. You don't see it. And partly that's because I'm much more interested in the actual terror, in the danger. But I was not interested in showing a literal violent act. I think we're just obsessed with that today. And you can so easily glorify it, especially in this kind of a film. I do not want to dramatize violence as a sensual act.

"In the whole of your audience, there may be five people who may be turned on by that, and I really don't want any part of that turn-on to violence. Film is such a powerful medium. A certain naïve or deeply disturbed person, or a very young person, is my responsibility if I'm making a film that deals with sexuality and violence. In *Klute*, there is not only a lack of literal depiction of violence, although it's talked about and indicated, but there is also a comparative lack of the actual sexual act.

"There are a lot of words, for a particular reason. It was the story of a woman who was obsessed with the need to seduce men. She was almost destroyed by that compulsion. And the words she used were part of her siren call. I indicate that more literally when she's going out on dates, when she's faking sexuality. When there's real sexuality with *Klute*, I show almost nothing. That was deliberate because you've seen the girl faking orgasms in pretense, but when it came to the real thing, there was no need for that kind of acting."

Turning to *The Widower*, Pakula explains, "It deals with two unlikely lovers. One is a young American boy who has withdrawn from life to a great extent, who refuses to compete. He has an enormously dumb and academic father. He has become seemingly very passive, disorganized, un-put-together. At the rather tender age of eighteen, he just seems to have given up. And on a bus tour of Spain, he meets a rather rigid, almost Victorian English spinster, a woman of great spine and discipline, with an enormous will, but who, in her own way, has withdrawn from life as much as he has. The one thing they share is their fear of being hurt. They're both afraid of exposure to life. In a sense, they are both virgins. And the film is about the coming together of these two unlikely people."

Born in Australia, **Gordon Gow** was a regular contributor to *Films and Filming* in the UK from the 1950s to the '80s. He also worked extensively as a broadcaster and is the author of *Suspense in the Cinema* (1968) and *Hollywood in the Fifties* (1971). He died in 2000.

Note

1. François Truffaut (with the collaboration of Helen G. Scott), *Hitchcock* (New York: Simon and Schuster, 1967).

Klute Review

Tom Milne / 1971

From *Sight and Sound*, Autumn 1971, 220–21. Reprinted by permission.

Editor's note: While film reviews are not the usual province of the Conversations Series, this one has been included because Pakula addresses points made in it during his conversation with Milne.

Levels upon levels upon levels. Like all good films, Alan Pakula's *Klute* tells several stories at once, not so much in layers which peel away one by one to reveal hidden depths as in parallel steps leading relentlessly up to the dark at the top of the stairs.

First story, and mainspring of the action: a highly respectable Pennsylvania businessman has disappeared, the only clue to the mystery being the fact that he apparently wrote an obscene letter to a call girl in New York, a slender lead which sets private eye John Klute (Donald Sutherland) off on his trail through the labyrinth.

Second story: the call girl, Bree Daniel (Jane Fonda), seriously determined to change her ways, is not only taking acting lessons but undergoing psychoanalysis because she is honest enough to admit that her wishes and her subconscious drives are very different things.

Third story, and this one sustaining many dimensions: the reverberation of the moment when Bree's guard of dry self-analysis drops to reveal something much more vulnerable, and she confesses, "You'll laugh, but I'm afraid of the dark." Initially, she tells Klute this because she has been frightened by a sinister, unseen presence on the roof; but it also underlies her nervous shying away from involvement when she realizes that Klute's wayward passion for her is beginning to change into tenderness; and finally, in the unstated, secret motif of the film, it illuminates her failure to realize that this love, which she at last dares to accept, *is* the darkness she fears.

Tangentially, at least, with its superb chiaroscuro apprehension (the color is perfectly dominated) of the darker, more mysterious corners of human perversities and bizarre locations, *Klute* seems to me much more authentically Chandlerish than all those films from *Harper* [1966] onwards which tried so consciously, and self-consciously, to reproduce the idiosyncratic world of the 1940s thriller. Perhaps because it doesn't try so hard. But more, I think, because it realizes that things have changed so that, to quote the Godard of *Le petit soldat* [1963], "The time for action is past . . . the time for reflection is beginning."

So *Klute* begins on a note of contemplative obsession. First, in a scene of mute, suspended puzzlement which exudes a sense of lingering trauma akin to Bertolucci's *Spider's Strategy* [1970], the missing man's family and friends are seen transfixed at a dinner-table with one empty place speaking volumes at the end, while the facts of the case are quietly recapped by a police lieutenant. Then come the credits, hypnotically superimposed over a miniature tape-recorder with a girl's voice droning on and on, quietly, obscenely, tantalizingly, half revealing another mystery one cannot quite grasp.

Almost immediately, strong plot-hooks are thrown out, establishing swiftly and elliptically that Bree, having failed to get a modelling job she has auditioned for, has gone back to prostitution, and that she is to be the first point of attack for Klute, who agrees to take the case because he happens to be a friend of the family, and because the police have failed to get anywhere in six months of investigation.

The wheels start turning for a splendidly traditional film noir: the dark, shadowy figure, sometimes heard but mostly sensed, behind windows and on rooftops, keeping a sinister watch on Bree; the seedy parade of pimps and madame, and the two call girls, one dead and the other a junkie, also soon to die, who may be the key to the mystery; the inevitable showdown in a dark, deserted tailor's shop with the homicidal maniac stalking his victim from a camouflage of headless tailor's dummies. All fine, rousing stuff, but, as the film progresses, one realizes that not only are these plot-hooks not grappling, they were never designed to grapple. Or at least, not in the traditional narrative sense.

The giveaway is an extraordinary scene—voyeur observing voyeur—when Klute, unable to persuade Bree to talk about her relationship with the missing man (whom she can't remember anyway), rents a room in the same apartment block so as to keep her under observation. Hearing her make an assignation, evidently with a client, he follows and watches through the window in bafflement at the strange and tender little charade which ensues. The "client" is a dignified, white-bearded old gentleman, and, as he sits at his desk gravely listening like a child being rewarded with his favorite fairytale, she tells him the story of an enchanted romance of which he is evidently the hero, she the heroine, at the same time performing a chaste striptease.

Despite the fact that, as Bree later explains, she was simply indulging an old man whose only pleasure now is in paying to see her body, the way the scene is presented leaves no room for sordid realities. Grace of movement and emotion make it a moment of magic, burying all other implications until one is left with an impression of pure innocence. And it is this innocence he has glimpsed which makes Klute fall in love with her, just as it makes her baulk at committing herself—she is too honest to deny any responsibility for her way of life—until she is finally and reluctantly persuaded by Klute's persistence that even she may love and be loved.

But just as Bree can never really solve the problem of the subconscious sexual drives which made her a call girl, so Klute can never really solve his problem, for precisely the same reason. True, he establishes the facts of the case, unearthing the murderer and the reasons why he killed the missing man and the two call girls, but only because the object of his own desires is threatened.

After witnessing the scene with the old man, Klute becomes obsessed with Bree to the exclusion of all else; and obsessed in a very real sense, as she half guesses when she wonders aloud how he can possibly love her after seeing her stripped down to her depths of fear and degradation.

By the end, the private eye and the girl are in each other's arms. But all is not quite as it once was with Bogart and Bacall, since what we have been watching is not the unraveling of a mystery but the creation of one. The i's are mercilessly dotted in the penultimate scene when the unhappy pervert-murderer, just before throwing himself out of the window, accuses Bree in a long soliloquy, not so much of self-justification as of explanation, which calls as its chief witness the same voice, teasing and tantalizing with sexual provocation, which was heard over the credits. You, he tells her, girls like you, you make us what we are. He then dies as Klute makes the traditional cavalry charge to the rescue, and Bree is safe again . . . or has John Klute taken his place?

The question remains unanswered by the film unless one goes back (and why not, since the film's construction is clearly circular, with Klute perhaps reported missing from his office . . .) to a remarkable earlier scene which then had a strange reverberation out of all proportion to its context in the film. Bree is alone in her room, preparing to go to bed. Clearly ill at ease and evidently going through the motions of a ritual, she lights a candle, sits down at the table, inhales deeply on a marijuana cigarette, and softly begins to croon a revivalist hymn to herself. The telephone rings: it is an obscene call, and she huddles even more deeply into herself. And as the camera moves out from close-up to frame the little pool of comforting illumination in the surrounding darkness (one is irresistibly reminded of the scene in *Night of the Hunter* [1955] where Mitchum and Gish, hunter and hunted, join each other in a hymn), the whole ritual is revealed as an incantation to keep fear at bay.

Fear of what? Fear of the dark, of course, the dark world we live in, the dark fancies of the human mind, the dark of the moon which is adumbrated in a love which hangs on a knife-edge of ambivalence. Truly, *Klute* is a film noir, one of black, tender despair for human relationships. It proves Jane Fonda to be a superb actress and Alan Pakula a director to be watched very closely indeed.

The prince of English film criticism, **Tom Milne** wrote regularly for *Sight and Sound*, the *Monthly Film Bulletin*, the *Observer*, and the *Times*, as well as authoring a series of books about filmmakers. He died in 2005.

"Not a Garbo or a Gilbert in the Bunch": Alan Pakula Talks to Tom Milne

Tom Milne / 1972

From *Sight and Sound*, Spring 1972. Reprinted by permission.

For several years, Alan J. Pakula was simply a name familiar from the credits of Robert Mulligan films. Born in 1928, he went to Hollywood, after graduating at Yale, as assistant to the head of Warner Bros. cartoons. There his stage work at the Circle Theatre brought a move to MGM as an apprentice in production. With Paramount, in 1957, he produced his first film, Robert Mulligan's *Fear Strikes Out,* and continued the association through *To Kill a Mockingbird, Love with the Proper Stranger, Baby the Rain Must Fall, Inside Daisy Clover, Up the Down Staircase,* and *The Stalking Moon.* In 1969, *The Sterile Cuckoo* (*Pookie* in Britain) signaled the arrival of a new director. Last year came *Klute,* and the rest, as they say . . .

"I never wanted to be a producer. It was sheer accident, and I was passive about it for so long it bewilders me. There were a lot of satisfactions, of course, but I've always wanted to direct, ever since I was seventeen—and that's fairly young to feel a mission, get so close to it, and then avoid it or seem to avoid it until middle age is starting to set in.

"When I went to Yale and majored in drama there, I remember directing a one-act Chekhov farce. I was working with much older actors—well, they were about twenty-five or so, veterans back from the war, and I can still remember the enormous sense of exaltation. I had never felt that happy in my entire life. I used to leave rehearsals and go down the street with great goat-like leaps, like something from a Thomas Wolfe novel. It was extraordinary—I just delighted in working with actors.

"I also thought of being a psychoanalyst, I think because I am basically enormously curious about people. The difference between me then and now is that at that age I found it much easier to categorize people. Now, the more I know about them, the more sense of mystery I feel, and I don't have any desire to pigeonhole people that way. The curiosity exists for its own sake, and I think that's really why I'm a director. And there's also . . . I remember at seventeen the feeling that people were finding things in themselves they could not have found without me. I was a sort of catalytic agent, and it gave me an extraordinary . . . sense of power, I guess you'd say. I suppose at the age of seventeen I suddenly felt like a father figure, and it was probably important to me, having had a dominating father. Besides which it was just pure fun.

"At that point, I was more interested in theater than in films. In the academic world, films were looked down upon a bit. Quite different from today—I'm on the other side of a generation gap there. Now there are times when I almost wish that films weren't treated with quite such reverence.

"The director as star is a direct outgrowth of this whole new seriousness about films, and, while it is marvelously healthy sign for the cinema and a great compliment to the director, my concern is that it can lead to a certain kind of self-consciousness. It can lead to people with particular talents and gifts being taken seriously as intellectuals, when one may have little to do with the other. It can certainly encourage directors to a sense of self-importance that is not unlike the old Hollywood, where you had an image to protect once you were successful. So many of the best films were done because someone just wanted to do them, without worrying whether it was really important enough. John Ford, I think, said that the most important thing is to enjoy it.

"You're getting me at a time when I'm selecting my next film. . . . I think finally that whatever I do is for very personal reasons. When I did *Klute*, I did it because I was attracted to the theme, the chance to do that kind of melodrama, exploring that kind of girl, that kind of relationship and search; but I also knew it would make certain demands on me in terms of cinematic technique and visual storytelling and control, which I thought important for me in my second film as director. I felt that it ran the risk of looking like a piece of tabloid, that it could easily turn into a B-film. It was also a film I thought I was strangely cast for, and all this was part of the attraction.

"The film I've just done, *The Widower*, which is not finished yet, is actually one I started work on before *Klute*. And again, it's entirely different. It's a very tiny film—when I say tiny, I mean intimate. Whatever it is or isn't, I don't think it has a false sense of itself or tries to be more important than it is. I think as a director—and as a spectator—I value a sense of scale almost as much as anything. Perhaps it's a reaction to Hollywood, where scale means that if you spend more than X-amount on a picture, it's a big picture, and it's got to *look* big. I like to make films with a sense of proportion, the size that belongs to the subject, and that's something you have inside your head.

"I started out on *Klute* feeling that it couldn't be more different from *The Sterile Cuckoo*, which deals with a much more innocent world in terms of style and everything, and this was one of the reasons for doing it. But halfway through I suddenly realized—much to my surprise because I consider myself a fairly rational fellow about what I do—that in both films I was dealing with a rather repressed male who seems organized and orderly, who becomes involved with a compulsive but enormously alive girl who acts out all her neuroses, is exciting, has a certain kind of wit and hysterical freedom that he is incapable of, and who lights up his world and almost pulls him into her self-destruction. Now, Pookie Adams and Bree Daniels are very different ladies, and certainly Jerry Payne and John Klute are very different, but there is a kind of essence in them that is alike."

By Indirections . . .

"I hadn't really thought about the elliptical approach you mention as common to both films. But it's true. I *am* oblique. I think that has to do with my own nature. I like trying to do things which work on many levels because I think it is terribly important to give an audience a lot of things they may not get as well as those they will, so that finally the film does take on a texture and is not just simplistic communication.

"For instance, the reason for that first scene in *Klute*—the family gathering—is that we are going into a world where families do not exist, an underside of people without roots that seems to exist divorced from the whole middle-class society. I guess that's kind of Hitchcock—where do you start that is going to be the opposite? And for me the opposite was to start with families and Thanksgiving and people who belong together. It is also the only sunny scene in the film. Everything is simple. Then you cut to the same tableau in darkness with the empty chair. I wanted it to look almost posed, like family pictures, romanticized as you like to remember family celebrations. People against that glass wall, against sunlight and all that foliage, like a group of warm plants in the sun; then the darkness, and you go into a world where people are enclosed . . .

"Then later, when Bree Daniels sings that little hymn in her room . . . that was not planned, by the way; it was Jane Fonda relaxing between takes. We had tried several things for that scene, and I wasn't happy with any of them. They were reloading the camera, and she was sitting there smoking, off in her own world, and I suddenly heard her singing that hymn. I whirled round, and she looked at me and stopped. 'Oh, God,' she said, 'you want me to use that!' 'Yes,' I said, 'that's it, that's what we've been looking for.' It's one of my favorite things in the film because it's the moment when you really feel her vulnerability.

"The panic comes after, on the telephone; here it's a much more ordinary kind of vulnerability. Which interested me. Because when you have a girl who is psychologically disturbed, and you put her into this kind of melodramatic situation which is a perfect reason to be in a state of terror, then finding those moments when you see what that girl could be underneath, finding unhysterical, seemingly relaxed moments, is the hardest thing to do, and the most important for me. I'm not very interested in characters who come in at the top of their peak emotionally and stay there; but when I can sense that . . . sometimes almost a sleepy part of them . . . then, ah! they exist *outside* the story.

"Several people wanted me to cut that scene, saying I didn't need it. And from a storytelling point of view, indeed, the story still would have played. Nothing would have been lost, except the character. But there was something else. That hymn she sings is one most Americans sing at Thanksgiving time in grade school—middle-class American kids—and it represents a whole kind of middle-class upbringing.

"When Jane asked me why I wanted her to do it, I didn't really know. I just knew it was one of the great moments for me. But it not only linked with the opening shot, it was also right for Bree. Because her family is never discussed, where she came from. I did have stuff in the scenes with the psychiatrist where she revealed more about her background, but I didn't use it because I thought, oh boy, it's going to become a two-penny analysis. But there, in the midst of all this—you've just seen her pick up a trick, you've heard people talking about her bizarre way of life—there's this unexplained thing which is almost like a past life. It's like Bridey Murphy, something coming out of that girl which has nothing to do with prostitution, nothing to do with her present life. It comes out totally unconsciously when she's smoking pot.

"In *The Sterile Cuckoo*, I wanted to suggest, not too directly, that Pookie Adams was a girl who belongs nowhere. In the script, originally, there was a whole sequence on her campus. But now you never see her college. You see her in boarding-houses, in buses, in his college, always coming and going. The only world of hers you see is the cemetery, some place where she goes to fantasize by herself and where she takes Jerry after the disastrous visit to the bar. Even the scene with her father adds to that because they never say a word to each other.

"The most dangerous thing about the film is that it almost misleads the audience. Because the whole of the first part, with the exception of the prologue and a few interspersed moments, is done in the rhythms of comedy. So when you get half-way through with the scene where they go to bed together, the audience thinks, well, this is obviously a fun film. A tender comedy, I guess Hollywood would call it. But then it changes: it becomes a sad little story of first love and first failure, of the people who survive and those who don't. There are still funny things, but it slows down deliberately—it slows down; it slows down; and then it just stops.

"Now if the affair had ended melodramatically, if she'd really been pregnant and gone for an abortion, then a theatrical kind of thing could have taken over the comedy. But it wasn't that: the reality of that kind of affair for me was . . . something completely unformed. It died, and there was nothing left. Originally, there was a scene which Alvin Sargent had written—and which, to his credit, I liked more than he did. It was a big, bravura scene to which everything was leading, and I shot it but never used it because it violated everything we were doing with that film.

"The scene is the one where Pookie comes back to the boardinghouse, and Jerry realizes she must be there and goes in. In the film now, she breaks down, he stays the night, and then just takes her back to the bus, and that's it. In the script, and what we shot, there is a dissolve. It's the middle of the night. He wakes up to find her gone. He looks around; there's an empty bottle of sleeping pills on the dresser. He panics, and there's a hysterical scene which ends with her smiling and saying, 'April fool, Jerry!' She opens her hand, and there are all the pills. And suddenly this gentle boy starts to hit her and breaks down sobbing, and she says, 'OK Jerry, *uncle!*' She knows she's destroying him and doesn't want to go on.

It was a good scene, but it was too big for the picture; it brought it smashing up to a Kazan kind of climax (no disrespect intended) instead of just dying away. Once he doesn't love her anymore, it's as though he has no right to express his anger. And the scene where he finally tells her he wants to leave her is one of my favorite moments in the film because she doesn't do anything. She just has her hand over her mouth and she looks at him, says nothing, and drives away.

"We're back again, in a sense, with the scale thing because I wanted *The Sterile Cuckoo* to have, again without stating it, a sense of looking back. The montage bits you don't like are part of that, an attempt at a kind of scene from memory. But I suppose they are Lelouchy. I feel the film gets unspecific and generally sentimental in those areas.

"Originally, the script told the story in flashback with voice-over, but I never shot that. It was based on a first novel by a young man just out of college and reminiscing about it, and I was trying to capture that sense of looking back. I would never have tried anything like the lyrical montage after the motel scene if I'd had two obviously film-romantic characters like Anouk Aimée and Trintignant. With this boy and girl in this romantic situation, I felt I could get away with it. But I forced it, perhaps. At my best, I'm oblique; at my worst, it slams in.

"On the other hand, the ending, the bus, that scene with the car, all that works for me; it *is* clouded with memory. And that motel with the funny little church next to it . . . it's almost like Land's End, a place made up by Pookie Adams. It's a world that boy would never find again. I don't know if you realize it but you never see a city in that movie . . . I didn't want to show any place that boy was going to go when he was an adult. In *Klute*, on the other hand, once you get into the city, you never see anything but the sense of being trapped in it."

A World off Balance

"I guess I'm attracted to a certain kind of limitation in the canvas, to films that take place in a limited world. With *Klute*, I cut off many of the compositions, reaching after very nervous compositions with Gordon Willis, the cameraman. On our first meeting, I said to him, 'One of the biggest problems of this film is going to be that we are using Panavision, and I don't want any open space. I want a sense of verticals. I want a sense of being off balance, people on the edge of the room, people constricted.'

"For Bree's apartment, George Jenkins originally designed three little rooms. I said, let's yank all that and just have a tunnel: I wanted her at the end of a tunnel. I also wanted it unfinished. Because you're getting her at a transitional period: she's halfway in and halfway out; she's nowhere. It's not the apartment she would have had two years ago when she was fully committed to the call-girl life. Nor is it the other . . . I mean, if she designed the apartment she'd like to have, it probably wouldn't be like this, and it probably wouldn't reflect her at all. This flat is not a cozy home, and one of the strange things about it for me is that here's a girl, she's very frightened, and yet she's in a rooftop apartment. There's a sort of ambivalence about the danger. Part of her walks right into it, is attracted to it, and the other part protects herself with five locks on the door. Part of her is trying to make it a home, but the other part is saying, 'Oh, I'll never finish it.'

"Again there were throwaway ideas in that. The fact that there was a patch of exposed brickwork. Stylish young New Yorkers will tear out the walls and go to the natural brick, because it's handsome. Obviously she started. She clearly has taste, and everything she has in there, in its own funny way, has a kind of taste. But nothing quite goes together; nothing is finished. The idea of the shawl put up over the bed as a canopy was Jane's . . . I'm not interested in puppets. I encourage actors like mad because I want their ideas and I can use them.

"She also wanted to live in that set and she did, in the studio up in Harlem, for three nights I think. I had her order all the books to help her find the character, and she put up the John F. Kennedy picture because I introduced her to some call girls and they all had one. She also ordered all the food in that ice box, mostly health foods. Again this is mostly throwaway, but these girls can be mainlining, and there they are saying, 'Yeah, but you got any wheat germ? I don't eat those nonorganic foods.' There are these rather comic attempts to take care of themselves and bring a certain order into their lives.

"Anyway, I wanted that sense of walls, of being able to pull back and have that girl trapped at the end of a tunnel, the sense of being locked in. When I first showed the film at the studio, one of the executives, a rather bright man, said, 'Well, the trouble with the film, Alan, is that it's claustrophobic. You've got to get some more wide-angle shots; you've got to let the audience breathe a little.' And I said no. 'I know this is not a cheap picture, but you're not going to get the whole screen for your money.'

"Even that garment place we found—it's a real location—has an unusually low ceiling, and it's very, very long. Again that was terribly important, although I wanted a quite different effect there. In a curious way, that setting for me was very romantic . . . the old patches of cloth and the sewing machines, all kind of silhouetted. It turns into terror at the end, but it starts out as a strange sort of romance in there. So much of the film up to that point is shot in a very cold way. Even, for example, the scene where she picks up the first trick. We shot that in a real hotel room.

"We could have built a set, but I wanted to get a sense of being forced into not having angles, of being forced to do a sort of cinéma-vérité photography. Well, to go from that kind of cold reality to that dress place, even going up in that elevator to begin with—which becomes terrifying at the end—is rather a funny, eccentric thing, and it's almost like being pulled into a storybook world. In the original screenplay by Andy and David Lewis, that scene was there, but the denouement took place in her apartment. The denouement was also quite different because there were no tape recordings, no recording of the murder. But there was that scene where she went and undressed for that old man; and that's when I thought, 'I'm going to do this film.'

"Jane asked me why I was so interested in that scene, and it's because it shows what essentially should be a totally corrupt sexual act, and yet it's in many ways the most romantic, innocent scene in the film. And that kind of contrast, that kind of paradox, interests me. I have a hunch that, of all Bree's clients, the old man might be the only one she deeply enjoyed. Ego satisfaction, ego reassurance. For a girl who undoubtedly had no fantasy life with her father—it's never said, but I'm sure hers is not a childhood with bedtime stories—this is about as close as you come to it. It's like a little girl playing at dressing-up, and there is a strange kind of storybook satisfaction.

"There was an attempt to extend the picture stylistically in that scene. For her entrance, there was that move down from his point of view, then a panning shot with her inside; and then another move down and she comes into this rather lush close-up. Very early on in the picture I said to Gordon Willis, 'That entrance should be just like von Sternberg photographing Dietrich.' The whole concept was misty and oozing rhythm, and then the almost liquid close-up. I thought the music was particularly successful there . . . something Michael Small has never really been given credit for. The music there has a deep sensuality and yet a storybook quality. It created an atmosphere in which romanticism did not seem out of place. That scene, you know, was shot with rats running around the floor. We had the place for the Jewish holidays—it was the only time we could get it."

Disturbing the Scale

"You mentioned the scene with the models at the beginning. Originally, the script had a scene in which Bree talked, and you saw the TV commercial she was trying out for. Well, you just can't satirize TV commercials anymore, so I did this scene instead. I said to Jane, 'I want to surround you with the most beautiful models I can get and put the prettiest next to you. I want the introduction to be as if you were just part of the chorus.' What I wanted was a sense of total anonymity. And they go right past her; all they say is 'Funny hands!' That was improvised—I didn't tell the actors what point I wanted to make. When I told Jane this was her entrance in the picture, she said, 'That's terrific. Because otherwise people would say, oh, Jane Fonda. What problems has she got? It's easy for her.'

"In contrast to that total anonymity, that sense of being nothing to these people, Bree is a star; she's Greta Garbo; she's Marlene Dietrich; she's all of it to that old man. As one of the call girls I talked to said to me, 'For half an hour I am the only thing that matters, I'm attractive to him and, oh, that sense of being *wanted!*' And there, Bree is with that moment, she's a goddess. That scene with the models was also an attempt to play with scale, disturbing the scale in the picture.

"The first time you move from that quiet little house and garden in the prologue is to an image of what is *supposed* to be: those three enormous photographs, much bigger than the girls lined up like soldiers on those little white chairs. It was also an artificial composition, taken flat on, an attempt to show a certain kind of pretension in that world, where image and reality are totally contrasted. I mean, those girls are tiny, but the fantasy they're reaching for is enormous. Probably nobody ever gets it; but there are so many things that have been said and said and said, and unless in some way you give the audience a sense of them without their realizing it . . .

"It's rather the same with the murderer, Cable, in his office, or the scene with the casting director. In a sense, all those offices and business places you see represent an attempt to be something more important than the person is, to make the person seem more important, and have little to do with any kind of reality in him. Finally, all these people are *playing* at being a television producer or whatever . . . and it's as though Bree were a kind of passive target for their egos. She's just something for them to play against, really; they're like old-fashioned star actors busy showing how marvelous they are. So it's something of that need to come back and say, 'I AM, goddammit. I am. I am important,' that drives her on. It's her way of hanging on to reality, compulsive though it may be. Then, when she goes to her client in the hotel room, in a curious way this faked-up act of sex has at least a reality of emotion from the man, and in a way that's something to hold on to.

"A lot of thrillers deal with the victim living in a nice safe world, and suddenly the terrible menace enters, turning it into a nightmare. Well, that has nothing to do with *Klute*, because this girl is trapped between two enormous threats. She is endangered by herself, by her own life, and she is endangered by the melodramatic bit. The tape recordings were an attempt to synthesize these two elements, to suggest that Bree Daniels really almost destroys herself. The irony is that, just as she is beginning to deal with her own problem, she is almost destroyed by a relic from her past.

"The tape recorder really came out of the fact that the end of the screenplay just had a man who came up to her apartment, started pouring out his life, and wound up by shooting himself. I was looking for a climax that had something more specific to the story . . . something more surprising, too. The idea of her hearing a friend's murder seemed more terrifying in its sadism. This man who records a murder he has committed is a man cut off from his own emotions, and he plays back the tape, trying to feel something. It's the final act of masturbation.

"He's very often shot through glass or against windows, a man isolated, dead, in the black-and-white world of his office. For me, a more essential truth than all the wild, uncontrolled passions in a sadist was the deadness, the feeling of something missing, of even perverse orgasms coming secondhand. The irony of a man who is a scientist, obviously involved in aeronautics and the moon thing and who can deal with all that, but is himself cut off from the most simple human behavior. The other thing that fascinated me about the tape recordings was that from the very beginning, her voice is weaving the web that is destroying her. You never hear the killer saying, 'I am going to destroy that girl,' or whatever; you just see that obsessed man going from murder to murder and listening to that seductive voice, that siren song calling him. So she becomes, up to a point, her own killer."

The Compulsions of *Klute*

"*Klute* really deals with compulsive behavior, and that's an area of John Klute we get into that is not totally developed, and it should be. Certainly the thing that you got came out of Donald Sutherland in the part, and I'm interested that you got it. It was not deliberate, and yet there *is* a complication in the man that was not designed. What Donald gave it was a kind of complication underneath, a cut through the straightness of the character so that there was something else in that man.

"Now, I discussed a whole subplot about John Klute with the writer in which he represented the kind of small-town American that Spiro Agnew talks about: a man who embodies the puritanical Protestant virtues, who believes that we control our destinies, is enormously honest, rigid in his code of moral behavior, and condemning of people who do not live up to it.

"This man, who obviously is repressed anyway, is forced in trying to find his missing friend into a whole world of compulsive behavior. It's everything he despises, and he feels attracted to it. In a way, there was an area where he is almost crushed by it because he falls in love with her, and [it invites] an examination of the why of what it releases.

"We discussed doing all of this in the film, but when we went into it the film began to lose a spine, something simple in the midst of all this convoluted storytelling that could pull the audience through it. So I rejected it. But somewhere or other it should be inherent; somewhere or other I felt there was something of the tortured puritan. And certainly Donald gave the subtext of obsession at times, which I think makes the character more memorable than if it had been played by someone more simplistic.

"The ending, too, is very tentative: the last line is 'You may see me tomorrow.' I think there is certainly no better than a fifty-fifty chance of Bree making it with a straight life . . . and I think a good deal less than that of her making it with Klute. The screenwriter would not have agreed with me: he had a happy ending. And Warner Bros. wanted the happy ending. But I didn't shoot it. What I love about that ending—which was improvised . . . the phone call . . . I didn't tell her how to react—is that it's done with humor, but for a moment she's attracted. It's still there. Part of her is going to miss the old compulsions; they're kind of cozy no matter how destructive they are.

"But one could do another film and tell exactly the same story from the point of view of the man. Because he has got to a certain age in life, and, when a friend whom he admires seems to have changed the whole pattern of his behavior, he's almost looking to find out how that can happen, what there is in me that can make it happen again. There is that kind of search in the film, but there was no time to develop it.

"I've been accused of being more interested in women's behavior than men's, but after all, this is only my second film. But I *do* relate to women. Let me tell you something that John Nichols, the novelist of *The Sterile Cuckoo*, said to me when I first met him. The book was written when he was a year out of college and is obviously very autobiographical, and, when we went on location to the college, everybody said this girl or that girl was Pookie Adams. What he said was, 'Well, there were a lot of Pookie Adamses . . . but the reality, which I realized when I was halfway through the novel, is that I was Jerry Payne, and I was Pookie Adams. Jerry was the stable, organized side of me that allowed me to function; and Pookie was the self-destructive, gifted part of me. Both surprised me and they're both me.'

"The same applies to me: I think I'm Klute, and I think I'm Bree Daniels at some points. I think I'm a man of great will, and also a man disturbed by compulsive behavior, someone surprised that at my age—forty-three—he's divorced. I did *Klute* at a very specific time in my personal life, and I was interested in that kind of ambivalence in a woman. Bree Daniels's problem, in a way, is the confusion of sexual roles; the paradox of the seemingly totally attractive woman who needs constant reassurance of her sexuality and who also finds ways of using sexuality to deny sexuality by proving that she can make a man feel without feeling herself. That she is therefore stronger than the man.

"The scene in the market, where Klute is buying fruit, and Bree is just watching him, loving him, surprised that she can love anybody, is, if you like, a kind of sexual reversal. First of all, Klute is a man who would buy fruit carefully and would know how, whereas Bree, for all that she's supposed to be—well, who *is*—very feminine, doesn't know how to act like a woman, as a lot of prostitutes don't. If I'd had a chance, I'd have shown Bree shopping earlier in the film, rushing through it, taking no care. Here is this girl, and the man has to teach her how to be a woman. It's like he's the father of a naughty child—when she steals the fruit—and he has to teach her not only how to be a woman, but also that the simplest action in life deserves care, a kind of pride and joy and feeling in it. They were both marvelous in that scene . . . I originally had dialogue there but they wanted to try something without, and I said OK.

"Areas of the film are improvised. For instance, the scenes with the psychiatrist. Psychiatrist scenes per se are such a cliché in films—they remind me of courtroom scenes: it's like nothing real ever happens there. The only justification is if you really feel a sense of self-discovery. If that doesn't happen—and it's an acting problem—then you can't do it. And it was very difficult. It was difficult because Jane was very true to character, and Bree Daniels is not a girl who is going to break down easily.

"Vivian Nathan, the actress playing the psychiatrist, was never introduced to Jane. She was installed at her desk, and, when she was ready and the camera was ready, Jane came into the anteroom, and, when I said 'Action!' she walked into the office for her appointment. And they talked. At the end of each take, I would talk to them separately, so they never met off-set. And then it got complicated, and it got kind of boring.

"What happened was that we would have session after session, and Jane would talk about her problems, but she never said she was a call girl. I suppose we got to about the seventh or eighth session. Then Vivian said, 'I keep trying and trying to get her to say she's a call girl, and she won't say it. I'm not going to force her because I'm not supposed to know.' I went to Jane, and she said, 'I keep *trying* to tell her, but every time I start getting to it, she changes the subject. She doesn't want to hear.'

"This went on all day, and everyone was getting pretty bored. But Jane was always in character. And then I got to a point where I felt I had to break her out of it, so as to get something exposed. So I told Vivian, 'You've got to be less understanding now. I want you to really go at her. Slam her for all those half-truths.' Jane came in, and Vivian started slamming her. And Jane got very cool, cooler than before, more poised, more relaxed, just the opposite of what I wanted. I was really sort of heartbroken, because it was about four o'clock, and I thought we weren't going to get it. So at the end of the take, I went to Jane and said, 'Gee, Jane, she really went for you. How come you weren't more upset?' She said, 'Overt hostility is the easiest thing in the world for Bree Daniels to deal with. She deals with that every day of her life. It makes her relax because then she knows where she's at.'

"She was so right! I went to Vivian and told her to forget what I'd said; it was a bad direction. This time I told Jane that, on her way to the psychiatrist's office, Bree saw a phone booth, that the compulsion to pick up a trick was as strong as ever, so she'd decided to quit analysis.' That's all I told her.

"She went into the office, sat down, got through all the how-are-you nonsense, then said, 'I can't come anymore.'—'Why ?' 'Well, I can't afford it.' She told about the phone booth and wanting a trick, and they talked a bit, and Vivian said, 'Do you feel I've failed you?' There was a pause, then Jane said, 'No, I feel I've failed you.' All this time Bree had been saying how much she hated people. And Vivian did something—if she'd told me she was going to, I'd have killed her—she suddenly dabbed her eyes. Jane looked at her and asked why she was crying. 'Well,' she said, 'all this time you've been telling me how you hate everybody, and you've just said a very nice thing about me. . . . Now that you're going to leave me, what are you going to *do*?' Jane burst into tears, and everything came pouring out, 90 percent of what I have in the film, and she said, 'You know what it is? I'm beginning to *feel*. And I'm just so scared.' It came out, the voice was shaking, it was happening, and my back went like *that*! . . . There was no way of directing that, everything pouring out . . . and then we ran out of film. Nobody talked. We just reloaded and went on.

"I don't understand anyone who says he just wants puppets. You *must* listen to an actor's instincts and give them consideration. But although areas of *Klute* were improvised within the form of a scene, and the script changed in terms of words and even scenes, it was the writer's idea to deal with that kind of girl and that kind of relationship in the form of a search.

"I felt that certain things in the script didn't work . . . for me. Too much was overt, verbalized. Finally, there was a point when I really felt I had to go out on my own. And then, in the course of the filming, things like the tape recorder and the improvisation with the psychiatrist . . . there were many things like that. But if Andy Lewis—he and his brother have screen credit, but it was Andy I worked with—had not been fascinated enough by that kind of sexual ambiguity and that kind of compulsion and decided to try to do it within a thriller form, there would be no film, and I would not have directed *Klute*.

The Widower [released as *Love and Pain and the Whole Damn Thing*]

"My new film is from a screenplay by Alvin Sargent, who did the screenplay for *The Sterile Cuckoo*. Both *Klute* and *The Sterile Cuckoo* dealt with one repressed person and one who was busy acting everything out. *The Widower* deals with two people who are totally repressed. And, in every other way, except their withdrawal from passion and from exposure to hurt, they are entirely different.

"She's an English spinster, really more Victorian than anything, a woman of immense will, enormous discipline. He's a boy, an American boy, who seems to have been filleted, boned out. He seems to have no sense of himself; he refuses to compete. And it deals with their metamorphosis together. It's a love story of the absurd. They're outrageously mismatched; but somewhere, underneath all of the surface mismating, there is something only each one could have done for the other.

"There is a shot early on in the film, a shot that must last . . . oh, I guess . . . over a minute and a half . . . and it's just a pan down rows of books. It starts at the top and keeps going down these endless academic rows, and over it you hear a man talking into a tape recorder, the boy's father, obviously preparing a speech for some august body, abstractions that would go with these books. And the camera just keeps going down, one case of books after the other, more books and more books and then, at the very bottom, like at the bottom of a well, there is this boy, and the father's voice just goes on and on and then says, 'Well, Walter, how are you?'

"And that's the boy. He's all secret and inside. And then he's sent to Spain because he spends all summer in movie houses, just sits there in strange passivity, and the father's not quite sure there isn't something wrong with him. Then comes his involvement with this enormously precise lady who protects herself in a different way. They're absurd together, ludicrous . . . but essentially, it's an outrageous little love story. In a curious way, of course, all three of my films have in common that they have ludicrous lovers. There's not a Garbo or a Gilbert in the bunch."

The Parallax View:
An Interview with Alan Pakula

Andrew C. Bobrow / 1974

From *Filmmakers Newsletter,* September 1974. Reprinted by permission of the author.

The sun was shining brightly through the brown curtains, shimmering off the glass table. The room was spacious, furnished tastefully but not ostentatiously: two couches, a glass table, and a large wooden one in the corner covered with books, papers, and a Sony tape recorder.

Although Alan Pakula looked much younger than I expected, he's no bright beginner. He produced *To Kill a Mockingbird* and half a dozen other films that now occasionally make the vast desert of late-night television a little less bleak. He's been involved in the film business for some eighteen years, even if *The Parallax View* is only his fourth film as director. And he's brought to his directing chores a wealth of experience, knowledge acquired firsthand and by example.

His success as a director is no fluke. He leaves nothing to chance—every frame in his films has to contribute to communicating his ideas. The end products are the result of careful and comprehensive planning.

Andy Bobrow: You have made several films, each with a distinctive style, different from the others but appropriate to the story. How do you develop the style in which you will make a film?

Alan J. Pakula: I have always felt one develops one's style for a film in the work itself. The first time I read a script, or if we start with a book or an idea, I begin to shape a conception. For example, I did not want *The Parallax View* to be a documentary. I was not doing an exposé of what actually happened in the Kennedy assassination, and I did not want to give the impression that it was a documentary about a specific assassination and that I had clues and answers to it. That would be irresponsible, and I am not in the business of muckraking.

I deliberately set out to stage a fictitious assassination for just that reason: so that it would be taken as sort of an American myth based upon some things that have happened, some fantasies we may have had of what might have happened, and a host of fears a lot of us have felt.

But although I do myths, I am interested in exploring some views of the world as it is seen through a distorting glass, which may point out certain realities more intensely. Essentially, I was doing a suspense-adventure film, obviously with overtones of things that have happened. But it had to be taken on its own fictitious terms.

For me, it was like a big poster with very flamboyant colors. I wanted to get at a lot of the bizarre contrasts in American life that many of us take for granted. And to do that, locations became an essential part of the making of the film. One develops one's style by answering a lot of questions. What are the locations going to be? What are the sets going to be like? The costumes? I sometimes think the main job of the director is answering questions, whether they be from the art director, the cameraman, the costume designer, the actors, or the scriptwriter.

AB: So what particular considerations did you have in mind when you chose the locations for the film?

AJP: I wanted to give a sense of the contrasts of American life and to set up the film immediately with some kind of bizarre theatricality. That's why I chose to put the first assassination in the Space Needle.

Locations are an integral part to me in creating the film. I had looked at some in New Mexico. I decided, for other reasons, not to shoot it there, but I was struck by the vivid contrasts. Look out into the mesas and buttes, pan a little way over and you're in a convention center in Albuquerque—which is another of those stone civic monuments to American industry, energy, and material achievement that are springing up in communities all over the country.

I wanted to deal with a lot of American monuments. When I got to the Space Needle, I designed the assassination around it. Looking with Gordon Willis for angles, we came upon a totem pole. It made just the statement I wanted to make about the incredible contrasts in American life, how many changes and civilizations there have been in such an uncomfortably short time in building this society, which may in some ways be reflected in the disturbances happening today.

I didn't want to *say* any of that, but I wanted to give some sense of it in the text of the film. Felicitously, there was the totem pole. It was like starting two thousand years ago. Then the camera moved a few inches, and you were in 1974. We cut to a Fourth of July parade, and again there was a whole mixture of times. The nineteenth-century fire engines came into it because there was a fire engine museum right near the Space Needle. I saw it while looking for locations. There was the American folk quality, which I wanted to get.

It's using what happens to be available on location. The Chinese girls' drill team that's in the parade had a sort of Indian costume, some of the kaleidoscopic color of American life that I was trying to capture. The whole end of the film, the climax in the Los Angeles Convention Center, is also an example of this. I knew I wanted to use a convention center when I saw the Albuquerque one. It was because it was this very American kind of monument; also because of the succession of huge spaces which we seem to have. There was an attempt to play with scale in this film, in the sense of people being manipulated, being very small figures in a large scale.

I had planned to do the ending with great crowds of people to make it seem that there was a political rally going on. When I looked at the convention center, it was empty. I was attempting to have the film function on a surreal as well as a real level, and the convention center had much more of a nightmare quality as an endless empty space than it would have had it been filled with the warmth of all those bodies. It never occurred to me to have it with a banquet, but they were setting one up as I looked around. It was like setting up a banquet in Grand Central Station. I said, "Marvelous, let's use it."

There was something dreamlike about those tables. We just put red, white, and blue tablecloths on them and made it look like he's caught in the middle of a banner, a flag, which again gave it a nightmare quality. There were a few men with golf carts traversing long distances setting up those tables. I was looking for ways of characterizing the candidate, of getting very specific, sometimes seemingly inappropriate and bizarre, American images. I don't think that I would have thought of him making his entrance in the golf cart without that. Suddenly, there it was. In many ways, so many things come out of keeping your eyes open during location scouting.

AB: Were other sequences shaped in this way? For example, in terms of original conceptions, was the dam sequence affected at all by the location?

AJP: It never occurred to me that we could shoot the dam with the water right in back of the actors. It seemed much too close until we found a location and suddenly there was a way of encompassing the water and them at the same time. I had originally designed the dam sequence in a different way, and I loved the way I designed it.

When I originally ran the film for audiences, it just didn't work. There was one shot reversed from the dam in which we see Warren Beatty and the sheriff in an exquisite rural setting, and then another view from the dam that looked just like a Japanese painting. It had a lovely willowy bridge and an endless canyon full of green—total peace and tranquility. It was like a dry riverbed with rocks.

I love starting out a scene with one kind of visual material and ending with another. What I wanted to do was play the whole scene against this pastoral setting, even though you knew there was a dam nearby. Then, when the dam starts to sound its warning sirens, abruptly reverse into the first time we see the dam there—a monolithic, threatening structure—and break the whole lovely pastoral image.

Conceptually, it made a great deal of sense. But the scene wasn't long enough to sustain it, and audiences became confused. They had no sooner absorbed the presence of the dam when they had to react to the fact of the water and the situation. They were so turned around that they were dizzy. If the scene had been just a little bit longer, I could have done it. Instead, I cut the scene down even more because the film depends so much on surprise. I'll always regret somewhere or other that I couldn't have done it that way and made it work.

To me, making a film, shooting it, and cutting it is constantly designing and redesigning. Always using the surprises of life that one gets in shooting—some good, some bad—helps me in terms of my very specific original conception. I am very much affected by location.

AB: I want to talk some about the newspaper office set, which looked to me like one of those 1930s movie newspaper offices. I half expected to see Cagney or somebody emerge from the shadows.

AJP: That was very deliberate. The film was designed as a myth, with archetypal people, characters, and places. It's full of alienated people wandering around in totally alienated worlds with a seeming absence of continuing relationships. On the other hand, the editor [Hume Cronyn] represents certain nineteenth-century American humanist values: tradition, rootedness, responsibility, an optimistic belief in the perfectibility of man and that we live in the best of all possible worlds in the most enlightened society so far created by man—a kind of old-fashioned decency and optimism. In a sense, he is an anachronism in this piece.

The art director, George Jenkins, did a lot of research into newspaper offices—it was supposed to be a medium-sized office, not one at a big paper. So we sent him out to some smallish papers. The newsroom did not differ that much from the newsroom of those papers. He brought me photographs, but they all had fluorescent lights, and the film is full of cold, hard, blue-white light, blistering, ruthless light. So I didn't want those fluorescent lights. I wanted old-fashioned yellow light. He said no, all the papers he'd been to had taken them out, and fluorescents were what they put in when they remodeled. But I don't care about the literal truth. I care about theatrical truth, and I wanted there to be a personal warmth in this office. If you got a sense of walking into the office with William Allen White in 1928, that was perfectly fine with me.

In the still photographs on his wall, I was trying to get a sense of a rooted man, one dedicated to the support of community life. This is one of the values you see in the film. He has only three scenes, and they originally were supposed to take place in several sets, but I arbitrarily put him in that office late at night, seeing him as a man whose whole life now is his work. I wanted something of a man who has stayed in one place, who is rooted, as compared with all the wanderers you see in the film.

In many ways, there is a stylization when you're doing a film with this complicated a plot. There is a kind of bold sketch work to indicate something about a character's life, what he represents in the story rather than just a literal rendering.

When I did *Klute* with George Jenkins, the same art director, I wanted a sense of Bree as a girl in a half-finished world, half in one world and half out of another. I wanted the sense of her being at the end of a tunnel, of a space not yet completed. She had a sense of style, but she is a girl who hasn't even completed that. She still hasn't finished anything in that respect. She lives in an unfinished moment.

I try, in using sets, to make statements about the characters, statements that work for the texture of the film rather than being totally documentary and realistic. I like to theatricalize.

AB: I'd like to know how you chose *Parallax View*. How did you get the idea? Did you read the book?

AJP: Originally it was a screenplay by Lorenzo Semple Jr. that had been bought by Gabriel Katzka, who is the executive producer of the film. It was sent to Warren Beatty, and it was sent to me. It was based on the book, but I had not read the book. I read the screenplay. That draft was about a cop, obviously changed in the film. I was interested in it, interested in the conception, interested in doing the kind of film that could make it work on a realistic and surreal level at the same time.

It really dealt with the man's relationship to society—for the first time in any film of mine, although *Klute* had something of that. The film has a kind of bold canvas, instead of being one with tiny, intimate details. It is a film with bold sketches and an almost expressionist quality, at the same time seeing things on the surface as being totally real. It dealt with the mythical American hero and a lot of American myths, some old ones but mostly contemporary ones.

In the script I read, there was no assassination at the beginning. The assassination that was talked about was one that happened during a motorcade in Dallas, just about naming the Kennedy assassination. But I said no, I'm perfectly happy to do a metaphor, a fictional reality.

AB: You weren't going for accuracy, then, since the film is not based on fact?

AJP: No, I wasn't going to expose new facts about the Kennedy assassination. The film was a myth; it was a nightmare based upon the terrors of our time. But it *is* a work of fiction. I think there is a difference between exploring certain terrors of our time and exploiting them, for me anyway, right or wrong.

AB: In that connection, how closely did you work with the writer on the rewrite of the screenplay?

AJP: I worked a good deal with the writer, David Giler, who came in and did a lot of work. He was the one who really begged me to make the main character an investigative reporter, as he had been in the book. And he was right about that.

I believe filmmaking is very collaborative. The auteur theory is a half-truth. The truth, the half-truth of it, to me, is that a good director has a very strong conception of the film he wants to make, but as long as you have to work with so damn many people, you might as well use their minds, their intuitions, and their creativity to contribute to whatever that conception is. That excites me. I'm not interested in being a puppeteer with actors or with anybody else.

It's a very secure feeling when you see the final cut, however, and you can decide what will and what will not be used, what fits the conception and what does not. Anything that requires so many people has to be a collaboration. If you work with a woman, for instance . . . if I'm doing a picture with Jane Fonda or Liza Minnelli or Maggie Smith, it would be perfectly absurd for me to tell them how they should feel as a woman every second of the time and not use what comes out of their intuitions.

AB: In general terms, then, how do you like to work with actors?

AJP: I work with actors in a very loose way, and I work in different ways with different actors. I work in ways that are right for them. Before we start a film, I discuss the conception of the film—what we're trying to achieve, what interests me—to make sure that, before we all commit ourselves, we are reaching for the same kind of film.

There are healthy disagreements about how to get to that point, but if it turns out that each one of you have read a script or a book and seen a totally different kind of film in it, then you are in for disaster when you make it. I believe, when I can do it, in using long rehearsal periods. But I don't always. *Parallax View* was very difficult because the film jumps around quite a bit and so much of it is not dialogue but action.

After talking with the actors, I see where their instincts take them. It's a curious thing about the creative ego: people do things better when it seems to come from their own mind, and not because they're being mean or small or petty. Something about creativity and the ego are closely allied. Sometimes they will fall in with what I had seen in the first place. Sometimes they will do things I didn't think of that are better than I might have thought of, or just as legitimate, and in terms of their personality would be better for them to do. Sometimes, too, they will do something that is totally wrong for the scene, and then we start to shape that. But I don't say, "You stand here. You move six inches to your left, and you move a quarter of an inch to your right."

For me, the essence of getting good work out of an actor is having some strong sense of that person, of his or her character, and getting to know them well enough so that you know what in them can contribute to the character they're playing. If I had done *The Parallax View* with Steve McQueen, I would not have tried to get the same performance Warren Beatty gives. If I did a film with Liza Minnelli, I would not try to get the performance that I would if Jane Fonda were doing that film. You must take into account that the character is a synthesis of the actor or actress who's playing the part and the character itself.

AB: In that sense, what do you look for when you're casting a film?

AJP: I don't have any rules. It's primarily intuition and instinct. For example, for the part of Lee Carter, the reporter, somebody mentioned Paula Prentiss, an actress I've always admired. In talking with Paula, something very interesting happened. I got a wholly different conception of the part, making her into a kind of vulnerable Raggedy Ann doll coming apart at the seams, so that when Warren sees her it's like a girl who is nervous and has cried wolf too often about too many other things. She became a character who would consume the audience's sympathy, hopefully to the extent that it wouldn't appear to them that something could happen to her as immediately as it does in the film. That part was really rewritten for Paula.

Klute and *The Sterile Cuckoo* are two films I don't think I would have made without their female stars. I don't think I would have made *The Sterile Cuckoo* without Liza Minnelli, and I don't think I would have made *Klute* without Jane Fonda, only because I didn't find anybody else who seemed as right to me. There are certain characters and pictures where you have second choices and certain ones where you just don't.

I had met Jane a long time before we did *Klute*. I knew her vaguely socially, superficially. Then I read a one-act script that was sent to me. Somebody was planning to do a series of one-act screenplays for women, with three different women and three different directors. One was for Jane. I read it, but I didn't want to do it. While it was an interesting idea, I felt that it was the kind of thing that would be a soap opera if it were done in a half hour; it needed an hour and a half and new development. But, in discussing the possibility of doing that film, we talked about life and the problems of women . . . many things.

Somebody sent me a first draft of the script of *Klute* shortly thereafter, and if Jane had turned it down, I don't think I would have done it. I couldn't think of anybody else who had that wit, that sexuality, who could play that kind of self-destructiveness and at the same time seem capable of being an extraordinary woman. While she played a call girl, it had to be somebody who appeared to have the potential of being a woman outside of that.

I interviewed many people for *The Sterile Cuckoo* and just couldn't see it without Liza. At one point I did a test of Liza for another studio. They thought that she was overacting, but in truth I had not directed in twenty years, and I overdirected the scene like mad. I had her crying and laughing and going through every emotional experience in life in five minutes. Liza, being a really gutsy girl, did it all, leaving the audience in the screening room in a state of shock and nervousness, longing for escape. What was wrong with the test was my fault, hardly hers. If anything, working with her in the test made me more enthusiastic because her range was as extraordinary as my lack of control in directing the test.

AB: Your four films to date cover a rather wide range of subject matter. Did you find that there was a problem in moving from, for example, an adolescent love story to a fast-moving political suspense thriller?

AJP: The next film I plan to do is a totally extravagant bawdy Rabelaisian farce. You might say that it has something to do with *The Parallax View* because they both depend upon a certain kind of cinematic daring, but that's all. It's an original screenplay by Stanford Sherman, a rural comedy. It deals with some people caught between sinning and salvation, between lust and guilt, trying to please the Lord and themselves at the same time. It's terribly bawdy. One of the major characters, the father, is very rough, very Falstaffian. It has nothing whatsoever to do with any other work I've done.

I don't do different kinds of films just to show people that I can do different kinds of films. I have a lot of interests in life. Each film is a new adventure, and to be repeating something I've done before doesn't interest me. That doesn't mean that I wouldn't work in the same style again. I started directing comparatively late.

The more I direct, the more I am fascinated by film, the more I try to extend myself to see what I am capable of, and the more different kinds of cinematic vocabulary I would like to master. The best way to do that is to work in different styles. Fortunately, studios pay me very well to do different kinds of films, so I've been taking advantage of it. As long as my successes outnumber my failures, they will pay me well to learn. When it reverses, we'll worry about it then.

AB: You were a producer for a long time before you became a director. What was it like making the transition?

AJP: It was terrific. Directing, for me, was completing and fulfilling what I had half done as a producer. As a producer, I knew I always wanted to be a director but also knew that there could only be one director. There's nothing more destructive than a producer who comes on to the set and starts interfering with the actors. There can only be one authority figure for the actors—one director. I always thought that when you want to direct actors, you should go out and do it yourself [as the director]; don't start trying to do it with somebody else's.

I have worked closely with writers as a producer, and I do now as a director. [As a producer,] I would certainly discuss the style of the film with the director, the art director, and all of those people. I would work closely with the director and the editor in the editing, as I do now with the editor alone. The one difference was that, when the film started shooting, the director was in charge, in charge of the set and the actors. So at that point I would withdraw. It was kind of difficult, but I knew it was necessary. But I would watch dailies and, if there was anything that I particularly liked or disliked, I would tell the director.

The terrific thing about being a director is that now I don't have to withdraw at any time. I really got involved in filmmaking based upon my enjoyment of working with actors when I was in college. And the one thing I didn't do for eighteen years of being in the film business was work with actors and the cameraman. I had started out interested in the stage, and now I find I am as fascinated by the camera as I am by working with actors. So for me, the transition was a joyous one, a totally joyous one, and I've never been happier than I am now.

AB: How helpful were your years as a producer and production executive when you finally got out to direct?

AJP: Obviously, being involved with the making of films, watching other people making films, and being a part of making films for that long a time were invaluable. At the same time, it would have been more helpful if I had directed the films myself. I think one learns from one's mistakes as well as one's successes, much more than through other people's.

I happen to believe—in fact, I have no doubt about it—that if I had started directing when I was twenty-one, when I was directing community theater, I would probably have done some things at that age that I am incapable of doing now, as I imagine I am doing things now that I would have been incapable of doing then.

That's why it is so incredibly important that young directors be given a chance. A film that I do about people younger than I is really quite different from a film that a young director does about his own generation, just as a film that I do about a woman would be quite different from the film that a woman director would do about a woman. I think we need more young directors, more women directors—we need more different kinds of directors.

AB: If you give two directors the same script, they're not going to come out with the same movie.

AJP: What would really be fun to do, if it didn't cost so much money, would be to give ten directors the same script and see what kind of films they came out with. There's something else that I've always wanted to do which is more sensible: keep all the footage from major films and give it, or dupes of it, to ten film students for each one to cut his own version of the film. It would be very interesting to see what happens.

AB: How closely do you work with the cameraman to establish the visual style of the film?

AJP: Very. The marvelous thing about working with Gordon Willis (and there are a lot of marvelous things about working with Gordon Willis) is that he remembers the very first things you tell him about your conception of the film. When I called him from Albuquerque while looking for locations for *Parallax View*, I told him I was thinking of a baroque style, bizarre contrasts, what I described earlier as a poster style. He never forgot that. Sometimes, right in the middle of a scene, he would say that what I wanted him to do was a violation of what I wanted the style of the film to be.

The director must have a conception of what he wants, otherwise the cameraman is just going to go aftereffects for their own sake. [Although] Gordon never does that. He always operates within a conception of the film. Whatever kind of disagreements we might have, they are always within the conception of the film. I work with the cameraman the way I do with the actors. When they have terrific ideas that I've never had, that's sensational. I don't like working with people who don't have a lot of ideas of their own.

There are sequences where what is best for the actors will come before the visual effects of the film, for me. There are other sequences where what is best for the visual effect of the film, the camera, will come before what is best for the actors. It all depends upon what values seem most important in terms of the storytelling. Again, I don't believe in iron-clad rules. I don't like to move actors around like puppets for the camera, nor do I like to come in and pretend that we're on the stage and that adjustments should not be made for visual storytelling. It all depends on the scene and the specific problem.

There's no question that the visual style of a film is collaborative. *The Parallax View* would look different if there had been another cameraman. The basic style of the film would be the same, but not executed half as well. That doesn't mean that Gordon didn't have lots of ideas. I trust he always will. But I would never want to work on a film where the basic visual conception did not come from me. I don't, however, look for cameraman puppets any more than I look for acting puppets.

AB: How about editing puppets? How much of a hand do you take in the cutting?

AJP: There I work very closely with the editor. I am obsessed with that, and in *The Parallax View* more so than before.

AB: Do you actually cut it yourself?

AJP: No. I'll sit at the Moviola, not all the time, but a lot. Sometimes I'll stop and start in the projection room, and other times at the Moviola. It all depends.

AB: One last question—how much preproduction planning do you do on a picture?

AJP: As much as I can. In the best of all possible worlds, you plan as much as you can; you plan the whole picture out and then have the freedom to violate the plan if what you've shot turns out to be better. I plan without being committed to every detail of that plan. But I'd rather do that than improvise on nothing.

An award-winning producer, writer, director, and film commentator, **Andrew C. Bobrow** is on the faculty of the School of Media Studies at the New School in New York City.

Under the Influence:
An Interview with Alan J. Pakula

Steven Soderbergh / 1998

Editor's note: This interview was transcribed from Soderbergh's on-stage interview with Pakula conducted on June 18, 1998, for the Director's Guild of America's Under the Influence Series, after a retrospective screening of The Parallax View *(and twenty-four years after Andy Bobrow's interview with Pakula about the same film). Printed by permission of the Director's Guild of America, Inc.*

Steven Soderbergh: I've heard that that it was only at the last minute that you came up with the idea to have the second assassination in *The Parallax View* take place during the politician's run-through rather than during the actual rally.

Alan J. Pakula: That's true. The original idea was that there was going to be this huge banquet, a big fundraising banquet, filled with people. And then I came in to look at the banquet hall in the location, and it was empty, apart from all these tables. I said, "God, just put red, white, and blue tablecloths on the tables. Keep it this way. Keep this endless, empty space here 'cause that's got a real nightmarish quality." The original idea was for a much more literal reality. And the surreal and nightmare quality began to extend itself.

SS: Right. There's hardly anybody there. That's a pretty bold reconception of a set piece. And it works.

AJP: *The Parallax View* was the second of a group of films I did that became known as "the paranoia trilogy." And it's like a nightmare, like a big flamboyant poster version of a nightmare. There are major parts of it that are as surreal as I've ever gotten. Like the last sequence, when we cut to the Supreme Court justices, and one of them says, "This is an announcement, gentlemen. There'll be no questions." Then he slams the gavel, and the justices just pop off the screen. That was deliberately designed.

SS: Was anybody shocked by that, when you said, "Hey, let's do it this way"?

AJP: Some untalented son of a bitch got ahold of it at one stage, and said, "Oh, no. They just popped off the screen. That's a mistake. We'll just have them walk off the screen." Maybe he did that because he thought television audiences are dumber than movie audiences, or whatever. But it was just totally changing what was there in the film, changing an optical that was very deliberately thought out.

Generally, though, I work with people who are beyond shock, and it's a basis you need if you're going to survive. People like George Jenkins, who's been production designer on many of my films, and he's a great artist. Just as Gordon Willis is a great artist, and the composer, Michael Small.

They're people who understand a concept and can make that concept grow. And you can improvise with them. As long as you know the story you want to tell and can stay loose, you can work with them and see if there are better ideas than you had eight weeks ago or six months ago when you were planning the film.

When we're looking for locations and starting to plan a scene, even when we're shooting a scene that we've rehearsed and laid out and staged weeks before, everything is still up for grabs. Maybe that day we have a better idea, and so we do it differently. For me that's a great part of directing.

There's no one way to direct. I mean, there was Hitchcock who planned everything out, and for him the shoot was boring because he knew exactly what it was going to look like. Still, I learned a lot of my film vocabulary from him. There's nobody who can better teach you the grammar and a certain kind of storytelling discipline, although his sensibility and mine are very, very different. And then there's John Cassavetes, who would just improvise everything. I'm somewhere in the middle, but I do like to shake it all up suddenly and say this is going to be very different.

SS: Were the details of the Parallax test that Frady does in the script? Was it described there?

AJP: All we said in the script was that it was gonna be a test. That was it. I had in mind a certain kind of psychological test that would identify an assassin, that would define and appeal to an assassin and whip his blood pressure up, and all of those things. That sequence for me was what we wanted to do, and that was developed totally in postproduction.

Jon Boorstin was my assistant on the film. Actually, he was a lot more than that. He was really much more of an associate. I told him that the idea was to create a fantasy of America, of happiness, of the ideal mother and father, and everything, and then go on to build up the rage of the have-nots for the haves, and of the people who feel deprived and used and manipulated and who feel that their parents have been castrated and destroyed and who feel that they've been threatened with castration.

SS: That must've taken a long time to create. The turn in it is so subtle, you know, as it begins to shift, and then the pace accelerates. It must've taken quite a while.

AJP: Right. It took months actually. Jon kept running out and getting pictures, going to endless magazine archives. And I had an epiphany when I was looking through the pictures he came up with. . . . Making a film is an extraordinary personal adventure when you're really into it.

As a child, I had these nightmares that I never forgot. They were the strongest images of my life. I'd be in bed, and there'd be these great rabbits. It might sound cute, but they were awful. They were long and about ten feet tall, and they had like no faces, just holes. And they'd come in twos, and they would grab me and take me away.

I never knew where that came from. Even when I took therapy in my twenties, I never knew it. All I know is that those rabbits and a terror of being kidnapped will haunt me for the rest of my life. And when we were going through Ku Klux Klan pictures, which I ended up using in the test, an infantile kind of chill hit me. I've seen Ku Klux Klan pictures for ages, but when you're working on a film, there's something of the child that is very much alive inside there. Then I remembered. I once heard my father talking about the Ku Klux Klan, about how they would take me away and kill me. So, I even had *my* assassin moment, you know, in working on that.

SS: Right.

AJP: And the whole idea of the music we used was to create the simple, warm folk romance of America, of a royal America of another time. Michael Small wrote it, and I thought it was very successful. And the central point about the film was that it showed that present-day America has become a world that was unrecognizable from the Old America. The Old America is represented by Hume Cronyn sitting at his office desk, just in one place. Frady, Beatty's character, is a wanderer who lives in motels, doesn't have a home. I also tried to play with images of America in the Western bar sequence. I was playing with all the old John Ford images.

Hitchcock said, "If you do a picture about Switzerland, you use cuckoo clocks and mountains." Well, in this one, someone was trying to say, "Here, look how America has turned out. This is not the place as we used to know it. It's all been tossed up and turned into a strange, kind of surreal dream." That was fun to do.

SS: Was any of that in the novel?

AJP: The novel has little to do with the film. I read the book. It had been sent to me by Paramount, and there was a screenplay—a totally different version of the story. What I was interested in was the theme of the book.

Over the years, I've done two different kinds of pictures based on books. One was around the time I started out as a producer: *To Kill a Mockingbird*, which Robert Mulligan directed wonderfully. Then there's *Sophie's Choice*. And *All the President's Men*, which, of course, is a true story, so you are going to be true to the book. But that's your goal: to adapt it in such a way that it will give an experience with the film that is comparable to the experience of the book. The basic idea for *The Parallax View* was taken from the book. But actually the film is very, very different from it, except for the situation that people who witness an assassination are dying.

SS: What was that process of making it like? The script's terrific. It really lays it all out well.

AJP: I'll tell you a story. The experience of making *Parallax* was surreal. We made it without a finished script that we liked in the middle of a Writers Guild strike. I wanted to postpone, but Paramount had a deal with Warren: pay or play. They said, "You're going to play."

So I said, "Okay, we're going to play. Away we go."

Out of this picture I discovered that, if you don't panic, anything's possible. But I never forgave Warren for one thing. He's wildly bright, and I have great admiration for him and great admiration for the picture he's just done [*Bulworth*, 1998]. I got married about six weeks before we started shooting. But on my wedding night—I can't forgive him for this—on my wedding night, I woke up, and I said to my wife, "You won't believe what I dreamed of. I spent half the night dreaming about Warren Beatty and all the script fights we were having." . . . It was always interesting fights I'd have with Warren, never dull ones, never stupid ones, 'cause Warren doesn't have a stupid bone in his body. But . . .

SS: What would these fights be about? A scene, or an idea . . . ?

AJP: Well, you have to understand that we were doing a film where we were very often rewriting scenes in the morning then shooting them in the afternoon. I remember Hume Cronyn coming up to the house on Sunday after having read one version of the script, and I said to him, "Well, we've had to make some changes, major ones." And he looked at me and said, "Alan, please don't make me improvise. Please." So I said, "You won't have to improvise. The scene will be written out for you, but it may only be finished the morning, or the night, before you go on." I don't recommend this, by the way.

However, there *were* certain basics about how we were making this film that were in place. The beginning was in place. What the story was about was in place. The central points about Parallax were all in place: the concept of the test, the dam sequence, the whole ending. . . . There was a lot of work to do, but the film, the basic concept for the film, was there.

Where you can go wrong in that kind of situation and where it becomes chaos is when you lose the overall concept, and you're just trying to make things work day by day. It then becomes a totally opportunistic thing, and you're not serving anything except trying to be entertaining every day. And that's a disaster. But, although the shoot was full of surprises, it was never like that on this film. You know, I played with images. I was being playful with images. I mean, even the guys on the little toy train . . .

SS: Right.

AJP: And there is a dream-like quality about this film. What you see is what the story is, about this tiny man in this huge world. And when the ambulances come in near the end and violate these red, white, and blue tablecloths, it's like America's being violated. All those things depended on the manipulation of space. If ever there was a film that had to be shot in 'Scope, for me this was it.

And while it reflects the paranoia of the time, it was also a time when things happened that one, no matter how paranoiac one was, couldn't have believed were going to happen. The three assassinations, seeing Jack Ruby shoot Lee Oswald right on your television set in front of you. Live! The Vietnam War. . . . This picture's very, very much a reflection of that. It's a cautionary tale, and it warns us to beware of thinking that we cannot be manipulated in ways that could destroy us.

SS: What I thought was really interesting was that the psychology of it was very well thought out, and the interaction between Jack Younger [the Parallax agent] and Warren Beatty is really terrific. Those scenes are amongst my favorites in the film. They're just in a little room, but this cat-and-mouse game that's going on is really terrific.

AJP: Two of my favorite scenes in the film too. It's wonderful acting. Walter McGinn unfortunately died tragically in an automobile accident a few years afterwards. He'd come from the stage, and he was this little mouse of a man. He played it almost as if he had a crush on Frady, you know. And it was very seductive in its way. It's like he's saying, "All I want to do is live for you and protect you and make sure that you have the success you deserve." And he gave it that dimension, which wasn't necessarily in the writing. There was some of it there, but the actor made it work. And that's what I knew he could do after I saw him on the stage.

SS: Well, it's in the cutting, too. You let him stare a lot, you know. You're just holding on him.

AJP: Absolutely. He can't take his eyes off Warren. It's like he's obsessed with him. I had a whole little subplot going. For all these actors, we had a whole little subplot going that you don't know anything about onscreen. And we talked about this sexual thing with him. I mean the fantasy job for him of going out and finding young assassins and deprived young men. And somehow, he draws out the evil in their lives, each in his own way. He also has his own tragic existence that has made him useful to the Parallax organization.

He really got into creating the Parallax character. He was full of surprises—you know I love surprises—and he really started becoming somebody else. I thought it was terrific work. It always helps an actor when he's working with another wonderful actor. And Warren is helped by wonderful actors in this picture.

But that scene was so dark. Gordon saw it in silhouette. I'll never forget when Warren saw the dailies the next day. He was so pleased when we shot the scene because, when he started telling his history of being a flasher, he cried real tears. He really, really got into it. And he was wonderful in the scene. But when he saw the dailies, he said, "Why did I work so hard? I'm nothing but a silhouette." But I thought the way Gordie shot it in the darkness made it memorable.

SS: Now, am I imagining things? Carol's wife is played by the actress who played the wife in the opening scene in *Klute*?

AJP: Yes.

SS: Is there some reason you keep getting rid of her husband?

AJP: Betty Murray was a model. She'd model for Coke ads, things like that . . . Pepsi ads, and all that. She was a healthy all-American woman. I met her because my first wife, Hope Lange, used to be married to Betty's husband, Don Murray. I met Betty that way. And when I was looking for somebody in *Klute* to be the healthy all-American wife, I thought of her. She wasn't an actress, but she had a natural quality and that kind of clean, fresh, wholesome look. And when I was looking for somebody for *Parallax* who had the same thing, I said, "Betty, you want to do it again? It's similar. That whole image of you is just great for this." I wanted that wholesome all-American image. Don Murray said to me a couple of years later, "Alan, did it ever occur to you that you gave my wife two parts and you killed off the husband in the first reel both times?"

SS: Can you talk a little bit about the development of your visual aesthetic, which, early in your career, obviously, is linked very heavily with Gordon Willis and with George Jenkins. I ask because it's so distinctive and, for a producer who then becomes a director, at least in my experience, it's rare that a visual sense that striking shows up.

AJP: I remember distinctly when I began to believe in my own eye. I had a meeting with Gordy at a bar in New York to discuss *Klute*, and I said, "This is how I see it." I started talking about the compression of this woman, and about verticals, and about "the heavy." I wanted her in corners, and I wanted him high up on buildings where there's nothing down below. Here was a man who had committed sexual crimes and killed prostitutes, and I said that what I really wanted to capture was the feeling that he's a man cut off from life. Everything's gone dead for him, and he's just totally isolated. And there were a lot of other things too. Then, weeks later, we're looking for locations, I said something, and he said, "No, that's not what you had in mind. That's not what you told me." He remembered everything I told him that night, and he gave me faith in myself. And, c'mon, Gordon is the master.

And I remember talking to George, who originally went with us to look at hookers' apartments. I said, "George, what I want to capture is the loneliness of this girl." He had already designed three rooms, but he just threw that away, and we went for that one room on top of a brownstone, just stripped away. And he put the bed all the way in the back, making it so it's like she's at the end of a tunnel. After that, I started thinking about space and the subjective use of space and the subjective feeling you get by what your relationship is to space.

Parallax was my second film with Gordon, and I have never done a film with Gordon where he hasn't remembered the first thing we talked about when we were preparing it. And, this time, I'd said to him, "It's a poster of a picture. It's a huge poster of a picture, and we're playing with symbols. And it's a cold world that uses symbols relentlessly and ruthlessly. And something's gone dead in this world and seriously wrong." And once that was said, everything was in place for him, and it affected all his work on the film.

I've said the best thing about direction is collaboration, but the worst thing about making a film can be collaboration too because sometimes your ideas get watered down. But if you work with the right people, like George Jenkins, like Gordon Willis, like Michael Small, your ideas just grow. These are people who give their own talent, who give the work more dimension, and who keep challenging you.

There's nothing more thrilling in a lifetime than when all of that's working, and nothing more hideous than when it's not, and you feel that suddenly you're working with people who have different conceptions than you about the film and that you're serving different masters. But when you do things like designing that last sequence in *Parallax*, designing it with George, getting the red, white, and blue tablecloths, all that stuff, putting it all in, getting those cards made, all that stuff . . . that's a joy.

But let me tell you a story about George. I would get angry at him because he was so obsessed. We were looking for a boat we were going to blow up ten days later. We hadn't had a chance to work that through yet because of the Writers Guild strike and all the problems that came with it. He had come over to my house on a Saturday, arriving well before I'd got around to breakfast. I'll never forget this. As I reached for my orange juice, he slipped these pictures of boats under my glass. I said, "George! Not before my orange juice." And the poor man was just saying, "I've got to get this ready for you." God bless him 'cause if he hadn't been so obsessed, this film never would've been finished.

And that kind of obsession is what you have to work with because as a director you're like a child who's dependent upon other people. All these people are doing their work for you, and they're all extensions of yourself as well as being artists in their own right. I don't like "yes men," so they have to be people with original concepts and visions who are willing to serve yours if they believe in it. They've been some of the best moments of my life working with them.

But I do not recommend making a film the way we made *Parallax*. I usually prefer working with four weeks of rehearsal. Every picture has its own life, and a lot of it you plan, and a lot of it takes on its own life and it tells you what it wants, and sometimes it defies you. And you just go with it.

This film is the most abstract of any I've ever done. It is most dependent on visual, abstract visual images and a soundtrack which has, I think, a remarkable score by Michael Small. Especially in the test scene. It is the only way the heavies are characterized. It whips people up into some kind of patriotic emotions, but, in the end, it seems to represent an old-fashioned Americanism, one that dangerous ideas can be hiding behind.

The whole idea of this film, what makes it a cautionary tale for the 1970s, is that it warns you that, hiding behind all sorts of patriotic symbols, there can be ideas that are not American, that are not democratic, that are not to do with freedom. It warns you that we can all be manipulated.

You have to remember it came out after the era of assassinations. And, when I was shooting the film, we would drive to work and hear the Watergate hearings on the car radio. America had become unrecognizable. In a sense, it became a Kafka America. We're in a very different time now, but this is the terror that is happening to our country.

A year and a half later, I did *All the President's Men*, which represented kind of a rebirth of the American hero. But not only did the hero not win in *Parallax*, not only did the heavies win, but you never know who they are.

The essence of the American Western, which is its triumph as a symbol of our society and of America, is that you can see your enemy down the street, and you can shoot it out. You know who the good person is, and you know who the bad person is. And what *Parallax* was saying is, "My God, this is more like middle-Europe of a certain period. We don't know who the good people are and we don't know who the bad guys are anymore, and we cannot depend on good triumphing over evil, in the optimistic way we did in America." That's what this film was all about. That's why I used all those symbols.

Obviously, all the things you see at the football games, you know: the cards with the faces of the American presidents, the red, white, and blue stuff, and the all-American high school band with a little schlepp playing the tuba who turns out to be the guy who's responsible for our hero being killed. It was fun developing that: a little scenario within the film. I used a golf cart because, again, the politician coming down in the golf cart makes you think of Eisenhower.

SS: Let's talk for a minute performance-wise. Obviously, you like to pitch things in a very naturalistic fashion, which in a film like this works really well.

AJP: Well, the actors are very naturalistic. The visuals, though, are not. That's exactly right. It's what I usually do.

SS: When you were doing theater, were you drawn to pieces that allowed for that kind of acting? Is that just a style that you like in general?

AJP: I like layered characters. I like to feel that there's more to that character than I can see on screen. Olivier once said about acting, "Great acting means no matter how much you give the audience, they should always feel there's some mystery left that they don't have." And I love acting that's like that, where you feel, "Wow, there's that character, and I think I know that character, but there's still other things that I can still find out about that character."

SS: Right.

AJP: And that's the kind of thing that interests me. I will go talk with an actor about things that are un-actable and say, "Look, let's talk about that now." Then we'll get on with it and play it moment to moment in the scene.

SS: Well, there's a great scene in *Parallax View*—and you do this a couple of times very effectively—where communication is taking place between some characters, but we don't hear what it is. But, still, there's a mood that's evoked that's very specific. Like with William Daniels in the scene in the boat, where clearly he's telling Warren Beatty what happened. But we don't hear what he's saying, and we just see those great shots of him partially obscured as he's looking out of the boat, and then he lies down and turns over. You'd never see that in a movie today. He'd have to say it all. There'd have to be a big close-up.

AJP: I love teasing an audience. And when you slam into big close-ups all the time, for me it's like being dumped on. I want to say, "Let me work at it a little." I like to give the audience just enough so that they'll have to start to come toward the picture. If you don't give them enough, they'll likely say, "To hell with this. I don't have to work that hard." But finding the right balance is exciting. It makes them participatory in it. I love playing with sound, and I love playing with dialogue. And there are also some things that are more interesting simply because they're *not* being said or shown.

You always see it afterwards in the film you've done. You say, "Oh, I could recut that and do that better." And, "Why am I holding so long on that shot?" Like the wide-angle one on Hume and Warren in the newspaper office. I waited such a long time to get in there. There was something about that space. It was an old newsroom. And, as I said earlier, Hume represents the old values.

I saw him really as a William Allen White character. White was a famous small-town Kansas editor in the early part of the century who represented all the great homespun decent American values. And I saw Hume as the decent conservative in that way, the representative of a different world that's just dying out.

As a matter of fact, we were originally going to have one scene at his house, and then I thought, "No, he should always be in the same place. He's the one anchored person here." And there's a pan down these pictures on his wall, and they're all pictures of an old America that's dying with him. So the set becomes very important to me, and a silence can direct your attention towards it.

SS: Normally, you'd see a newsroom bustling with activity, but it's dead. It's like a funeral home.

AJP: It's dead. Exactly. Exactly. The picture is full of ideas like that, and it was better not to spell everything out. Because, in this kind of a story, if you really spell it all out constantly, it'll fall apart in your hands. So, yes, if you look at Hume's office with its old-fashioned look with all the solid wood and compare it with the Parallax building, which is glass that is totally reflective, what you see is a symbol of what's happening to the film's world. And the film is full of big picture postcards of America like that, and like the huge powerful dam with the tiny figures in front of it. For me, that's what this film is about.

SS: This is one of those very influential films from the 1970s that really found their audience after the film had been released. I gather, though, that you weren't thrilled with how and when the film was released through Paramount. Can you remember what happened then?

AJP: I remember I wasn't thrilled, yeah. I think they found it a tough film to sell. Warren was shooting *Shampoo* [1975] at that time, producing it. And when *Parallax* came out, he wasn't available to promote it. *Chinatown* [1974], a wonderful film, came out around the same time and was produced by the head of the studio, Bob Evans. But I don't think that was the problem, and I don't blame the studio.

I have to tell you something. I think if you kill off the American hero like we did, that's taking a commercial risk. So I have to take full responsibility for that. That was my decision to end the film that way. I felt passionately about it. I thought, without that ending, the film would be totally compromised. I still feel that. But what's interesting to me now is that all of those things that I think created trouble at the time have since become very acceptable—and more than that—very interesting to people.

It's a film that, as much as any I've done, has taken on its own life. It's one of the first I'm asked about when I visit universities. I admit that I had expected more people to say, "Wow!" after they saw the film on its initial release than I felt I got. The reviews were mixed. But since then, it's taken on a whole other aura, and audiences have seen it differently.

SS: Well, I could go on all night but . . .

AJP: One thing before we end. You know, I'm being asked questions by one of the most original filmmakers of our time and . . . you look at his films, and they have a total integrity, and they're true to his vision in a way that I find remarkable.

When I saw his first film—it was *sex, lies, and videotape* [1989]—I turned to my wife and said, "You know, I see a lot of films I admire, but I never think, 'Gee, I wish I'd've done that film.'" But that's exactly what I thought then. It fascinated me. So, thank you, and I wish you well.

Since his feature debut with *sex, lies, and videotape* (1989), **Steven Soderbergh** has become a widely admired American film and TV director, producer, screenwriter, cinematographer (as Peter Andrews), and editor (as Mary Ann Bernard). He is the subject of *Steven Soderbergh: Interviews*, edited by Anthony Kaufman, in University Press of Mississippi's Conversations with Filmmakers Series.

Mr. Pakula Goes to Washington:
Alan J. Pakula on *All the President's Men*

Rick Thompson / 1976

From *Film Comment*, September–October 1976. Reprinted by permission of the author.

Alan J. Pakula, forty-eight, grew up in New York and majored in drama at Yale with "semiusual fantasies about becoming an actor." Later, he directed plays at Hollywood's Circle Theatre, including Anouilh's *Antigone*. As a production apprentice at MGM, Pakula spent eight months reading scripts and writing synopses for writer-producer Don Hartman, a veteran of Danny Kaye comedies and the *Road* series, who then became head of production at Paramount. At twenty-two, Pakula went along as assistant head of production.

At twenty-eight, he began to produce a series of films directed by Robert Mulligan (the only director Pakula produced for): *Fear Strikes Out, To Kill a Mockingbird, Love with the Proper Stranger, Baby the Rain Must Fall, Inside Daisy Clover, Up the Down Staircase*, and *The Stalking Moon*. In 1969, he began directing with *The Sterile Cuckoo*, then *Klute* (1971), *Love and Pain and the Whole Damn Thing* (1973), *The Parallax View* (1974), and *All the President's Men* (1976). He considered a career as a psychoanalyst but did not pursue it. He describes himself as "an analytic buff."

This interview took place in June and August 1976 in Pakula's offices at MGM, where he is preparing his next film, *Comes a Horseman Wild and Free*, original screenplay by Dennis Lynton Clark. Set in Montana in 1946, the film will star Jane Fonda and James Caan.

I am grateful to Richard Jameson and Howard Suber for suggesting key questions—**RT**

Alan J. Pakula: When I came on to *All the President's Men*, there was a first draft of the screenplay by William Goldman, and Bob Redford and Dustin Hoffman had been cast. Bob Redford was the producer.

Rick Thompson: Had Redford cast himself?

AJP: Bob had no choice. He wanted to see this film made.

RT: Why?

AJP: Bob's interest was on a lot of levels, I think. He's an activist in terms of things outside the industry—ecology, for example. I'm sure the triumph of the individual over the vastness of the government appealed to him; that's the extraordinary appeal of Woodward and Bernstein's story.

I had just made a film, *The Parallax View*, which someone at the *Atlantic Monthly* said had destroyed the American hero myth. If that's true, *All the President's Men* resurrects it. One film says the individual will be destroyed; it's Kafkaesque that way, Central European. The irony of the film lies in the contrast of all the pop-art American motifs, indicating the innocent, open society; you get the feeling we used to associate with Central Europe of the individual destroyed in a secret maze by forces of which he has no knowledge.

The Woodward and Bernstein story is the antithesis of that. Film students have asked me how I could do one and then the other, and I say, it's very simple: *Parallax View* represents my fear about what's happening in the world, and *All the President's Men* represents my hope. Like most of us, I'm balanced between the two.

Bob is fascinated by how the system operates. I have a theory—Bob knows it—that he has a tendency to make how-to pictures. The first picture is *Downhill Racer* [1969]—how to be a champion skier; *The Candidate* [1972]—how to be a political candidate; *Jeremiah Johnson* [1972]—how to survive in the wilderness; *All the President's Men*—how to be a successful investigative reporter.

Bob was far more interested in making this film, seeing it made, than he was in acting in it. He was not crazy about the part of Bob Woodward; he's very fond of Woodward, but he wasn't crazy about playing him. He thought it was a very difficult and possibly thankless role.

RT: The Redford we saw on the television documentary about the making of the film doesn't seem at all like Woodward, whereas Hoffman really fits Bernstein. Woodward is such a poker player compared to Redford.

AJP: Forget about the TV show. That was Bob Redford, not Bob Redford playing Woodward. In the film, Bob plays it very close to the vest. He's very cautious, very concentrated, very contained.

RT: When they interview someone, one reporter is the tough cop, and the other is the con cop.

AJP: Bernstein's the con cop and Woodward's the tough cop, the one who goes right to the questions, bluntly; it embarrassed Bernstein sometimes. And, unlike the man who was in *The Sting* [1973], he plays no surface charm; Bernstein does all the charming things.

RT: How did you think out the way you would characterize people in this film? Characterization seems to operate through behavior—acting—and also through environment, through the décor you place your characters in.

AJP: That's terribly important. In the beginning, you start with reality; doing a real thing. Besides reading the book, I had spent a lot of time with Bob and Carl, as had Bob and Dustin. I went over the characters with Bob and Carl, reminisced about them; they described the characters, sometimes in more detail than in the book. We tried to go with reality wherever possible.

I felt the film demanded the same kind of discipline that is necessary for investigative reporting. At all times, the prayer was that audiences would sense a great deal more about the characters than was verbally revealed on the screen.

One of the greatest problems with doing this kind of story, where the narrative demands are enormous—and the narrative demands *were* enormous—is that every scene must add to the solving of this mystery or show you the conditions under which it was solved.

RT: An incredible amount of exposition.

AJP: Incredible. I don't think there's a more verbal film that's ever been made, not even *Claire's Knee* [1970].

RT: Do you find that sort of characterization, in which more is implied than said, common to *Klute* and *The Parallax View* as well?

AJP: Yes. In any detective story when your main character is going to a series of characters who last for only one or two scenes in the film, you are in danger of winding up with characters who are just lifeless puppets serving the narrative. Usually, this is disguised by some obvious surface color—which may account for the number of broken-down, alcoholic nymphomaniacs one finds in detective stories.

The average detective story lends itself to that kind of obvious color, because in most detective stories the solution of the mystery—which is who killed so-and-so or who stole what money—invariably leads you to the bottom of society, to the people who do not live like everybody else, the people who have not made it, the people whose lives have been destroyed, the people whose lives have a good grotesque quality about them. It's a director's dream: the audience is not going to get bored.

All the President's Men is the opposite of that. If it's a detective story, it's a middle-class, establishment one. It was essential not only to preserve the sense of that in the film, but to emphasize it. Instead of the world of nightclubs with broken-down torch singers, crap games, gunmen, the night world, the world of people who don't come out in the daytime, people who never seem to raise their heads up into the middle class, Woodstein's search takes them to just the opposite: they're in the world of people upon whom the sun shines, the people who cut their grass, the people who pay their taxes on time, whose lives are ordered, whose houses are neat, whose world is precise, the people whom most of your audience envision as themselves.

We had to emphasize that. It's what the story is all about: establishment corruption, the most threatening and dangerous kind. I said to Gordie [cinematographer Gordon Willis] that a lot of this must take place in the sunlight. We have to go for ordered, formal compositions; the compositions and sets have to visually give you a sense of their lives.

For example, Hugh Sloan has only two scenes in the film—well, three, but one's on videotape. He's a major character, and you have very little time with him. Again, we started with reality. We saw the exact apartment he lived in at that time. The exterior used in the film is the building Sloan lived in at that time. Sloan lived in a new suburban development of row houses designed in a Disneyland version of eighteenth-century federalism. There's a clear contrast between this sunny little community with its sentimentalized architecture—federalism with the guts out, this protected little enclave for middle-class people on the way up—and the gray world Woodward walks into after the second Deep Throat scene, that no-man's-land of huge stone power dwarfing the individual in a most threatening way. That contrast dramatizes one of the most important themes in the film: the complacency and abuse in the removal of most of the society from the dangers that are being revealed to Woodstein and the audience.

We built the interior from the real floor plan. Carl and Bob described the way it had been furnished: it was like visiting your grandparents, they said; it looked like old people, with wingchairs—that to them is old.

Sloan's first scene takes place in the daytime, and there's sun on the wingchair, soft light through gauzy curtains; the sun's on him, but not on them on the couch. There he sits—a very formal portrait. We shot a medium shot and a close-up; only used the close-up for one line as the tag at the end of the scene; never used it for the rest of the scene because in the close-up you lost the formality, that whole sense of a modern version of the young Virginia squire, decent, aristocratic, sitting in his wingchair with a nineteenth-century convex mirror behind him, almost ready for Gilbert Stuart to come along and paint him. In the midst of this precise tableau with the shaft of sunlight, all these cheap, corrupt little facts come out—in counterpoint to what we see, and indeed in counterpoint to a simple, traditional kind of decency that we sense in the character of Sloan.

An essence of investigative reporting is getting people to talk about things they don't really want to talk about, or at least are deeply ambivalent about. How Woodward and Bernstein will get them to talk, and if they will get them to talk, is the key to much of the suspense in the film. If you don't have a sense of the character—why it's difficult for him to talk, what his attitude about all this is, what kind of person he is—then none of the suspense works. Unless you know what his feelings are and what might work on him, then there's no fascination in seeing how the reporter handles it, how he gets the information.

RT: You must have chosen to include scenes in the reporters' apartments as well.

AJP: You get a sense of the character. There was a major decision made in this film, and we kept fighting against it and testing it: dramatize them through their work and don't linger on their personal lives. We even shot a scene between Dustin and a girl; and we spent endless time working out scenes of Bob with a girl, but we didn't shoot them. The film is about their work. The reason we were filming the story of Woodward and Bernstein was because of what they accomplished and how they accomplished it. The challenge became to reveal them as people through the way they worked.

RT: Generically, it's a job film.

AJP: That's a decision Dustin is unhappy about to this day. He feels it left out the whole personalized sense of the characters.

RT: Because both actors were so involved with their real counterparts? Because Dustin wanted to play Carl in a larger, mythic way?

AJP: No, more than that, I think Dustin loves detail, and it meant leaving out an enormous amount of detail. There were fascinating things we found out about them that there was no time for. But Bob and I felt we could not stop the relentless narrative drive of the film—to stop parenthetically, kick off our shoes, and relax with the characters. Dustin felt we didn't take enough time to play the reactions of Woodward and Bernstein, particularly Bernstein. We felt it would have made for a more leisurely film, endangering the line of tension that holds the whole experience together.

RT: You sneaked a lot in—the bicycle wheel is there.

AJP: In terms of their getting the story, always their work, you had to sneak everything in. In directing any film, you spend a great deal of time first accumulating information and then discarding information. Both these areas of work were more difficult than on any film I've done before.

I spent my first months of preparation finding out everything I could about the subjects and characters, and amassing details and ideas—a constant accumulation. The next step was ruthlessly boiling it down: discarding, discarding, discarding, and hoping that somewhere in that boiling process, something of the original richness was still there, even if no longer verbalized. One hopes the initial accumulation will give the film a texture, a resonance the audience will feel.

I told Bob I didn't know how I could do this film if I couldn't go to the *Washington Post*; there's no way I could get that sense of reality. It's a how-to picture, and if you don't believe how they did it, the film is nothing. That was the bottom line for everybody playing reporters or editors: whatever they knew or didn't know, they must know their work, must know how to be a good reporter and a good editor.

I think we feel the reporters' ruthlessness in the film. In dealing with an administration, part of whose tragedy was that the end seemed to justify any means—and some of those ends were pretty crummy too—Woodstein certainly did not hesitate to have *their* end justify some very questionable means. Their end was to get the story, not to save the country.

When I was first doing research, Nora Ephron told me that investigative reporters are not interested in making great moral statements; they're not working from moral outrage. And it's true; they're obsessed only with getting that story. To *reveal*: that's their job, that's their hunger, and it has to be a desperate hunger for them to succeed.

An investigative reporter exposes the secret wrongdoings of people with great power. People with power are never taken at face value. They must always be seen whole and clear for what they are not: they must not be looked up to unquestioningly as the child looks up to the parent. The investigative reporter performs a great service to society. But it's a highly unsentimental line of work. They're a far cry from the simple, kindly heroism of Capra's films: there was no way we could make *Mr. Woodstein Goes to Washington*.

RT: The film is about two obsessive individuals—you don't see them do anything else; you see them doing this at 3:00 a.m.

AJP: No question: it *is* obsessive. Without that obsession, there would have been no way that anybody would have made those breakthroughs. Somebody said that if Woodward and Bernstein had been happily married, Nixon might still be president.

RT: Within the newsroom, the only two of their colleagues they use badly are women.

AJP: I know. It's based on two incidents in the book.

RT: And they do use those two women in sexual ways.

AJP: One of the people at the *Post* was disturbed by the fact that the two *Post* women were shown using their sexuality. I think what you say is more to the point: it's not the women who come off questionably; it's the reporters who come off questionably because they're exploiting them. But when you're obsessed, it's for the story. From their point of view, the women are reporters, and if anybody should understand, they should. And if they don't, well, the story's more important.

RT: How subjectively did you intend viewers to relate to Woodward and Bernstein? Were you careful not to be judgmental? Were you inviting viewers to be judgmental?

AJP: My initial fascination with the subject was: What would it have been like to have been Woodward and Bernstein when they first revealed the story? So obviously I intended the viewers to relate to Woodward and Bernstein. We tried to make the film the way investigative reporters write: to present the realities and let the audience draw the conclusions to be drawn.

When we previewed the film, we found that in the cities, the audience would relate very strongly to Woodward and Bernstein, but in places like Kentucky, there would be strong relation to the people they were interviewing, people they trapped.

RT: They seem to know how to use people: they're not inventing the technique on the spot; they've done it before.

AJP: It's not the good old Mr. Smith hero, who was so simple he didn't know how to disguise how he felt. This is a very different kind of man, not in the classic mold. Obsessed with the work at hand, they'll do anything to achieve success in it. They're more related to the detective character than other American types. Look at the Bogart characters: they weren't doing it for good or to save the world; it was out of their own fascination with it, their own amoral feeling about the case.

RT: That's apt, as the Bogart character in those films is quite willing to bluff or misrepresent himself to find out what he wants to know.

AJP: Absolutely. He wants to get his story; he wants to solve that mystery. They're both amoral in a way, not much to do with the old-fashioned American hero compared to the manipulating European.

RT: Are you interested in film noir, those postwar crime melodramas with the world coming apart at the seams behind the plot? That picture of the world in chaos and disarray, as well as the use of visual style and signs to carry most of the film's "meaning," could relate to *Klute*, *The Parallax View* . . .

AJP: Oh sure. In *Klute*, the fact that you are in this nightmarish world, this underbelly of society, right away makes it much more theatrical. The most interesting things to photograph, I suppose, are extreme things: the very rich with huge houses; the very down-and-out people, alcoholics and derelicts, the people who can't make it but who are desperate.

RT: Because they're not real to us?

AJP: That's right. You see very few middle-class detective stories. Carvel was the setting for Andy Hardy; you never see *The Carvel Murder*.

RT: Hitchcock came close with *Shadow of a Doubt* [1943].

AJP: There's the great exception. It's a wonderful film. And that's why it's unlike any other film of its time, when you think about it. It's stunning. I never get tired of seeing it. In *Klute*, you see, I deliberately open on a middle-class setting—Thanksgiving Day, sunlight, the only family we ever see in the film—to point out the alienating nature of the rest of the film.

There's titillating escape in going to see films about murders, and the fact that you've gone into a world of people who dare to live like that has always had a great theatrical pull. *Klute* has that in it. Those films of the 1940s had it. Sure, it was a film of the alienated people, but the fascination for an audience was spending two hours with characters that let their ids go awry. In *All the President's Men*, we couldn't offer them that. There's no shock in seeing how Sloan lives, or how the bookkeeper lives.

RT: Faced with the scene from detective films where the client tells the detective he's off the payroll and off the case, Woodward and Bernstein would do what the dick does: keep on going.

AJP: Exactly true; they would. It has about the same moral base as the detectives had. When Bob first talked to me about directing the film, I said to him that one of my concerns was that he and Dustin were in the film, particularly him—I'd wanted to work with them both for a long time, so it had nothing to do with their talents. The essence of this story is that two unknown reporters are catalysts in bringing down some of the most powerful people on earth. If you have two huge stars, right away that makes its own statement. Particularly Redford. While Dustin's a star, he's a character actor as well; he's not an obvious hero star. Bob is in the classic mold—one of the few first-rate actors who is. He looks so competent on screen in everything he does.

It doesn't matter that Bob can have trouble opening a bottle of club soda in real life, like all of us; on screen, it looks like it would pop open if he just waved his thumb at it. That's trouble for this film. But now I am convinced that one of the shrewdest things done in the making of the film was the casting of Bob Redford and Dustin Hoffman—and I had no part in the casting.

I told Bob, "If you come on as stars in the newsroom, we're in trouble." The key to that is Ben Bradlee because the star of the newsroom at the *Washington Post*, without question, is Bradlee. Look at Ben in that half-hour television documentary the other night on the making of the film: Ben comes out of it as the star. He has that thing: he holds the screen down. If Bob and Dustin went in there as stars, and the Bradlee part went to a secondary actor, no matter how good, who didn't have the sort of personality that could overpower them, if they seemed more above the title than he—it wouldn't work.

RT: In all newspaper films, the editor is top dog.

AJP: Yeah, but it's true in real life. More often than not, especially in magazines, the Clay Felkers have a quality that turns writers on. So casting that part became very important.

RT: So your strategy was to set Bradlee as the center . . .

AJP: A center who can push them down. For example, the major "star entrance" in the film is Robards's. Up until he comes on, there's almost no camera movement . . . very little. When he comes out of his office, arbitrarily out of nowhere, we move with him down half the set: we give him a star entrance out of Belasco, all stops out. And you say, "Here comes the king."

Jason's greatest successes have come playing failures, men who could not deal with reality, whether as Hickey in *The Iceman Cometh*, or in *Moon for the Misbegotten*. The poetic failure. Poetic failure is the antithesis of Ben Bradlee, who thrives on success, on being of and in the world and trying to be a controlling factor in the world. He loves dealing with reality. Whatever poetic qualities there may be in Ben privately have nothing whatsoever to do with the Ben Bradlee who's in that office and portrayed in this film. Jason and Ben are very different people. Jason's full of soul, which is one of the least-needed qualities to play Ben Bradlee. We finally went with Jason's belief that he could do it—and he knew Ben; he understood the part and its problems.

RT: You must have thought about characterizing Bradlee as positively as you did. He's the only character in the film who is totally admirable; he doesn't screw anybody, etc. You could have placed him more ambiguously had you wanted to.

AJP: First of all, he's not sentimental. His concern is not about hurting people unnecessarily. It's "Is the paper going to be in danger?" He never says, "Poor John Mitchell, poor so-and-so." He is concerned about the truth and corroboration of the story. If the story turns out to be untrue, it's going to be bad for the *Washington Post*.

RT: How did you deal with the problem of fairness in depicting real people?

AJP: In terms of accusations or charges, nothing was ever said that wasn't corroborated in the book, or in their notes for their stories; that just could not have been done. That became our guideline: Woodward and Bernstein had their two-source rule, and this was our rule.

RT: What did you see as the purpose of the film-illustration of the book? A "lest-we forget" parable, what?

AJP: In the beginning, to be really absurdist about it, it was climbing a mountain because it was there. I wanted to tell that story because it was there. On a childlike level—one of the most important levels on which this picture operates, that primitive storytelling level—I was fascinated by what it would have been like to be Woodward and Bernstein. These two untried young men discovering the story which became the most important investigative story of our republic, that had an enormous effect on our society, and eventually resulted in the resignation of the president of the United States. This goes right back to why you make pictures, why you want to be a director. It goes back to that childhood fantasizing, putting yourself into a world you would love to be in.

Second, the methodology of investigative reporting fascinates me and of course, as I think *Klute* and *The Parallax View* represented in different ways, the relationship between the individual and power. And, as I said to Woodward and Bernstein, if *All the President's Men* had been a work of fiction, I never would have made it. I wouldn't have believed it.

RT: The modifying point is that the power of these two individuals is hooked up to the power of a great institution, the *Washington Post*. In the case of *Parallax*, it's impossible for Warren Beatty, without a major paper behind him, to accomplish what Woodward and Bernstein do later.

AJP: I don't think the *Washington Post* would have had the story without Woodward and Bernstein. In that way, it was very much their story. The *Post* backed them, that's true; but it wasn't like the power of the *Post* or the power of Ben Bradlee could really get them that much help. If anything, it sometimes made it more difficult in terms of people being frightened of speaking to them. But the fact that it was published certainly had a lot to do with the courage of the *Post* at that point.

RT: Any qualms about political criticism for releasing the film during a presidential election year?

AJP: Bill Safire came out and said the book, *The Final Days* [published in 1976], and the release of the film were a vendetta. The realities are that Bob Redford wanted to make this film before that and there was no way to get it ready in time—he wanted to make it earlier, not later. From the point of view of Warner Bros., who controlled the release date, they were also financing President Nixon's memoirs—they paid him a large sum of money for paperback publication rights. The fine, even hand of American business!

My own feeling is that this kind of corruption, this danger to the electoral system, can't be restricted to one party. I think that people who are attracted to enormous power share similar strengths and vulnerabilities. It's certainly not limited by party. I don't think Woodward and Bernstein would have decided not to pursue the story had it been LBJ in power, and I don't think we would have refused to do a movie if it had been about a Democrat.

I don't think you worry about the political effect of a film's release in that way if you believe that the film does deal with reality and has its own integrity. I don't think any of us were trying to be kingmakers by the release of this film.

RT: What about the data-technology close-ups that run through the film? Television screens, typewriters, Xerox machines, library slips, special copy-paper sets, and, at the beginning of the film, those .44 Magnum typewriter key letters filling the screen?

AJP: The use of the television set is something apart. The typewriter keys, library slips, lists of people who work at CREEP, notepads on which Woodward scribbles his notes while he's phoning, pencils, pens, were all part of a conception of the absurdity of the weapons in this war story—that what brought down perhaps the most powerful people on earth were these little slips of paper, and pens, and typewriter keys.

Actually, the opening shot of those typewriter keys sets the whole use of objects in the film. I thought of that in Washington a couple of weeks before we started to shoot. If there was ever a picture which says on the most primitive level that the pen is mightier than the sword, this is it. Letters as bullets; typewriter keys as guns; little things becoming huge in their power: it becomes those little things against those enormous buildings and against those people behind the television screen that you can't reach.

So when the typewriter keys come down, we had whiplashes and gunshots mixed in with that sound; not enough so you can tell, just enough to get that CRACK! Originally, I didn't want to see the Bros.' trademark before that because I didn't want to see any letters before the typewriter keys: the first letters you see are weapons. We tried to magnify those sounds—the little scratchings of pencils; it's like little rats who scratch their way under those huge buildings and that huge power, burrowing in.

RT: Some of your shots are intricate presentations of the idea of scale. The Library of Congress reading room shot, for instance, where you have several abstract ideas of scale at once: how small the library slip is, yet how much it contains both in terms of importance and in terms of sheer data—that shoeboxful of them containing millions of discrete data bits, all very tiny. You pull back, [and] there are the men, and what they contain, their complexity, how big they are in one sense but, as the shot continues, how small they are in another; and then the library is so large. It's something like Charles Eames's film, *Powers of Ten* [1977].

AJP: That was the essence of the Library of Congress shot. Some people say it was a tour-de-force for its own sake. I don't think it was. I tried to do several things with it. Starting with those little library slips as clues, filling the screen at first, enormous in their size, and then pulling back to the top of the Library of Congress, where the reporters are so small, gave me a chance to dramatize the endless time it takes to do these things, without being boring about it. It also gave me a sense of how lost they are in this thing, how tiny these figures are in terms of the enormity of the task and the heroic job they're trying to achieve.

There's also something about the Library of Congress that moved me, particularly in that shot in the hallway, something I didn't expect audiences to share, a personal thing. That pseudo-Renaissance hallway they walk through to the reading room and, indeed, the reading room itself have a romantic conception of power behind them, also a romantic ideal of the human being: the antithesis of what's going on in this film.

RT: It's an architectural difference, among other differences.

AJP: I love to use architecture to dramatize a society, very much so in *Klute*, even more so in *Parallax View*; that was really creating a whole sense of a world through buildings. In *All the President's Men*, the power of the administration is dramatized through the buildings. It's strange because you don't see the power: you don't see the president except on television.

RT: An idea that comes from that is that the buildings don't belong to the men in them: the buildings will be there forever; the men will come and go. That doesn't come from the data of the building's appearance, of course; it comes from our prior knowledge.

AJP: There's never been a film I know of that has depended so much on the basic knowledge the audience has and that uses that, takes it for granted. That's deliberate. That's what surprised me when the picture was such a success in England and at the Berlin Festival.

RT: You made *Klute* and *The Parallax View* for wide Panavision proportions while *All the President's Men* is in 1.85. Why?

AJP: We shot with Panavision equipment on *All the President's Men*—Panavision made some special diopter lenses for us, but we didn't use squeezed [anamorphic], we used 1.85. That was Gordon's decision. I said, "Fine, as long as I get a very sharp, hard look." I would have fought it on *Parallax View*, with its wide scale and space.

RT: And where several key scenes are so horizontal.

AJP: Absolutely. *Klute* was a very vertical picture, and *Parallax View* was very horizontal. One has people trapped in tunnels, pressed, claustrophobic, the world pushing in on them; the other has people lost in space. In *All the President's Men*, an essence of the work, investigative reporting, is concentration and patience: sitting on the phone, talking to people you don't see, locked in for long periods of time. It's the opposite of physical movement. And to have done a lot of camera moves would have broken the concentration rather than intensified it. So there is comparatively little camera movement in the film. When the camera does move, as they become more manic toward the end, it seems very theatrical by contrast.

The new film I'm working on will have a great deal of movement because intense physical movement and work are a major part of the characters' lives and story.

RT: Do you think about composing your frames in terms of negative space? Charged space? You seem to compose more spatially dramatic shots than other directors working now—the way you place characters, often off center or off balance, using passive and active space.

AJP: There's a great deal of that in *Klute*, where I was going for tension and compression. That sense of negative or potential space—in film you have the other element, too: it moves. Part of the tension is the constant change in spatial relationships, which I love to do: the spatial relationships between the characters and their world changing during a scene as well as the spatial relationship between characters changing during the scene, all of which comes out of trying to convey some subjective feeling to the audience.

I hate camerawork for its own sake. If you don't know what to do with a camera, then don't do anything—just as I tell an actor, "If you don't know what to do, don't do anything until you find what's needed; start with nothing." When you start imposing something to make it interesting, the whole concentration of the film falls apart. It becomes dishonest, and the audience senses it.

The decision about how to frame a picture comes from how to intensify that experience for the audience, to give it to them without telling them that you're giving it to them. I once said of *All the President's Men* that I didn't want the film to editorialize: they wouldn't say so-and-so is bad, so-and-so is good; rather, they would say, so-and-so did this, this is what happened. But actually, the camera keeps pushing the audience to a point of view all the time. In the middle, that crowd at the convention screaming, "Four more years! Four more years!" while Woodward is at the typewriter—that's giving the audience a whole sense of what's happening.

And at the end, Nixon on the television set, taking the oath of office while they're both typing away: visually, the audience is pushed into very specific feelings, but they are not stated verbally. It deals on a more primitive level on the one hand and on a more sophisticated level on the other; it's more unconscious for them; they don't even know what's happening to them in some way.

RT: It bypasses verbal formulation.

AJP: Yes. I'm bored with people who say films have to be all visual. I've often wondered what would have happened if radio had started before silent films, and if films had come out of radio. I think we would have had a whole different sense of what's pure and what's impure. It's absurd to say that film is only visual and that to use a lot of aural effects makes it an impure art. That's nonsense. It's trying to compare being painterly and being literary: two different things. Sound is as much a part of films today as visuals. You try to orchestrate the soundtrack very carefully for an effect because people do not hear at the same level all the time. The ear edits. That's one of the great tools you have as a director—what you do with the soundtrack.

RT: You have a set of shots which counterpose the television screen and Woodward's typewriter carriage.

AJP: That scene is during the Republican Convention, when Woodward is sitting at his typewriter writing about the delay of the GAO report—the Republicans are trying to hold it back until after the convention. He's trying to write that story, and on the television is the renomination of Richard Nixon. There's one shot of the keyboard of the typewriter in the foreground, with his fingers typing. In front of him is the television set. His hands and the typewriter are *bigger* than the television screen.

Anyway, that was the original shot I thought of having. We were setting up television sets around the room so there wouldn't be just one, stagily set in front of Bob Woodward. I was bothered that the original shot made Woodward's hands and the article he was writing much more powerful than the nominating convention on the television screen. So we put a TV set way in front of Woodward so that the cheering people at the convention would fill three-quarters of the screen while Woodward typing would be a tiny figure in the background, thus dramatizing the David-and-Goliath struggle I wanted. That shot became the climactic shot of the scene. The reversal of scale from the previous shot, where Woodward's hands were bigger, dramatized the true nature of the conflict.

The president is never shown except at the height of his power. There were people who said, "Why didn't you give him the defeat? Why didn't you show him down and out and give the audience that satisfaction?" That's not what the film is about. The godlike quality the audience has at the end of that last scene, seeing the man take the Oath of Office for the second term as president of the United States, at the height of his power, and those men with their little typewriter keys against the gunshots of the cannon salute. Thank God they had the twenty-one-gun salute because it set up the typewriter keys as weapons. And the reporters don't look up: just that same, driven . . .

RT: Nixonian concentration.

AJP: Yes. But the power of that shot depends upon the audience knowing what the president at the height of his power doesn't know, what even the reporters typing away don't know: that, in two years, what they're writing is going to force him to resign.

I never planned the twenty-one-gun salute against the typewriters until [associate producer] Jon Boorstin brought in the tapes, and we were playing them to decide on which one—of the inauguration—we would use. We got to the twenty-one-gun salute, and without that we wouldn't have thought of the effect: it all came together that day.

RT: You put Woodward and Bernstein through their paces in space: a lot of strange positioning in the frame, unusual compositions, making them move in odd ways. Woodward particularly seems more ill at ease in space than Bernstein, from the scene where Bernstein rewrites his copy onwards.

AJP: Woodward was the new man in the room. Bernstein had been there awhile, for years; in reality, I think, he was going through a bad time just then on the paper. Carl is a man who works hard when he's turned on, and if he's not turned on by something, forget it—a syndrome I know very well. Woodward had come in six or eight months before and was turning out page-one copy regularly: totally driven, he calls himself a "workaholic." That tension inside Woodward helps hold this picture together; it comes out of that tense, obsessive drive for the story. Almost always, he doesn't relate to the world he's in unless it relates to the story. The way he walks: it's not where he is, unless that space has something to do with what he's thinking about. It's like he almost doesn't belong there, in that space.

RT: What about the emotional or dramatic use of color? There are times when it seems that, out of the normal, low-key fabric of the film, you go KAPOW! The scene in Bernstein's apartment when Woodward comes over to say, "We're bugged!" you frame Woodward in the entryway, silhouetted against hot chrome yellow, everything else dark, shadowed. And that's the moment when fear comes to the front of the film.

AJP: When I came on the film, I went back to do the research, trying to keep my mind free of as many preconceptions as possible. Hoping reality would make the work more organic.

The first thing I did was hit the *Washington Post* newsroom. I shudder to think what it would have been like if the *Post* hadn't moved into its new quarters, which it had done about a year before the Watergate story broke. Their old offices, I gather, were like most old newspaper offices. It would have been a great loss to the film. I can't tell you that I would ever have thought of conceiving of a newsroom like that if the *Washington Post* hadn't had it; but given that newsroom—it was the whole key to the style of the film.

The colors of the *Washington Post* are hard. First of all, it's hard fluorescent light through the whole room. I said to Gordie, "I want it hard; don't soften it. I want to make the audience uncomfortable." The truth is uncomfortable. We're obsessed with the truth, so there should be harsh light. There is one major cut when you cut back to the newsroom from Bradlee's lawn at night when your eye is literally shocked. I wanted that.

My concern was that Technicolor [the lab] would balance the prints for a nice sense of flow, soften it down to a smooth, ivory thing. I told them I wanted the audience to recoil; it's back to exposing the truth.

Plus there are those incredibly harsh, tough, poster colors—hard electric blues—in the *Post* newsroom. And that idea of being put in the middle of a modern poster, the total lack of subtlety, a kind of cruelty about it, the lack of rest for the eye, became the center of the visual conception of the film.

The *Post* newsroom is in the business of communicating the truth. They do it in a place without shadows, where everything is exposed; you can hide nothing in that room. That reality gave us a very apt visual concept. In contrast to it, the world that's trying to hide itself becomes that much more dramatic. I wanted to show the total accessibility of everyone at the *Washington Post*—you see everything Bradlee does behind his glass wall; if he scratches, the whole office watches him—compared to the inaccessibility of the president.

A light that exposes everything with hard, tough, exposed colors became terribly important to the center of the film: exposing the truth. Then obviously you have the dark and the hiding as a contrast.

RT: Do you think of yourself as an actor's director?

AJP: I always love working with actors: it was my first love. It's not so much anymore. I enjoy it. In many ways, it fascinates me because it is an exploration of character—the kind of thing that interested me in being an analyst, except you're not doing it for therapeutic reasons. You're doing it to find out what there is in that person that'll be right for that character. An actor cannot give anything to a part that is not somewhere inside him. All an actor has to work with is himself—his own observations, his own feelings.

RT: Are actors grasping? Do they want something from you?

AJP: They want any help they can get from anybody to be better actors and give better performances. That's why every actor says, "I want a wonderful director. I want a very strong director." And invariably, they want it on the one hand, while they doubt and question it on the other. Usually, the ambivalence they bring to a relationship with the director is the very ambivalence they have about themselves: moments of enormous belief in themselves and moments of grave self-doubt.

That's very often projected on to the director. Sometimes you're swept along in the moments of great belief, and you can do no wrong; other times, you're swept along in the moments of self-doubt and can do no good. It's a hell of a rollercoaster ride. Somewhere in between, you try to keep your equilibrium about what work you're doing is good and what is bad.

RT: This film, *Klute*, and *The Parallax View* have been called a paranoid trilogy. What is paranoia for you?

AJP: I think that paranoia is a terribly misused word, the sort of word that's used constantly today, unclinically and incorrectly. I use it to represent an excessive fear of the unknown, the unseen.

RT: The unknown is always threatening?

AJP: Not always, but there is that kind of unknown—a child's fear of darkness, night fears, fears in some way of being punished—that is indeed threatening. That there is something out there that you can't see, that could destroy you. Not a realistic fear of the unknown, but one that comes out of internal fears for oneself—one's internal anxieties being directed on to something outside of oneself.

RT: It's a personalized fear—something trying to get you.

AJP: Very personalized. In *Klute*, it was much more personal, so that the whole suspense thing of Bree's being followed by this man and her anxieties about herself all come together. One of the fascinations of melodrama is that it takes so many of our fears of the unknown and gives us a chance to act them out in a group situation where we are safe. The word "paranoia" might be more sensibly applied to *Klute* than to *All the President's Men*, where the characters are more rational.

What most melodramas do is take that irrational fear of the unknown we all have, then externalize it, make it something to be afraid of; then the hero and heroine are saved, and we've triumphed over the fear, facilitating that kind of catharsis.

In both *Parallax View* and *All the President's Men*, the fear has to do with a growing sense of living in a potentially threatening society. The fear in *All the President's Men* comes out of the dealings with Deep Throat. After those dealings, we have the sense that the safe, open society we supposedly live in is full of dark unknowns that could be threatening us—the kind of thing we associate with foreign societies. That's very much what *Parallax* is all about, and that's why at the end of it, we used all those cheerful, open, American images—red, white, and blue tablecloths and banners, all those little cheerleaders putting up their little presidential faces—a vision we've all grown up with about America, underneath which is the mysterious unknown.

RT: You reserve that fear until the end of *All the President's Men*. You don't let it break through to the surface earlier in the film.

AJP: The only places you feel the fear before that, I guess, is when they're talking to secretaries and when they're interviewing people in doorways.

RT: You're seeing the effects of anxiety.

AJP: You're seeing the effects of anxiety. Yes, but you reserve that till the end because, if we didn't, then the whole picture would have been hyped and unreal. Deep Throat is the key to the whole thing: a man who was that disturbed and that frightened, who was obviously close to the center of the government—that's what releases that fear.

RT: How did you decide to present Deep Throat in such a strong way—close-ups, dramatic dark lighting, dominant composition?

AJP: I had great concern about that. When I talked to Bob Woodward originally, I kept asking for assurance that there really was a Deep Throat, that he wasn't apocryphal, because the whole idea of meeting this unknown source in garages in the middle of the night, flags in flowerpots, changing cabs, all that was out of style with the rest of the story. I kept saying, "It's almost like a gift to some film director. Did it really happen that way?" Because, if it didn't happen that way, I wouldn't do it that way. My first reaction if it were a work of fiction would be to say, "Is it going too far?" Bob reassured me that it did happen that way. Given that, I said, "Alright, its gift to us is that it does dramatize another sense of danger in these things at a different level than anything else in the film." The idea is that Deep Throat is so afraid of being followed that Woodward begins to be frightened, wondering what was going on.

RT: The pace of the film seems very effective in that there's a certain rhythm for the beginning and the middle and then, BAM, the film's over. It's one of the most hard-minded choices in the film, making the end pointed, hard, abrupt, rather than letting it diffuse.

AJP: Absolutely. To leave the story while they were still the only ones battling it out, at least in the vanguard, when the story had been revealed to them in its outlines. I liked the irony of ending right after their greatest defeat, the Haldeman story: they were right, but their story was wrong. That was Bill Goldman's concept before I came on the film, and the more I worked on the film, the more I came to trust it: the two of them and Bradlee against the world; everyone saying, "They've obviously gone too far," while we know it goes further than that. That's much more dramatic than seeing them proved right all over the place. The one thing we did do was put in the teletype at the end, and that came later—after the first preview.

RT: It fits well with the beginning, the typewriter keys.

AJP: And again, it's relentless: the weapons of words keep hammering out the fate of these people.

RT: And it's impersonal.

AJP: Absolutely. A good investigative reporter is not on a personal vendetta.

Born in the United States and now based in Australia, **Rick Thompson** has written extensively for publications in the United States and abroad, and his work has been widely anthologized. He also taught cinema studies at UCLA, the American Film Institute, and Australia's La Trobe University.

Making a Film about Two Reporters

Alan J. Pakula / 1976

From *American Cinematographer*, July 4, 1976. Excerpted from a talk given by Pakula at the Ninth Motion Picture Seminar of the Northwest, held in Seattle, Washington. Reprinted by permission of the American Society of Cinematographers.

I was out of town and unreachable when I was supposed to be asked about the title of my talk today. When I arrived here, I was told it had been given the title "Making a Film about Two Reporters." That amused me, because somebody else had called the film the same thing. Ron Ziegler, President Nixon's press secretary, went to an early preview of the film and, when asked what he thought about it, said, "Well, it's just a picture about two reporters." I was amused to see that the Ninth Motion Picture Seminar of the Northwest had confirmed his statement.

In many ways the title is apt because to me the essence of the experience of the film is the whole Walter Mitty fantasy of what it would have been like to have been Woodward and Bernstein. These two reporters, when they discovered the Watergate mysteries and broke through the cover-up, affected all of our lives and our whole society.

When Bob Redford asked me to direct *All the President's Men*—it was Bob's idea to make the film—I said, "The experience of making the film fascinates me. How to do it, I have no idea at this point. But since I've always been a producer, and have always produced the films I've directed, let's make damned sure we agree about the kind of film we want to make."

So we sat down to see what it would be like to be these two reporters, Woodward and Bernstein. It's been a fascinating adventure, recreating two men's lives. And the whole experience was colored by the fact that they are very much alive.

I went to the *Washington Post* and spent months at Bob Woodward's desk. He was upstairs doing *The Final Days* with Carl Bernstein. I had Woodward's desk in the newsroom and I had my own Walter Mitty fantasy. I was a reporter for the *Washington Post*. I would attend all the meetings. It was marvelous.

There was another problem in directing this picture, and that was that you could hear the drums rolling in the background, signifying that this was an important event. There is no way of writing importance, and there is no way of directing importance, and there is no way of acting importance. We were going to do a film that would show what it was like, and it had to be totally unselfconscious.

I was very concerned that the actors might hear a symphonic orchestra playing John Philip Sousa every time they walked onto the set, thinking, "Here is our great contribution to American history!" So I tried to lessen the environment so that it was as if we were all play-acting after school because actors would come on to the set, and they would say, "I must give my all for this film." The fact is that, for most actors, "all" is just too much. Laurence Olivier once said that an actor should hold something in reserve, and some actors should hold a lot in reserve. It was a problem I've never had to this extent on any other film, and I don't think I ever will again because of the very nature of the event.

Everything portrayed in the film was dictated by trying to make it an immediate experience, trying to say what it was like at that time. Originally, Bob Redford had seen the film as possibly being made in black and white, in what I suppose you would call "a classic documentary style," but I didn't want to do that. To me "documentary" does not necessarily mean black and white; it does not necessarily mean grainy; it does not necessarily mean hand-held cameras. Or, at least, "reality" does not mean that to me.

I felt there had to be a very, very specific visual storytelling approach to this film. I wanted to use color, and, from the time that I first walked into the *Washington Post* newsroom, I knew we had to use color because reality just gives you wonderful, wonderful gifts.

Woodward and Bernstein were enormously helpful, but there was that difficulty about the fact that they were alive, and I would say to them, "You know, Bob and Carl, it would be a lot easier if this had happened one hundred years ago, and you were long since gone—not that I wish you that."

But there is always the danger, when dealing with living people, of doing a Wax Museum of a film—of getting such perfect imitations that there is no essence of reality. I made anybody with a major part in the film who was supposed to work at the *Washington Post* spend time at the *Washington Post*. Bob Redford had been there long before I had, and Dustin Hoffman went out on his own investigative reporting case. It's amazing that when Dustin disappeared into the newsroom it would take me ten minutes to find him because he looked like every other reporter there. He's extraordinary that way.

After the research was done, the most important thing was to make it our own, and at that point I had to say to Woodward and Bernstein, "Look, you're wonderful. You're terrific, but we have to make it our own, and if you watch over us you are going to be the real people and we'll just be doppelgängers, and these actors will keep thinking of themselves as imitations of real people."

So we built the set of the *Washington Post* in California, and that was quite wonderful because when Ben Bradlee came from Washington to visit our set, he was a visitor to our *Washington Post*. The real Ben Bradlee of our *Washington Post* was Jason Robards, and Bradlee was just a visiting Ben Bradlee. This was terrific for the actors. It gave them a sense of security to make it their own. If I had had other actors playing Woodward and Bernstein, I would not have looked for the same performances. I did not want imitations. You use things in Bob Redford; you use things in Dustin Hoffman; the parts become an integration of the actors and the characters. It's the only way I know how to work with actors.

Fortunately for us, the *Washington Post* had just moved into its new newsroom six months before Woodward and Bernstein started their investigation. It was a relentlessly fluorescent-lighted room, huge and totally white, a very hard white. The colors of the chairs were poster colors, hard electric blues, hard oranges and reds, hard greens. The lighting was ruthless, and for a world of investigation, it was just marvelous because it was a world without shadows, a room in which nothing could be hidden. That was the essence of the visualization of the whole activity of trying to expose things that people were trying to hide, and that became the visual focus of the film. This room with its glaring light was the hub of the film, and from there we would go out into the dark places with their dark secrets.

The director of photography, Gordon Willis, and I worked for visual counterpoint. For example, there is a scene with Jane Alexander, who plays a bookkeeper—a perfectly wonderful actress—and Dustin is interviewing her. We shot this in a tiny little house in suburban Maryland. It's a set we could have built in any studio, but it also had a porch, and it had those wonderful eastern trees. We shot a second sequence between Woodward and Bernstein and her, in which they are questioning her and asking her all of these really tatty questions about the scandals, the cheapest kind of human activities being explored. But against her fear, through the screened porch, it's all sunlight. It could be an impressionist painting. It's incredibly romantic looking. The world looks perfect, but inside it's all crumbly.

Gordie and I had worked on two other pictures together before *All the President's Men*. They were *Klute* and *The Parallax View*. He had also worked with Francis Ford Coppola on both of the *Godfather* films. After *Godfather II* [1974], a critic in Minneapolis had called him "The Prince of Darkness" because of his reputation for very dark, moody photography. But we needed a "Prince of Light" as well on this film. And before I asked Gordie to do the film, I talked to him about my problem of wanting to see lots of counterpointed action, lots of scenes with action going on in several planes deep into the background. It meant much use of wide-angle lenses. It meant a lot of the total opposite of all the flare photography that is being done today. It meant going back to a crisp, hard, sharp style of cinematography.

Visual style in films is always dictated by content, and in this case, it was to represent how reporters see and how they look at things and their perceptions. In order to achieve that style, Gordie used a lot of split diopters, which are essentially bifocal glasses, in a lens sense. Split diopters make it possible to shoot with enormous depth, but they make it very difficult for the actors.

For example, Bob Redford has a six-minute scene filmed straight through in one setup, with no cuts. The camera moves imperceptibly. It starts on a medium close-up of him, and in the background, there is a group of people in the newsroom watching George McGovern on television as he dumps Thomas Eagleton from the ticket. In the foreground, there is Bob Redford obsessed with his own story and finding out how money that was given to the Committee to Reelect wound up in a Mexican bank account. He pursues his story, going from one phone call to another and another.

We wanted that counterpoint of action in several planes, which meant using a split diopter. Bob had his plane in which he was in focus, but if his hand moved half an inch too far, he would be out of focus. The prospect of this disaster didn't thrill him, but it was very important to the style of the film for us to be able to watch him shut out the whole world. That's the obsession of the investigative reporter, an absolute obsession for exposing the secrets that people in power want to hide.

All the President's Men is not a moralistic film, despite the fact that it is an incredibly heroic story in outline. It deals with the power of the individual—in this case, two individuals, two really unimportant reporters, who bring down the most powerful people on earth. Their reasons were not heroic. Investigative reporters are quite amoral. They are obsessed, just like people who climb mountains "because they are there." They are obsessed with exposing untruths in high places.

I have my own little tacky theoretical hypothesis about why I call it the "*Catcher in the Rye* syndrome," that syndrome of the adolescent when he gets to that age when he suddenly realizes that Daddy is imperfect, with all of his Achilles's heels, and suddenly the great disappointment that comes out, and the enormous anger and disillusionment that is expressed. There is something about investigative reporters constantly exposing the untruths and hypocrisies of the people in power that relates to that.

All of these things came out in the making of the film. I had an enormous problem in trying to get full three-dimensional characters on to the screen because the narrative demands of the story were just so relentless. Hitchcock has always said that, in a suspense film, it's so much easier to use established stars, because you have no time for deep character exploration. Yet I did not want the people the reporters interviewed to be merely narrative tools who just served the story, so I spent endless time with the actors in discussions of the characters they were playing. There were things never verbalized in the film that, nevertheless, added to the suspense, and it's curious that while it is a huge story in the historic sense, the picture is made up of many tiny mosaics, with one tiny little thing leading to another tiny little thing.

The essence of investigative reporting is making people talk about things they don't want to talk about, and, unless the characters being interviewed are specific, and you understand what their frustrations and hang-ups are, there is no suspense in the scene. It's the classic tip-of-the-iceberg theory, which is, hopefully, that the actor has all of that going to texture his performance and, even though his background is never discussed, the audience will feel a dimension it would not feel otherwise.

I have talked about visual style being dictated by content, and I really believe that. Otherwise, it's just a tour de force, and I have no use for that. But visual and audio style are very closely related, and, to me, the sound is almost as important as the photography in the making of a film. The essential conception that fascinated me, and that dictated much of the visual and audio style of this particular film, was the way little absurd elements combined to bring down towering people in power.

If ever there was a story that demonstrates that the pen is mightier than the sword, God knows it's *All the President's Men*. In this case it's the typewriter that becomes the weapon, and, in order to dramatize that, we opened the film with a typewriter key that is as big as any gun in the world, slamming letters onto a blank, white screen. While we used a regular typewriter, we mixed with its own sound a bullet shot—the firing of a gun—and the sound of a whiplash.

I spent a lot of time doing that sort of thing because it does make a point. We pushed up the sound of pencils and the scratching of pens, as they make their little notes. And one phone call or piece of information leads to another so that it was like the sound of little rats scratching their way into these huge walls of power, bringing them down in a way that all the guns in the world could not.

One amazing problem we had was that of visually dramatizing the people the reporters were against. The antagonists—the "heavies," if you want to call them that—are never really seen in person in the film. The picture deals with the reporters' point of view, and they never meet the people in the higher-up places. So there were two methods we used in order to visualize power. One method was that of showing the antagonists on television sets. There's something about seeing people on television or film that makes them godlike, untouchable, beyond your reach. That worked very well. The other method we used for dramatizing them visually was through the Washington, DC, buildings in which they held power. The buildings look like postcards—lovely, graceful, humane in their proportions—but they're really citadels of power.

It was Bob Redford's idea to do the film a year-and-a-half before I came on to the project. He had spoken to Woodward and Bernstein as far back as 1972, long before the film script was written. By the time I came on to the picture, Bob had already committed Dustin to play the other role—so it was Bob and Dustin definitely. I said to Bob, "One of my great concerns is that we have two top stars playing two unknown reporters. How do we do that?"

I was more concerned about Bob than I was about Dustin because Dustin has an "average man" quality. He's a character actor. People don't think of Dustin as being larger than life. But, as I told Bob, "You have an air of enormous confidence on the screen. If what you do comes across as a star performance, the film will be destroyed."

As a result, the star performance in the film, in terms of personality, is Jason Robards as Ben Bradlee—and that's the way it was supposed to be. That was the key to solving the problem. Woodward and Bernstein are supposed to be two young, unknown reporters. They must disappear into the newsroom. They must be working for a man who totally overshadows them—and editors do have "star" personalities. God knows Ben Bradlee does. I said to Jason, "If you don't overpower those two, the film is out the window."

Fortunately, Bob and Dustin had enormous respect for Jason, and they understood the problem. I mean, they would watch Jason walk away with a scene—and do it happily. Other stars would have had another director the next day. The other key for Bob in keeping that problem under control was his character's curious relationship with Deep Throat. In their scenes together, the relationship is almost that of teacher and acolyte. He is intimidated by Deep Throat. He's afraid of making a fool of himself. That worked well, but the problem of having big stars playing unknown reporters was one we had to deal with all through the filming.

One of the biggest problems of the film was to dramatize what investigative reporters actually do. The essence of it is the sheer, stubborn, agonizing patience they demonstrate in going over and over details. How do you dramatize that without tedium? That's why, in the Library of Congress sequence, the camera keeps going up and up and up, until they become infinitesimally small figures. That shot took so long on the screen that we finally telescoped it with two dissolves. Otherwise, we would still be going up right now. But it was a way of dramatizing visually the kind of endurance it takes to be an investigative reporter.

At the beginning, though, I deliberately kept the camera very locked in because I didn't want to soup up the film with random movement. For example, Bob

Redford plays a very tightly closed, compressed character. He is obsessed, and it's that obsession that drives the film. But you couldn't do any colorful things externally at that point because that would have put the film down the drain. I wanted to keep the character of Woodward very compressed, with an energy that was ready to explode at any point, but temporarily held in.

There is the sequence, for instance, where he's on the phone making a series of four or five calls, trying to find out who the hell Howard Hunt is, with only voices on the other end of the phone. I didn't want to show the people he was talking to because you had to see what it's like to be a reporter trying to get people you can't even see to communicate with you and tell you things they don't want to tell you. We shot the setup for the first phone call and it was fine. Bob said, "Okay, call me when you're ready for the new setup for the next phone call." I said, "We *are* ready. It's this same setup—and the one after that, and the one after that, and the one after that—because we've got to show what it's like to be a reporter, locked in, trapped with that phone, making call after call, holding on, talking to unknown voices, trying to get that story to build."

Therefore, the movement is very controlled, and then gradually, as the film starts to progress, the camera begins to move with them. As they get more manic, the camera gets more manic, so that near the end of the film there is a shot of Dustin when he thinks he's gotten confirmation of Haldeman being named as one of the heads of the one of the secret funds. We started at one end of the newsroom, and we flew. One of the best Disneyland rides we've ever had was on that dolly.

We went with him from the end of the newsroom as he ran all the way to Bob's desk, which was in the middle, and then he and Bob ran all the way to the other end of the newsroom on a diagonal until they hit the elevator. They ran through two sound stages. At that point I wanted to dramatize the fact that they were so manic that they were out of control and getting unreliable. But up until that point, I wouldn't use camera movement or cuts just to say, "A series of phone calls is boring, so I'm going to concentrate the audience's attention by using flash for the sake of flash."

World without Shadows

Richard Combs / 1976

From *Sight and Sound*, Summer 1976, 153. Reprinted by permission.

"It was possible to do *All the President's Men* after *the Parallax View*," says Alan Pakula. "I don't know if it would have been possible to do *The Parallax View* after *All the President's Men*. One reflects for me a kind of despair and fear about our society; and the other reflects a hope. One of the reasons I was so attracted to doing *All the President's Men* is the very reason I did *The Parallax View*. And the fact that they're antithetical in resolution is part of the attraction."

A prophecy of doom that largely fell on deaf ears, *The Parallax View* was an almost abstract meditation on a climate of distrust and disillusion that had yet to find an articulate cause in Watergate. "I think that the 1960s, which were very traumatic for the States, starting with the assassinations and then the endless Vietnam War, left many Americans with a fear of the unknown within the society that they'd never felt before; an almost Kafka-like fear that seemed more appropriate to Central European and Asiatic countries than to the States. And *Parallax* was an almost nightmare reflection of that."

Two years later, there is instructive irony in the fact that Pakula is reaping much more substantial rewards for revealing a light in the gloom with *All the President's Men*. "The pivotal center visually of this film is that newsroom—that hard, white light, that world without shadows. You can hide nothing in that world. And what do they do there? They expose truth."

The contrasting styles and functions of the reporters in the two films say a lot about their divergent aims. "*All the President's Men* is much more rigidly controlled in style because of the very nature of the work itself. It's about the mechanics of gathering information, and that becomes the action. The action is rather cerebral." A large part of that action involves putting information together at the peculiar remove imposed by a telephone receiver, an instrument that has served Pakula often before in dramatizing a communication block ("Somebody said I should have a free phone service for the rest of my life"). But here it is particularly crucial in "trying to get the reality of their experience, the endless tedium of being locked in one place with a phone and a pad and trying to figure out what leads to what. And when Dustin's with Jane Alexander, that bookkeeper, it's like you're caught together in time, and that's the essence of that kind of confrontation between the reporter and the person he's interviewing. You're just locked in there, and if the camera had started to move, it would have broken the whole hypnotic quality."

For all that Pakula regards *The Parallax View* as being very different in style— "much more picaresque, much more surreal, kind of American baroque"—it can also be seen dealing in the imagery of individuals locked in place and time, though with much more sinister implications. Its central metaphor, the "parallax view," is "the compression of time in America, the layers of time just being compressed on to each other, so it's almost like earthquakes are bound to come out of it in so many ways—human earthquakes." Thus, Warren Beatty's reporter works for an editor whose comfortable, shabby office represents, Pakula says, "much more simple American values, almost nineteenth-century values. It represented a family, a man who was rooted, a whole American tradition that was dying, an anachronism, as compared to this totally cold and enormously bizarre world that Beatty goes after, and in comparison to his own character, which is the totally rootless modern man." The film "takes a lot of those American myths, all the movie versions of the indestructible hero figure, carried almost to the point of kitsch, and says this is what has happened to them. The American hero character who can do anything, who can survive anything and expose the truth in the end, has been destroyed. We can't believe in him anymore."

A similar strain of "visual wit" can be seen working through *All the President's Men*, despite its more cleanly functional, almost documentary procedures. "In most detective stories, people go to the underbelly of the world, where lives are in chaos; and in this one, just the opposite. You go to the sunlit world of people who belong, whose lives are orderly, and who pay their taxes on time. All looks right with the world, and yet there's chaos; there's something crumbling underneath it. On that porch on the side of the bookkeeper's house, I said to Gordon Willis, 'I would like you to do this as if you were doing an impressionist painting. I want it lyrical.' I wanted dappled sunlight coming through the trees. And then within that, all they're talking about are these little pieces of decay. Sloan, the young man, sits in his wingchair, and there's a kind of round, eighteenth-century mirror in back of him, and it's all like a little reproduction of an eighteenth-century world. And it's thrown away, but it's that orderly world; it's the American dream gone awry.

"I do love objects as symbols in certain ways. And that's why the film begins with the typewriter keys—the typewriter as a weapon. Words as bullets. These unlikely weapons finally brought down this enormous power behind those huge intangible buildings. We got so lucky when we saw the tape of Nixon, and it had the twenty-one-gun salute, because then I could have the guns against the typewriters. There's the battle right there."

Veteran English film critic and historian **Richard Combs** is a longtime contributor to film magazines around the world and to a host of anthologies on the cinema. He currently teaches at London's National Film and Television School.

The American Film Institute's Dialogue on Film: Alan J. Pakula

American Film / 1979

From *American Film*, December–January 1979. Copyright © American Film Institute.¹ Reprinted by permission.

"A man and a woman committing themselves to a life together is one of the most heroic acts in the world." That was Alan J. Pakula's recent observation as he spoke about *Starting Over*, the movie he is currently directing. Heroism infuses Pakula's latest film, *Comes a Horseman*, with Jane Fonda and Jason Robards, as it does his last film, *All the President's Men*, with Robert Redford and Dustin Hoffman.

But heroism of a more prosaic kind—the sort people bring to trying to live their lives—informs earlier Pakula movies. His first film, *The Sterile Cuckoo*, with Liza Minnelli, deals with a college girl staggering through youth with a burden of vulnerability; *Klute*, with Jane Fonda, explores the brassy pluckiness of a young prostitute.

If the notion of heroism, prosaic or otherwise, suggests a certain old-fashionedness, Pakula would not deny it. His ideas about what a film should be are grounded in a boyhood of Saturdays spent at the movies in the late 1930s and early '40s. His films have the carefully crafted look of Old Hollywood; the details are meticulous. For *All the President's Men*, not only did he construct an exact replica of the *Washington Post* newsroom, but—in a Stroheim touch of excessive realism—imported to Hollywood the contents of the newsroom wastebaskets.

But more important to Pakula than appearances are performances, both large and small. Fonda's work in *Klute* is an extraordinary tour de force; but also memorable is a bit part in *All the President's Men*, a dour, ungainly FBI agent given to sore feet. Pakula simply explains that he loves to work with actors.

Question: Do you regard your latest movie, *Comes a Horseman*, as a departure for you?

Alan J. Pakula: In certain ways it does seem very different from anything I've ever done. I've never done this kind of outdoor film before. It's the first time I've worked on a film in which the characters are so related to the land where they live. The land is a kind of central character in the film. Yet it's also a love story; in that way, you can compare it to some of the other pictures I've done. And it's a film about work, as *All the President's Men* was about work—in this case ranching instead of reporting. I have a deep respect for people who commit and risk their lives for work they value and respect. And it is an attempt to deal with a classic film genre to explore character, as was *Klute*.

Question: What was it about *Comes a Horseman* that led you to direct it?

Pakula: There was the great attraction to people who fight against powerful odds for freedom and dignity, who live for values beyond the obvious material ones of today. In a way, the picture is a return to heroes, to people who are not smaller than life. That was a very strong appeal. Another attraction was the chance to explore a woman in the American West as a heroic character.

In most Westerns, the woman is in a calico dress, running after the hero on the horse, saying, "Nothing is worth dying for," or she's a gun-toting Calamity Jane. The idea of dealing with a heroine in the West, very much a woman yet willing to fight with the same passion as men, was a great attraction. I thought there was no one better than Jane Fonda to represent that kind of strong yet vulnerable American woman.

Question: What are some of the other themes you tried to deal with in *Comes a Horseman*?

Pakula: *Comes a Horseman*, which takes place in the West in the mid-1940s, is about people who are anachronisms. They really could be living in the nineteenth century. It deals with ranchers, and it deals with classic—or hoary—American themes. If the picture succeeds, they'll be classic, and if it fails, they'll be hoary. [It deals with] themes like the obsession with land, the obsession with freedom, the mentality of two different kinds of people who settled the West.

One kind: the people who really wanted the freedom and their own piece of land and who didn't want much else; the other kind: the expansionists who have a dream of power, the romanticists, the empire builders. The inevitable clash between them is still going on, after generations, in 1945 when this film opens. It also deals with a personal obsession of mine: guilt—and people who are haunted by a past, one that's not even just their own, but the past of generations.

Question: Did you try to convey any of these notions in your visual conception of the film?

Pakula: I had a conception which wound up costing much too much money; if I had had any idea of what it would cost, I wouldn't have followed through. The relationship of the people and the land is what the film is about. I wanted the valley it takes place in to have a haunted look. Most Westerns are in bright sunlight. But I said to the cinematographer, Gordon Willis, "It's a *Wuthering Heights* in the West in terms of visual feeling. These people are all haunted. I'd like to start out in bright sunlight, and then I'd like to go to grays if we can get them."

We decided the night-work photography had to be day-for-night, which is an old-fashioned stylization that's difficult to do well. I wouldn't have even dared mention it to anybody except Gordon, but he's so incredibly skilled. If we just did regular night work, you would see nothing of the land and its relationship to the people. In straight night photography, you can light up only the immediate area, and you lose a sense of the environment. It was important to me that we never divorce the people from the land in any of the exterior scenes.

So we did a lot of day-for-night. We were shooting in a valley which the Colorado Film Commission—thou shalt not listen to film commissions—had assured us has perfectly dry, stable weather in the summertime, even though it was called Wet Mountain Valley. Hollywood people can be very gullible; the weather kept changing.

We'd have an hour and a half of sunlight; we'd have an hour and a half of thunderclouds; we'd have an hour of rain; we'd have another hour of sunlight; we'd have some more thunder, then rain. We had a kaleidoscope of God's weather every day. For several days, we even had incredible hailstorms, and we were hailed in. Day-for-night photography requires back lighting, and the constantly changing weather and light meant endless waiting, which was murder on the actors and the budget.

Question: When did you first decide you wanted to direct films?

Pakula: I decided to be a director when I was seventeen, and I directed my first film as I hit forty. My first experience as a director was when I was at Yale as an undergraduate: I directed a one-act farce by Chekhov. At that time, I was in love with the theater.

I'll never forget the moment after the first day of rehearsal when I felt the actors were finding things in themselves they wouldn't have found without me and doing things, for better or for worse, they wouldn't have done without me. This sense of being a catalyst, this sense of power, was overpowering. I remember bounding through the campus with great, goatlike leaps, feeling like someone out of Thomas Wolfe who'd just discovered the ecstasy of life. The ecstasy returned about twenty years later.

Question: What first brought you to Hollywood?

Pakula: I came here to direct a play, a production of Anouilh's *Antigone* at the Circle Theatre. Charlie Chaplin's son Sydney was in a production of Camus's

Caligula at the theater, and Chaplin himself came in to redirect it in the last week. He was, of course, a genius, but I have never seen a director tense up an actor more than he did.

I'll never forget what he did. One of the young California actors was struggling with Camus, and there was not much relationship with Camus left by the end of rehearsal. Chaplin stepped in and showed him how he would play it. He looked into an imaginary mirror and began playing the mad emperor. The joyous, yet hideous, Pan character he created in front of your eyes was overwhelming. It was stunning. Then he said to the young actor, "Now, you do it." The actor, of course, was paralyzed.

Question: How did you get into film?

Pakula: I met Dore Schary, who was head of production at Metro, and Don Hartman, a producer-director-writer who had done some of the *Road* pictures [1940–1962] and some of the early Danny Kaye pictures. At that time, there was still an apprentice program; the studios still thought in terms of tomorrow. So I became an apprentice, and I was assigned to Don Hartman. Six months later he became head of production at Paramount, and he asked me to go along with him. Suddenly, at the age of twenty-two, I found myself as assistant to the head of production at Paramount.

I wrote overly long memoranda on every film the studio made. I thought I knew which pictures should be made and which shouldn't be made. I've kept some of those memos, and the memos get a little less secure as the years go on. Suddenly, a picture I knew would never make it is a huge hit. For example, I read the script for *Rear Window* [1954] and said, "It's not that much." Then I saw the dailies, and I suddenly saw Hitchcock's visual mind at work.

I learned there are certain movie scripts that sell very quickly because they read very well, but they don't play very well; and there are certain scripts that are not written to be read, they're meant to be made. Most front offices can still be fooled today by something that reads in a tour de force kind of way, that works on a kind of literary level.

I was working with writers and sitting in on major meetings, and it was fascinating. I saw Audrey Hepburn's original screen test for *Roman Holiday* [1953] and was in on the meetings in which six or seven grown men were trying to decide whether Audrey Hepburn's teeth should be straightened. Wisely, they were not.

Question: What led to your working as a producer?

Pakula: I became a producer because I wanted to be a director. Don Hartman was a lovely man. There *are* very decent people in this great jungle. I kept saying, "I want to be a director," and he kept saying, "Why don't you end up being Irving Thalberg and work as head of a studio?"

I said, "I want to be a director."

He said, "If enough people tell you you're drunk, lie down, for God's sake." So I lay down for five or six years, stayed in the front office, and became a producer because nobody thought I could work with actors because they had never seen me work with actors. The only reason I had ever come to Hollywood in the first place was to work with actors.

Question: What finally brought about your move to directing?

Pakula: I'd taken an option on a book called *The Sterile Cuckoo*. Alvin Sargent was writing the screenplay. I was going to use a young director, and then I thought, "It's ridiculous to use a young director. Why don't you use a man who's not quite so young, but certainly is inexperienced: yourself?" I think the joy of working with Alvin made it difficult for me to give the script to another director. But suddenly life came into focus again. Life takes on a new dimension when you're doing what you feel is really right for you.

Question: Did you face any particular problems as a new director?

Pakula: One of the biggest problems I had when I first started was that I wanted to see everything. The screen test I directed with Liza Minnelli and Wendell Burton for *The Sterile Cuckoo* was the most overly directed piece of film, I think, in the history of modern film. I had them do everything you could possibly do in a lifetime in five minutes of film. They cried, and they laughed, and they were happy, and they were unhappy, and they were ecstatic, and they were suicidal. Name it, and they felt it in five minutes. That they recovered was amazing.

The people who were about to finance the film saw the screen test and said, "We wonder if Liza is right for this." Well, the poor girl had been so overdirected. The crew had all applauded, I might add, during the middle of that test. There's a certain kind of virtuoso work that wakes people up when they're tired, and Liza got applause for the very things that were wrong with the test. It was too virtuoso, and it was too show-offy. But Liza, who is a director's dream, was giving the director what he asked for.

I remember when I was cutting that test. It was the first time I'd ever cut a piece of my own film, and I suddenly regressed. I wanted to see everything, and I found that when I started directing *Sterile Cuckoo* I still wanted to see everything. One of the primary lessons of filmmaking, which is easy to follow when you're dealing with other people's work, is that what you don't see gives focus to what you do see.

Question: Your early films deal very much with personal relationships. Do you think that's where your real interests as a director lie?

Pakula: I gave a talk at the British Film Institute right after I did *Klute*. The young man who introduced me said, "Mr. Pakula makes films about the pursuit of happiness as pursued by people who have an inordinately difficult time pursuing it." I laughed because there was a lot of truth to it. Then I did *The Parallax*

View, and I did *All the President's Men,* which has nothing to do with the personal pursuit of happiness and deals with man's relationship to society, or to a specific society. Certainly both films have political, social overtones. I now find I am interested in combining both.

Comes a Horseman is a kind of Dreiserian Western that deals with very specific American myths and with very specific personal relationships among three people. All I know is that one part of me once wanted to be a psychiatrist; another part of me would have been very happy being a historian. I am very interested in political society, and I am very interested in the personal pursuit of happiness.

Question: You went from *The Sterile Cuckoo* to *Klute.* Are they entirely different movies for you?

Pakula: When I was doing *Klute,* I thought, "Oh, boy, I can't be doing a film that's more different from my first film." *The Sterile Cuckoo* is about the loss of innocence, and it's an innocent film in certain ways for all the tragic implications in it. *Klute* is hardly an innocent film, and the style is so different. But I happened to realize that there was a major similarity. The major similarity is that they both deal with middle-class, controlled, repressed males—one a boy and one a man— both falling in love with self-destructive, witty, vibrant, spontaneous, surprising women who almost destroy them, in the process of destroying themselves.

As different as the films are, that same theme is in them both. In *Klute,* I wanted at first to explore the character of *Klute* more deeply than I did. He is a square man who has lived his life by simple rules, almost Victorian rules. He suddenly finds himself falling in love with somebody who is all the things that he despises. In some way, he has to learn compassion for the human condition and to realize his own complexities. This was meant to be a secondary theme in the film, but there was not enough time to explore his character as fully as hers without making the structure of the film patchy and unstable.

Question: How did Jane Fonda come to do *Klute*?

Pakula: It's a film I would not have done without Jane. I had met her a long time before, but I never really talked in any depth with her until a couple of weeks before I was sent the screenplay. I had just done *The Sterile Cuckoo,* and her agent sent me another screenplay that I didn't want to do.

But I met Jane, and we talked for several hours about a lot of things—about women in our society, about sexuality in our society. It was just a wonderful, freewheeling discussion. I came out of it thinking, "I'd love to work with that woman." About two weeks later, the *Klute* script was sent to me, and I called her immediately.

The first-draft script by Andy and David Lewis, despite the fact that it clearly represented the film I wanted to make, had a certain tabloid flavor in areas. After I sent her the script in New York, I flew there to talk with her because I thought she might be put off. "I don't know what I feel about it," she said. We talked for a half hour; she had an interviewer waiting, and she had to get rid of me. She said, "Look, do you really want to do it?"

I said, "Yes."

She said, "OK, I'll do it." Out of such little statements things get made.

By the time we came to do the film, Jane had changed considerably. She had become politicized, and she came to the set with this great passion—about everything, really, and I was concerned that her mind was not going to be on the film. She was very involved in so many causes. But she has this extraordinary kind of concentration. She can spend the time when somebody is lighting a film making endless telephone calls, raising money, whatever, and seem to be totally uninterested in the film. But when you say, "We're ready for you, Jane," she says, "All right, give me a few minutes." She just stands quietly for three minutes and concentrates, and then she's totally and completely in the film, and nothing else exists. And when the scene is right, and you have it, and you don't need her anymore, she goes right back to the phone, and that other world is total. It's a gift a lot of good actors have; she has it to an extraordinary degree.

Question: What help did you have on the lifestyle of a call girl?

Pakula: First of all, the character of the call girl was very well written in the first-draft screenplay. I have to presume the writers were there before me. Our technical adviser was a twenty-three-year-old call girl. She was really very helpful.

I sat her down with Jane the night before we shot a scene in a hotel room. The girl said, "The first thing you do, no matter what, is get your money. You get it before, because you're not going to get as much afterward. The second thing you do is make sure the man thinks he is different. You need the money because you can't afford to take him for free, but he is different from any other john you've seen, and he really turns you on. You get more money that way." This young girl said, "Mr. Pakula, they all believe you—psychiatrists, judges, doctors, politicians. I've lost all respect for men because they all believe they're different, every one that comes along."

I thought, "Directors, too?"

Question: To turn to your more recent movies, are there connections for you between *The Parallax View* and *All the President's Men?* Both seem to deal with exposing something hidden.

Pakula: *The Parallax View* showed a very different view of America. In America, most films are about good and evil. But the difference—in the American myth compared to the European myth—is that, in America, the evil is always known. For example, in the Western, which is a classic American story, evil is the guy at the other end of the street with the gun during the shoot-out. It may take you a while to find him, but you find him, and you see him clear and sharp.

He's recognizable, and he's out in the open, and you can kill him. It's an open society; it all hangs out.

Parallax said that's not true anymore. We live in a Kafka-like world where you never find the evil. It permeates the society. Underneath all the pop images in *Parallax*—the flags, the banners—the truths are unknown. We live in a world of secrets, a world in which we can't even find out who is trying to destroy our society. It was saying, "This is the world we live in. It's a different America. There are things we'll never know about and that are hidden. It is not an open society anymore."

In a curious way, it was a pre-Watergate film. Two years later, I made *All the President's Men*, which said "No, it can all be exposed. Everything's changed. Suddenly everything's opening up." I never would have made *All the President's Men* if it was fiction. No one would have believed it.

Question: You had worked as your own producer before *All the President's Men*. How was it to find someone else, in this case Robert Redford, as producer?

Pakula: I didn't know what was going to happen. I said to him, "The first thing we have to do is really make sure we both have the same concept of this film before I do it." We started out by saying, "What are the films we don't want to make?" I didn't want to make *Butch Woodward and the Sundance Bernstein*. You know, Bob Redford and Dustin Hoffman loving and laughing their way through the East as they bring down the president of the United States. It might make a mint, but we would look in the mirror and not like what we saw.

Fortunately, Bill Goldman in his first draft had wisely selected the portion of the story that should be told and had already eliminated another potential danger: an attempt to give an entire historical overview and its ramification. We would have had the longest montage in film history. The film we were making, like the book, would be, in the simplest Walter Mitty terms, "What was it like to have been these two young men who broke through this cover-up and discovered these facts that eventually led to the exposure and political destruction of some of the most powerful people on earth?"

But to get back to Bob as producer: I enjoyed working with him because I respected his passion and total dedication and responsibility to the film. Without him, *All the President's Men* would not have been made into a film. It would have been a different film made without me—possibly better, possibly worse—but it would have been made because of his determination.

Question: Did you have any qualms about casting Redford in the role of a young, inexperienced reporter?

Pakula: I'm a great admirer of Bob as an actor. I saw Bob when he was twenty-one years old in a small part on the stage, and I was deeply impressed. But I was concerned about casting him because I felt the extraordinary quality of the story, as a piece of American folklore, was that it was a version of Jack and the Giant, of David and Goliath. They were two young and comparatively inexperienced reporters who partially bumbled their way into the story.

But I felt that Bob has an incredible sense of competence on the screen. I told him this, by the way, when he was trying to open a bottle of wine for me and couldn't get the cork out. He was laughing at that, and I said, "You know, what you are in real life and what you are on the screen are two very different things. You may bumble your way through opening a bottle of wine, but nobody will believe it on screen. They'd think it's just bad acting."

Question: In *All the President's Men*, while Woodward and Bernstein are generally sympathetic characters, they also have another, less attractive side. There are touches, for example, of blind ambition.

Pakula: That was deliberate. I'll tell you who was quite insistent that that side get in, and that was Woodward and Bernstein themselves. They were afraid that if they came out as Warner Bros. World War II heroes—like Errol Flynn—they would be the laughingstock of all their journalist friends. That was their great terror. "How do we face all the journalists we know without being these cardboard heroes?" They never fought those touches; quite the opposite.

Interestingly, at one preview in Denver, the audience was really with Woodward and Bernstein. The next night, at a preview in Louisville, the audience was more on the side of the people being questioned. The audience was thinking, "Why don't those damn busybodies leave those poor people alone?" Woodward and Bernstein represented smart-aleck busybodies to them.

Question: The absence of a private life for the Woodward and Bernstein characters has been noted. For example, no girlfriends. Why?

Pakula: We were endlessly constructing scenes with girlfriends. Both Bob Redford and Dustin Hoffman felt the scenes should be there. Otherwise, they feared, the characters might become automatons. Finally, we sat down and talked about it. The reality was that neither of these men was deeply involved with anybody at the time of the story. What was important was their work. They were totally obsessed.

All the President's Men was a story about work. We were telling this story because of what these two young men had accomplished. Their personal lives had little to do with it. The film is dependent upon a gathering tension. If you stop it to show a happy romantic life, or an unhappy romantic life, then that kind of parenthesis will pop the tension. At least that was my feeling, and Bob in the end agreed.

I am fascinated with telling stories about work. I guess you could say *Klute* is a story about work. *Comes a Horseman* is a story of ranching, in a certain way, even though hopefully it works on other levels. But getting the ranching right was very important to me. If Jane Fonda and Jimmy Caan had not worked as hard as they did to get the ranching right, there would have been no picture. And if Bob and Dustin and Jason Robards had not worked so hard to get the reporting and editing right, there would have been no picture.

Question: Tension is certainly present in a lot of your films. Is it what Redford, as the producer, wanted from you?

Pakula: Supposedly, it's the reason Bob hired me for *All the President's Men*. He felt a tension in *Klute* that he had not felt when he read the script. He thought I had this strange, threatening quality in some of my work. I was a little concerned about that. I said to him, "Bob, yes, the story gets into an area of paranoia, but it cannot get literal. You may want something from me that I will not give as fully as you want me to give, because if it gets very literal it's going to be hyped up, and if it's hyped the picture goes out the window. The terror is kind of unknown, and it builds, but it mustn't get too specific."

This question of using tension is interesting. You're operating out of something inside yourself that is very subjective, namely, fear. I think to scare other people, you have to understand what scares you. It has a lot to do with who we are and who we're not. The master of tension is Hitchcock. As we all know, he had a very nervous childhood. His father, who had a friend who was a police chief, once played a joke of putting him in jail when he was about seven or eight years old, as a punishment because he'd done something naughty. Well, it scared the hell out of the poor kid, and it gave us a great body of work. And I'm sure that was just one incident.

Question: Did you have a specific look in mind for *All the President's Men*?

Pakula: One of the first things I said to Gordon Willis was, "I want very deep focus in this film. I want it sharp and hard. It's about reporters who try to see everything, who are always looking. So you've just got to have that kind of mentality behind the cinematography." Now, we got lucky with the *Washington Post*, which, six months before Woodward and Bernstein started getting on the story, moved into a new building with fluorescent, white offices, a world without shadows. We shot in total fluorescent light, which was rather difficult for Gordon, who is known for his great dark, moody photography. But I said I wanted a world where nothing is hidden.

The hub of this film is that newspapers and investigative reporters try to expose the truth about everything. Nothing can be left secret or hidden. So the fact they work in a room where the light is that ruthless, where there are no shadows so you can't hide anything, is terrific.

The world our detective-reporters go through in *All the President's Men* is a world of sunlight. It's a world where the sun shines, the grass is mowed, houses are clean and bright and cheerful and orderly looking. And in the midst of all this orderliness and sun and middle-class bourgeois cleanliness and brightness and cheerfulness and Disneyland happiness is decay. I wanted that counterpoint.

Question: What was your reaction to the possibility of libel suits from *All the President's Men*?

Pakula: My father called me and said, "Hey, Alan, I'm reading this book. Boy, if I were you, I'd make damn sure that I had some indemnification in the contract." My wife and I had just bought some Spanish antiques, and I could see them all ending up in San Clemente. So I got a clause in the contract saying that if the film I delivered was approved by the Warners legal department—and we were constantly checking with lawyers all along the way—I would be indemnified from any libel suits.

Question: Was there any thought to having an actor portray Nixon?

Pakula: We only dealt with people Woodward and Bernstein actually saw. They never saw Nixon. They always dealt with the little people. But when Walter Matthau saw *All the President's Men*, he said to me, "Alan, have you read *The Final Days*? Boy, I'd love to play Nixon." I don't know if he was kidding or not. I'm sure he could do it. I guess he'd be playing the biggest Bad News Bear of them all.

Question: *All the President's Men*, like *The Parallax View*, ends with a sense that it isn't all over. A deliberate ploy?

Pakula: You're leaving with the third act hanging in your hand. That was deliberate. I said to Warren Beatty before we did *Parallax*, "If the picture works, the audience will trust those sitting next to them a little less at the end of it." And the ending of *All the President's Men* *says* the books are never closed. Something could happen to the system any time, and there is a certain kind of watchfulness and vigilance that is always going to be required. It's a continuing possibility.

Even *Klute* is never over. You don't know what's going to happen to the call girl. Originally it ended with her and Klute laughing and loving their way down the street in a classic Frank Capra ending—except that Frank Capra was wise enough not to do those happy endings with complicated people like call girls. Jane Fonda said, "There's no way I'll have anything to do with that," and she was right. So it ends somewhat hopefully, but enigmatically. I have a tendency to do that. In *Sterile Cuckoo*, you don't know what's going to happen to that girl. Liza thought she was going to be fine, and I thought that was important for her to feel. However, I didn't agree with her.

Question: Before starting a film, do you examine the work of other directors in the particular genre? For example, did you look at newspaper movies for *All the President's Men*—or did you avoid them?

Pakula: I told Bob Redford, "I can't do this film unless I can spend time at the *Washington Post*. Otherwise, you're going to get all my childhood memories of all the old newspaper pictures, and Ben Bradlee will sound like Rosalind Russell. I have to become familiar with the reality." The *Post* let me be there, and I never ran any newspaper pictures.

Before I did *Comes a Horseman*, I ran some Westerns by the masters. It's just a way of checking your vocabulary, checking out your knowledge of grammatical construction. It never hurts to run a few Hitchcock pictures before you start a film too, even if it has nothing to do with suspense or melodrama, because for the sheer visual vocabulary, he's the master.

I'm doing a contemporary American comedy next, based on a book by Dan Wakefield, called *Starting Over*. The screenplay is by Jim Brooks, who is one of the people who conceived *The Mary Tyler Moore Show* [1970–1977]. It's the story of a man in his late thirties whose marriage breaks up and who's starting over. I suppose it's the man's side of *An Unmarried Woman* [1978], and it's with Burt Reynolds and, curiously enough, Jill Clayburgh, who's now on the other side.

I don't want to see a lot of pictures about divorce and things like that, though I would love to run some old comedies. I'm going to run some old Lubitsch pictures. I just want to be in touch with a great comic talent. But for *All the President's Men*, I felt what was important was not to have secondhand reality and, as much as possible, to base it on the reality I knew from the *Washington Post*.

Question: What approach do you use in working with your actors?

Pakula: I work very privately. Redford and Hoffman and Warren Beatty used to do imitations of me taking them aside and whispering. It's like I'm more a conspirator than a director. But the reason I do it is that I don't like to criticize people in front of others. It's something very private. I carry it to extremes, perhaps. But I have no one way of working with actors, and that's one of the reasons I like the rehearsal period. I like to see how actors work and what works for them.

When I worked with Liza Minnelli, I would do what I found worked for her. Halfway through the film, we were in a very difficult scene, and she was having trouble with it. She suddenly said to me, "Alan, if you could just tell me the story of the picture." I knew that Liza knew the screenplay backward, but I said, "Alright." I took her to my trailer, and I told it as you'd talk to a nine-year-old child, in the most simplistic terms: "Once upon a time there was a little girl, and she didn't have a mother, and she didn't know how to be a woman and she wanted somebody to love her, and she tried so hard . . ." I told it in those simple terms. For whatever reason, that helped her at that moment, and occasionally I'd do that with her.

Now, if I had sat down with Jane Fonda in *Klute* and said, "Once upon a time, Jane, there was a little call girl . . . ," she'd think I was out of my mind. I don't think that would have worked for her at all. Everybody has different ways. Dustin loves to talk. He wants to examine and reexamine a scene. Bob Redford likes to examine it and say, "OK, let's go. Let's do it." He's very intuitive; he's very quick.

Dustin, who is overwhelmingly inventive, is examining how many angels are on the head of a pin, and Bob is ready to start the take. The rhythm is going to be different, and you start to think, "Oh, boy, by the time Dustin is up, I'm going to lose Bob." That was a problem. But we all reached for an area of balance. Fortunately, they both like to respond to the work of other actors. And that made everything much easier—and for the director much more exciting.

Question: As someone who started out in theater, what particularly draws you to film?

Pakula: The best of film for me—and the worst of film—is that it is such a collaborative process. You are dealing with incredibly different kinds of people, and, even worse than that, you are dependent upon incredibly different kinds of people. I pride myself on having a specific vision of what I want a film to be. But, unlike an author or composer, I am dependent. I am working with a writer, with the actors, with a set designer, with a costume designer, with the cameramen. I am working with endless numbers of people. It is enraging at times, and it is also the most exciting part of it at times.

There are some directors who use actors as puppets. They believe there is one conception for the film, and everybody else is a puppet to carry out that conception. I believe the making of a film is a life process; no matter what the conception is to begin with, there will be changes in the making of the film. The film must come alive in spontaneous and surprising ways. That means surrounding yourself with people who are gifted in what they do. In the end, if the film is successful, it is a synthesis of so many people that it is impossible to remember who did what and when.

One of the things that amuses me about reading many critics is that they'll say, "So-and-so did this, and so-and-so did that." I can't remember a week after I shot a film who did what. It's an extraordinary process that goes wrong and goes right every moment of the day. There is an essential lack of privacy in making a film. That's why, when I get in the editing room, it's all so wonderful. Suddenly there is this kind of medieval cell, and you're a kind of medieval monk, and you can work in peace on your film.

Question: You cite collaboration. But many directors prefer to give the impression their films are virtual solo flights.

Pakula: I was on the jury at Cannes this year, and I saw twenty-three films— a couple of extraordinary films and some not-so-extraordinary films, some films with directorial stamps on everything but the actors' foreheads and, at their worst, full of style and without content. Directors have been glorified lately, and it is a mixed blessing. It can lead to self-conscious work and attempts to take ourselves too seriously. There can be a lingering too long on shots, too long on moments of performance—of which I can be as guilty as the next.

It's what directors would never have done in the old Hollywood. Then they said, "Tell that story. Tell that story." There's something that was wonderful about that; they weren't setting out to make greatness. That's the unfortunate thing today: sometimes films look as if they're made on granite instead of celluloid.

When I came back from Cannes, I cut seven minutes out of *Comes a Horseman*. I started playing over some of the scenes, and I thought, "Oh, you hang too long there." You're saying, "Hey, look at that," and, "Look what Gordon Willis and I did there," and, "How about that moment that Jane Fonda has over there?" It was a healthy experience for me.

Question: You've mentioned Hitchcock several times. Are there other directors whose work attracts you?

Pakula: Renoir is the one I would say I feel closest to. But there are so many. There is no way to have made a sound film after 1940 without being influenced by *Citizen Kane* [1941]. My tastes are very catholic—Ingmar Bergman, Fellini. I've run *8½* [1963] several times. Fellini's technical skills are extraordinary.

But I think I've probably been most influenced by all those films I saw when I was eleven, twelve, thirteen, fourteen years old, sitting in a movie theater on a Saturday afternoon, when the life on the screen seemed more real than my own life outside. So I would say my films are a product of my childhood in that I'm attracted to a certain old-fashioned, 1930s and '40s kind of storytelling.

Question: Can you pinpoint a topic—or theme—that you want to explore in your future movies?

Pakula: I think the attempt of people to survive with some strength and dignity and honor in their personal lives and their work in a world where values are constantly changing at every level.

Question: It's not entirely a new area for you.

Pakula: Yes, but that's like saying that because I've done one battle scene, I don't have to think anymore about war.

Question: Do you sometimes consider getting away from films for a time as a way to renew yourself?

Pakula: I think a sabbatical should be a required part of a filmmaker's career. I told my wife that last year, but this time I think I mean it.

Question: Do you ever think, for example, about getting back to the theater?

Pakula: Yes, I do think about it, and I've been exploring it. I like working with actors, and I'd like to explore areas that I wouldn't explore in films. I'd be interested in doing Chekhov or attempting Shakespeare. But, as with all future plans, I fantasize. I shall believe it when I do it.

Note

1. An inquiry into the arts and crafts of filmmaking through interview seminars between fellows and prominent filmmakers held at Greystone, under the auspices of the American Film Institute's Center for Advanced Film Studies. This educational series was directed by James Powers.

Lichtenstein, Legends, and Leviathan: Pakula on *Rollover*

Alan J. Pakula / 1982

From *Monthly Film Bulletin*, September 1982. Reprinted by permission of the British Film Institute.

Rollover, in general, was not well received in America. Critics complained that it was difficult to understand. But one of the reasons I chose to make it was to explore a world rarely seen on film. I found the very strangeness of the monetary world, the newness for audiences of its jargon and rituals and the way it operates, one of the strong attractions of the material. And, no matter how complicated that might appear, I thought the underlying themes—personal and financial success and failure, ambition, and the fascination with success and power of both the leading characters—were most accessible.

I thought the film was taken too literally by some critics, where I had hoped that its obvious stylization would make it work as a cinematic fable. In many ways, it is the most stylized film I have made. The opening shot of the trading room, with the wall lighting up, was designed as an overture to establish that kind of heightened reality.

My own notes refer to the film as American baroque. It deals with two characters who believe themselves capable of controlling their worlds, who believe in themselves as brilliant manipulators possessing all the skills and drives that make the successful think they can control whatever they do. Both the Jane Fonda and the Kris Kristofferson characters—master manipulators—discover that they are themselves being manipulated. The film deals with hubris, the hubris of a certain kind of simplistic individualism.

Both these characters represent a very specific kind of American archetype. Lee Winters (Fonda), the successful film star who becomes a successful industrialist, is a woman who has created herself. The entrances she makes, the décor of her house, and the way she plays it are all elements of the actress's character. Personal environment was very important to me. Her house was designed to make a statement about her, to help create an identity for her. It's an identity that comes through fantasies of films she has made, through films she has seen.

The emphasis on the Western side of Hubbell Smith (Kristofferson) came after Kris was cast. There are major figures in several banks in New York with Western backgrounds, whose great hobbies include ranching. Again, I was using an American film archetype: the man from the West who—according to the legend—will solve anything, who must inevitably triumph. And, of course, there is an irony in the counterpoint between the simplicity of good and evil in the Western legend and the complexity and abstract, impersonal quality of the world of finance. America is the land where people can dream of creating or recreating their own identities. The role models are very often carry-overs from the legends which their own and previous generations have seen dramatized in the cinema.

The film was shot in a hard-edged, cold style. In many ways, there is an airless quality about it. *Rollover* deals with a class of people who, while making decisions that affect the whole society, are themselves often cut off from society. They are people living behind glass walls far above the crowd or insulated in limousines. They deal with abstractions more than people, but their abstractions affect entire populations. The Currency Trading Room at the bank was deliberately a windowless set, cut off from itself. The walls are walls of numbers; changing numbers seem to be the only reality.

The large party at the Museum of Natural History was staged there for several reasons. First, to show the power of the social group involved in the party. It is as if not just vast public buildings but the leviathans of the sea can be commandeered for their amusement. I went to a charity party in that room once, and I was struck by the bizarre conjunction of elegantly dressed people, representing the most "refined" element of their civilization, and these huge, captured giants of nature. Yet underneath, of course, they are both caught up in the "big fish/ little fish" syndrome.

If *Klute* dealt with the "underbelly" of our society, one might say that *Rollover* deals with the "overbelly." But the people in both films are cut off from humanity; they live in an airless, dehumanized world. *Klute* and, perhaps even more so, *The Parallax View* are related in point of view and style to *Rollover*. The Warren Beatty character in *The Parallax View* and the Jane Fonda and Kris Kristofferson characters in *Rollover* share the same sense of hubris: the American belief in the power of the individual. The interior of the bank examiner's little house is the only example of how most of the society lives, and its intimacy of scale is there to serve as a human counterpoint to the interiors of the major characters.

In certain ways, *Rollover* has—like *The Parallax View*—a pop-art quality. The hero and heroine embody traditional hero and heroine qualities rather than whole characters. In a melodrama dealing with such complex issues, this kind of stylization seemed to me appropriate. And it also, of course, made a point: it was a reminder of the simplicity of certain American success myths.

The picture has a deliberately emblematic quality, hopefully at times witty, not unlike *The Parallax View*, where the use of the Space Needle for the assassination at the beginning and the use of the empty convention hall for the assassination at the end—with the red, white, and blue tablecloths and the high-school students doing patriotic card routines—were similar attempts to make statements in an emblematic mode. In *All the President's Men*, where Woodward and Bernstein are dealt with in a much more realistic manner, they do not have this stereo-typical heroic motivation, only a personal obsession which drives them towards their discoveries.

Some people who admired *Rollover* accused me of trying to have it both ways in the touch football scene. They felt I was violating the style by trying to humanize the characters in a sentimental way. There is also the question of whether the Hollywood-fable quality of Hub and Lee's relationship made the apocalyptic ending unbelievable. *Rollover* is a tall story. But we live in a world where tall stories have been surpassed by reality. As for the hope at the end of the film? Well, the essence of characters like these is American optimism. To deny them that at the end would be to deny their essence.

Pakula's Choices

Jonathan Rosenbaum / 1982

Originally published as "Les choix de Pakula" in *Cahiers du cinéma*, no. 23, April 1982. Translated by Jacqueline Lesage. Printed by permission of the author.

At the beginning of February 1982. In Pakula's office, on the top floor of the Gulf + Western skyscraper overlooking Central Park. On the walls, a plethora of drawings and photos of the locations and décor in which *Sophie's Choice* will soon be shot: in Manhattan, Brooklyn's Park Slope, Fox Studios, and, for the European part of the film, maybe Zagreb. The film is based on the bestseller by William Styron—the author of *Lie Down in Darkness*, *Set This House on Fire*, and *The Confessions of Nat Turner*—and our conversation centered on his adaptation of Styron's last novel (and masterpiece).

Jonathan Rosenbaum: As I adored the novel, I need to ask how you intend to treat its more literary traits: for example, the fact that the narrator, Stingo, is himself a writer. Will that play as important a role in the film as it does in the novel?

Alan J. Pakula: The fact that he is a writer and an artist is very important. The form of the scenario is very similar to the novel, except for a few structural differences. The point of view is that of a mature man as he looks back on his youth and recreates the life of these two people whom he loved so much but couldn't save. In a sense, the movie is the history of a mystery: by which he tries to solve the enigma of these two complex and extraordinary people. And, while observing this process, in a way one is witnessing the work of a writer. In addition, there is also the narration, absolutely the work of a writer, which comes from the book.

JR: At first, one may think that, with all the flashbacks, the chronological structure of the film will turn out to be rather complex. A middle-aged man sees himself back in the summer of 1947, from where there are flashbacks to earlier times—in particular, the memories of his friend and neighbor, Sophie, memories of Poland, of Auschwitz.

AJP: Well, in the film one never sees the narrator. Even though the narration is in the present tense, one does not *see* the present where it comes from; basically, one only *sees* two periods. The process of memory does free you, in some way, from a certain literality. However, one should not forget that the book is written in a classical narrative style, like a nineteenth-century novel. And I have respected that. One of the first lines of the book, "People call me Stingo," is a direct reference to the first line of *Moby-Dick*, "People call me Ishmael." And the themes are typically nineteenth-century themes—about a young man coming into contact with good and evil, love and death.

JR: Did you consult William Styron about the script?

AJP: Yes, I spoke with him before I did the first draft. Then, before the rewrite, a few months ago, I spent time at Bill's farm in Connecticut. He has been very collaborative and constructive.

JR: If I'm not wrong, it's the first time one of his books has been adapted for the screen, isn't it?

AJP: Yes. It's curious: all his novels were supposed to be adapted into films, but nothing has ever happened. For *The Confessions of Nat Turner*, all the sets had already been built, but because of the civil right protests, Fox studios decided not to go ahead with it. So, it means that *Sophie's Choice* will be the first of his novels to be adapted into film—well at least I hope it will [*Pakula touches wood*]. At the moment, we have started rehearsals, and they're taking place on the sets. This will help the actors get into character, a bit like therapy in action. Filming will start in two and a half weeks, and we will leave for Europe early May. I think the German parts will be shot in German with subtitles, and the Polish ones in Polish (also with subtitles).

JR: One of the fascinating aspects of the novel is that it is practically impossible to imagine one of the three main characters—Sophie, Nathan, and Stingo—without the other two.

AJP: That's true. It's why we have rehearsed with the three characters—played by Meryl Streep, Kevin Kline, and Peter MacNicol. . . . Meryl has been taking Polish lessons for the last five months. Monday, when we started rehearsing, the first thing I noticed, as we read the first lines, was her Polish accent—it was simply "there." Of course, she did a huge amount of work during those five months, but the character is nothing like the Meryl Streep I know. And yet she didn't seem to be hiding "behind" the character of Sophie. It's truly remarkable. I couldn't feel any effort on her part, which means that she must have worked really hard to prepare herself for the role.

JR: In quite a few of your films, there is a recurrent pattern: the female characters are obsessed by death, and some innocent men fall in love with them. *Sophie's Choice* seems to fall into this pattern.

AJP: You're right, of course, although it's totally unconscious on my part. Someone pointed out to me that, in many of my films, a young man falls in love with a complicated woman, loses his innocence, and is almost destroyed by her. In some ways, you could almost say that it is the story of *The Sterile Cuckoo*, my first movie, and while filming *Klute*, which I believed to be totally different, I realized that I was going to fall into the same pattern. It is a theme I find it hard not to return to. But I think I am interested in characters who are not *only* self-destructive but also have an extraordinary gift for life. That's certainly true for Sophie.

Apparently, some people with a great gift for living also have a great one for self-destruction. Maybe you could say that I have in me something essentially romantic—a childhood dream where I am a knight on his white horse saving a damsel in distress. I am also interested in the complexity of sexual love because this is the story of a man who saves a woman, but destroys her too. I am fascinated by this dichotomy. And in *Sophie's Choice*, what I find fascinating is the symbiosis between two people who end up betraying each other.

Jonathan Rosenbaum was the *Chicago Reader's* main film critic from 1987 to 2008 and has lectured on and written numerous books about the cinema. He maintains a website archiving his writing at jonathanrosenbaum.net.

"I Am Very American in Many, Many Ways": An Interview with Alan J. Pakula

Tom Ryan / 1983

Editor's note: This interview was conducted at the Regency Hotel in Melbourne on March 15, 1983. For the local publicity team (UIP), Pakula's visit to Australia and the interview provided opportunities to promote Sophie's Choice *to Australian audiences. For me, it was a chance to talk to a director whose work I'd admired ever since I first saw* The Sterile Cuckoo.

Tom Ryan: One of the most striking things that occurs to me about your films is that they're all in a sense about America and what it means to be American. The iconography, as in, say, *The Parallax View*: the totem pole and the Seattle Space Needle, the barroom brawl that comes straight out of a Western, the way the Warren Beatty character sees himself as a crusading hero . . .

Alan J. Pakula: Absolutely. I've always very much drawn to these kinds of things. Very much so.

TR: And your characters become embodiments of a kind of American consciousness, an innocence about the way the world works, a naïveté that will ultimately doom them if they can't move beyond it. It's the case with Klute, Frady in *The Parallax View*, the characters in *Comes a Horseman* and *Rollover* . . .

AJP: Yes, it is. And the irony with *Rollover* is that Hubbell and Lee think that they're on top of everything but are the most naïve characters in the film.

TR: Yes indeed, although that film troubled me because it left me feeling that you'd let them off the hook at the end.

AJP: Which you question?

TR: Not exactly . . .

AJP: Too sentimental?

TR: In a piece you wrote for the *Monthly Film Bulletin* [see page 94], you say that "the film deals with the hubris of a certain kind of simplistic individualism." With which I don't want to argue. But, as I see it, the optimism you allow at the end of *Rollover* is a bit like giving *The Parallax View* a happy ending.

AJP: I think that showing the hubris and endorsing it are two very different things. Also, although it may seem unlikely considering the nature of all of my films, I'm not a total pessimist. And I am very American in many, many ways, and part of that includes the fact that, after I have my morning shower, there is, most of the time, an immediate, ordinary day-to-day moment when a certain optimism exists within the boundaries of what is, essentially, my pessimistic nature. That's *my* irony.

I mean, I write about characters who are torn by opposites. I am very much of that way, which is a strange mixture of a very American optimism and a rather dark, European kind of pessimism.

One could also say something else about my characters. In all of my films, there always seems to be one major character who's disillusioned, who's trying to come to terms with reality. Whether it be a male or a female, whatever the situation, there's almost always that element of disillusionment.

There's a constant loss of innocence in my films, which, I think, is very American. Why it's there, and why I'm so attracted to it, I don't know. I don't deliberately take on a film because it's about that, but it's obviously what I'm constantly attracted to.

TR: *Rollover* is one of the films you didn't write, although I understand that you were closely involved in how the screenplay got to the screen. Its dramatic logic leads you to a certain place, which in this case is the economic destruction of the Western world. But the film has a little coda, which you chose to add—rather than not to add—which seems like a betrayal of what's gone before.

AJP: Well, it's not exactly a happy ending. It's very much these two people finding themselves in a total disaster and starting off on something else that could be even more of a disaster. I mean, I'm not commenting on the morality of what they're going to go on to do, but I think it's very American to really just get on with it, to do something, whatever it is.

Whether or not I approve of that activity, I'm looking at a society that, more often than not, is distinguished by the fact that it is active rather than analytical. There is something about it that makes it say, "Let's just get on with it." That can sometimes be quite wonderful even if the best and the worst traits in people can often be all intertwined.

Getting on with it has a really admirable kind of gallantry, and guts, about it. It's a quality that I aspire to. If a picture succeeds, the first thing that I try to do is forget about it because you can't live in the past. And if a picture fails, you have to say, "OK, this is why I think it failed," try to understand why, and get on with it. There's always the danger, though, that, at the same time, getting on with it can be a way of avoiding things, of just not facing anything.

In Sydney last Sunday, I saw a production of *Uncle Vanya*, a play that's the antithesis of my films, the antithesis of what I consider to be American realities.

I'm fascinated by Chekhov, and I relate very strongly to the way his characters are constantly paralyzed by indecision and paralyzed by a sense of the moral degradation of the society they're living in. They're the antithesis of the characters I deal with, you know. They are many things, but they're not paralyzed.

TR: That notion of people going on and just getting the job done seems to be a central quality of your films.

AJP: The essence of the journalists in *All the President's Men* is their obsession with their work, and I think that is very, very American. Their work is their life. And, yes, it's probably true of many of my characters.

And all of my films are really stylized, full of American movie archetypes and icons. That's very deliberate too: like the Space Needle and the barroom brawl that you mention in *Parallax View*. I was criticized for that, but it's the kind of thing that's always interested me. I think *Rollover*'s probably one of my most stylized films.

TR: That becomes clear in the sequence on the staircase, with the lovers . . .

AJP: Yes, exactly. I mean, it's meant to be outrageous, designed to draw attention to itself.

TR: Which produces a real tension with the thriller elements of the film, which, by comparison, operate in a more realist way . . .

AJP: Yes. I have a tendency to mix my genres in a way: to work within a style and, at a certain point, to deliberately undercut that style, or find a counterpoint to it. It's very risky, I guess, and some people find it offensive. I find it interesting. In a way, it's about the dissolution of reality: the characters in the film think of themselves as total realists, but they really live in their own world of total illusion. Hubbell is the archetypal Western hero in a situation he doesn't really comprehend.

TR: From Klute through to Woodward and Bernstein, the closer you look, the more ambiguous your heroes seem to become.

AJP: The first script I saw for *All the President's Men* before I became involved with the film was by William Goldman, but it was a script I couldn't go with. And the film I finished up making was much more dependent on Woodward and Bernstein's book. It was a heroic story because what Woodward and Bernstein *did*, what they accomplished, turned out to be heroic.

The reality, though, was that these were not good guys against bad guys. The film is about how journalism functions. They were good journalists who were responsible about what they did in terms of trying to get their facts right because if they didn't, they'd be in trouble. But they were not knights in shining white armor who were out to do good. They were journalists obsessed with a certain job, obsessed with achieving success in a certain job. And therefore, I tried not to glorify them.

In certain ways, they were quite immoral in how they went about doing their job. A lot of that came through as we went back more and more to the book. I didn't want to sentimentalize them, and I didn't want to sentimentalize the American press. I was showing how journalism works and how it can play an extraordinary role in a free society. But that important role doesn't mean that one should sentimentalize the people in it.

TR: To move on to *Sophie's Choice*: would you say that, while Stingo might be a kind of innocent, he's also an ambiguous figure?

AJP: Stingo is the camera. I mean, he is the camera's storyteller. He's also a catalyst for what happens, and, as such, he becomes passionately involved with what's going on. It was very important to keep him straight because the other two characters were just so colorful, so rich, so exotic. It was important to the film's sense of truth that he be there, that you would believe in his existence and that he'd give you the chance to enter the film through him. But there was always the danger that you'd become so concerned with his problems that it would distract you from what's going on with Sophie and Nathan. So I think we were always walking a kind of tightrope.

TR: Yes. I think one of the things I think that the film contrives so well is a kind of counterpoint between the often-exhilarating masquerade that the book calls "Nathan's comic mode" and the reality that's the characters' experience of a kind of evil that, perhaps, might better remain concealed. Which is all then ripped away from us when we find out at the end that Nathan is a paranoid schizophrenic.

AJP: Perhaps, perhaps. But you see my feeling is that, however exhilarating the sham, I like things that are real. The uplift of the sequence on the Brooklyn Bridge is Nathan's gift to the boy, something that he can't otherwise grasp. And the fact that Nathan turns out to be mad does not make every part of the masquerade a sham. I mean, that boy does go on with a greater sense of himself as a novelist thanks to Nathan.

I did not mean to suggest that it was all April Fool, that nothing was real about Nathan because nothing he does could be taken seriously. It's the same when Stingo becomes disillusioned with Sophie and is confronted by all those lies. . . . There are so many lies, but that doesn't mean that there's no truth.

People are complex beings. It's very easy to reject somebody because there are lies swirling around them. The reality is that lies and truths exist side by side in people, and it's very hard to sift through it all and very hard to judge them because of that.

Not unlike the characters in *Iceman Cometh*, or in many of Eugene O'Neill's plays for that matter, the characters in *Sophie's Choice* are people who do not, cannot, face the truth about themselves. They are running from the truth about themselves; they're afraid of being destroyed by the truth about themselves. It's almost as if Sophie's room is like a treehouse away from the world, a place where they can create the illusion that, while they're there, they're safe from it.

Stingo becomes important to them because third parties are always very important to people like them, couples like them. They can play the masquerade for him. They can look into his eyes and see that he believes the masquerade, and that allows them to believe it even more strongly themselves. They can see it through somebody else's eyes. The terror that the truth will destroy them is part of the tragedy of those characters.

There were two things about Nathan: he was also born gifted but he was also born a paranoid schizophrenic. In certain ways, he was like one of God's rotten jokes. He gave him all these incredible gifts, but then, at the last minute, he said, "Well, I'll just take that little part away and replace it with this other thing that makes him unable to function properly, artistically, and tear him apart with his own powers."

But beyond being a gifted paranoid schizophrenic, Nathan is also a man who, even in his rational periods, which are considerable, or have been in the past, refuses to admit that he's a paranoid schizophrenic. It is unbearable for him to admit his feelings. That destroys him probably even more than the paranoid schizophrenia.

If he could have sat down and said to Sophie, "This is who I am. I am a man who suffers psychotic episodes. I am a man who could go mad at any time," there might have been a chance for them. But death was preferable to the truth. It was unbearable, and he instinctively understood that. So he's destroyed by his inability to admit and face the truth about himself. And that's a basic theme in a lot of my films.

TR: And what you've said about Nathan here applies equally to Sophie? The masquerade allows her to keep at bay her knowledge of the impossible choice that she'd been forced to make?

AJP: Exactly. Again, Sophie is a woman who is so horrified by the truth about what she'd had to do that she's trying to hide away from it. In reality, she's totally the victim, although not in her own mind. She sees herself not as a victim but, by making the choice she had to make, as a perpetrator.

The horror of what had been done to her, first by her father and then by the Holocaust and the Nazis—and it's one of the most obscene parts of the Holocaust—meant that the victim has been made to feel responsible for her own victimization. She's made to feel responsible for what happened to her child; she's made to feel responsible for what's happened to herself: that it was her own cowardice and her own mistakes that were to blame. That became her reality.

What I find absolutely fascinating is the romance that she and Nathan are sharing. They're simultaneously destroying each other and saving each other. She found a man who needed her as much as she needed him. He found a woman who needed saving, allowing him to play God, the father, the savior. For the first time in his life probably, he felt really in control, able to do something really extraordinary. And she was genuinely with a man she absolutely adored and who also needed her. At the same time, he found somebody—unconsciously—that he could also destroy. And Sophie found somebody who awakened her, which she desperately wanted, but who also found existence as unbearable as she did.

The remarkable thing about Sophie is that she stayed alive as long as she did. Both she and Nathan, seemingly two opposite beings, found in each other somebody to live with and love with and fight for life with. At the same time as the darkest part of themselves was pointing towards death, the other part of themselves was pointing towards life. The conflict that continued between them still haunts me.

TR: What you've described here points to a mythic dimension in *Sophie's Choice*, one that's already present in Styron's novel. That also leads one to think of all of your work in that light.

AJP: Well, what makes me really interested in characters and in telling their story is that they have to work on other levels as well. If a story doesn't work emotionally, then there's no point in telling it. Those other levels have to be there without you working for them because if you start working for those wider resonances then you're likely to end up drowning in pretension.

TR: I'm referring to the kind of innocent-gaining-experience thread that connects Stingo, the Wendell Burton character in *The Sterile Cuckoo*, the Timothy Bottoms character in *Love and Pain and the Whole Damn Thing*. There's even a similarity in the way they look, even if their personalities are different.

AJP: Yeah, even the Klute character . . . though he is an older man.

TR: Yes. And Jane Fonda in *Comes a Horseman*, Beatty in *Parallax View*, Woodward and Bernstein . . .

AJP: I think Stingo brings this into sharp focus: a simple person coming into a world that he never dreamed was so complex and being stunned by that complexity, stunned by the fact that a capacity for originality and life and wit and passion can exist, to the most intense degrees he's ever seen in a person, side by side with such destructiveness. That kind of paradox in people never fails to surprise me. I find it fascinating, as much in myself as anywhere else.

TR: You spent a long time working with Robert Mulligan. How much of you is there in the films you made together?

AJP: Well, there's a hell of a lot of me in those films, but there's also a hell of a lot of Robert Mulligan in them. One of the reasons that I worked with Bob at that time was that our sensibilities are very similar, and our working relationship was very much an indication of that, although Bob and I are very different men. Some of my films, I think, are reflections of the similarities that we share; but there are others that seem very different too.

TR: Stylistically, *The Stalking Moon* (1968) looks as if it could have been the point from where your films take off, especially in the way the imagery is composed, in the use of the wide screen. But also in small details, like the intimate Gregory Peck/Eva Marie Saint dinner-table discussion, which turns up again in *Comes a Horseman*, with variations of course.

AJP: Yes, it is a very similar scene. I recently saw the film again on television. *Stalking Moon* is the story of an Indian scout who's about to retire, who's seen just about everything, but then with the woman he encounters a dark side of his world that he's never encountered before. I don't think that this aspect of the story was ever developed as much as it should have been. I mean, that was there, for me, but it could have been much richer.

TR: Can we talk a bit about the visual style of your films? Charles Lang shot *Stalking Moon*, and the use of the wide screen in that film seems to give it a lot in common with *The Sterile Cuckoo* [shot by Milton Krasner]. And then there's Gordon Willis.

AJP: I should start from the beginning. I'd originally been more interested in directing in the theater than in films. So I'd always wanted to work with actors. But the thing that concerned me most when I became a film director was that I was frightened about working with the camera. Once I started directing, the visual storytelling, as well as the storytelling from sound and the stylization and effects, became fascinating to me. And it turned out that I had a feeling for it that I didn't know I had. I knew I could work with actors, but I didn't know that I'd enjoy the other side of things to the extent that I did.

With *Sterile Cuckoo*, there were certain things that I tried that I didn't feel comfortable with and things that I knew I got right. The very first scene I shot in my life was that scene in the telephone booth with Liza Minnelli, the one that probably got her the Oscar nomination, which I shot in a single take. I knew there should be no cuts in that scene. I also shot the boy's end of the conversation, but I thought to myself, "You know, don't. Stay with her; stay with her; that's what it's about."

So there were areas of that film that worked very well, and other areas that I look back at today and find visually naïve. I mean, there's a montage, and it just doesn't work. I used long-focus lenses, and I use them a lot, but I would never use them in that way again. If I were doing that film today, I'd never use them like that because of the way they're sentimentalizing: you lose the specific personal detail, which frustrates me now when I think about it. I know why I used them; I know the kind of thing I was trying for.

But then I got to *Klute* and met with Gordon, who's very special. I explained to him my conception for *Klute* and the particular kind of claustrophobic feeling that I wanted to create for it and the sort of stylization I was looking for. He never forgot what I'd asked him for, and, when I started to become very opportunistic during the shoot, he said to me, "That's not what you originally told me you wanted to do." And he was right.

I learned a great deal from Gordon, and he helped me to trust my instincts. *Klute* was, for me, a big advance visually, in visual storytelling, a huge advance. I mean, we were playing with scale. I still love the scene where Jane Fonda goes to the model agency, and there are these three huge photographs of models, very stylized, hanging on the wall. And there she is, lined up under the photographs with these hopeful models, you know, like little dolls in chairs. I wanted to show the dehumanization of the world she lives in, where she means nothing. All in one shot. Then the ad team comes to her, and one of them says, "Funny hands," and then moves on. After that, off she goes: she needs a trick because at least with a trick there's someone who needs her. There was stylization with that whole film, and I felt I was getting to control the camera and to understand how it could work.

TR: It's a very bold film visually. The way you sometimes fill most of the screen with black with a tiny figure off to the side of the frame, all you can see.

AJP: Exactly. But the next film I did, *The Parallax View*, was, to me, the most interesting visual work of all, the sheer visual storytelling and the coldest film I've ever made, about a plastic world and people who were as totally alienated as they are in *Klute*. This time, there were no families and, really, no love either. It was in *Parallax* where I used all those American icons, starting out with the Space Needle, you know, that *thing*, meaningless, a totally meaningless symbol of America. Of American know-how.

And I think the reason I was drawn to that film was the opportunity it gave for visual storytelling. Everything's reflections, glass, nothing you can hold on to, a strange, dead world, except for Hume Cronyn's office. That was very much a picture of the 1960s, a 1960s world, even though it was filmed in the 1970s.

In terms of its style, *All the President's Men* is a more realistic film, more controlled.

TR: It's a dark-light film.

AJP: It *is* a dark-light film. As soon as I saw the *Washington Post* office, I knew I was in business: all the fluorescent light, a world without shadows. Everything is open. That hard light is the light of truth.

TR: But you shot it in normal ratio. It's as if the parameters of the world have closed down.

AJP: Yes, yes. Also I wanted to get those fluorescent lights on them. And there were those hard poster colors that the furniture had, which was actually from the *Washington Post*. As it was then, they were in an old building. A brand-new office on a big scale wouldn't have suited me half as well.

And a lot of the film was shot in bright sunlight. What was fascinating to me was that most melodramas go probing dark worlds, exploring dark corners. But this was about middle-class crime. This was about people who lived in the sunlight, who lived in the open air, like that bookkeeper in his cheerful world and the well-kept porches and lovely flowers and trees growing on the residential streets. With Sloan in that modern condominium townhouse that's like a parody of eighteenth-century architecture, it was almost like a Disneyland complex, where everything's neat and tidy and precise and where all's right with the world. Except that it's not. It was wonderful for me.

By that time, I knew how to use what the camera could show, and that's curious because I almost didn't direct. Looking back now, I think there are certain similarities shared by my films, visually, but there are also certain areas of difference.

TR: Which brings us to *Starting Over*. It looks very different from all of your other work?

AJP: I feel that *Starting Over* probably has the least visual style of all the films that I've done. It's a very intimate piece, and I wanted the style to reflect that. Jim Brooks and I talked that through when we were working on the screenplay. He's a wonderful man. He'd come out of television, out of *The Mary Tyler Moore Show*, and he'd just become a director. Actually, the film he's making [*Terms of Endearment*, 1983] was based upon a book that I sent to him. I really wanted the camera almost not to exist in a way. You know, it was strange. It was almost like the style of that film was no style at all.

TR: But one is very conscious of the lighting. As in the dinner-table scene near the start where the Burt Reynolds character first meets Jill Clayburgh at his brother's place, where it's really very beautiful.

AJP: Yes, yes, yes, yes, yes, yes . . . yes. That's true. It's rather romantic in that way, and the film was rather romantic. I had different, more complex ideas for the style of the film, but I was worried that I'd just drown it, I'd actually drown it. It's kind of frustrating, you know, because coming out of *The Parallax View* and *All the President's Men* . . .

TR: And *Comes a Horseman*.

AJP: Oh, yes, *Comes a Horseman*, which was a very specific style. I had to hold myself back, you know, always hold myself back. I'd have to tell myself, "Watch out you; just watch out." It was frustrating in many ways. I was always holding back on impulses to do certain visual things because I feel that style, if it doesn't reflect or illuminate content, is then just showing off.

TR: Finally, to come back to *Sophie's Choice* . . .

AJP: For me, it was a way of genuflecting to what I believe is one of the greatest novels in the English language. When I first read it, I was awed by it and, in adapting it for the screen, it was vital for me to adhere as closely to its spirit and sensibility as I could.

TR: If I've got it right, it's as if visually and dramatically it starts off very close in and then gradually expands to give us a much wider view before it closes down again with Stingo coming back across the bridge in a quite different shot from the earlier one of the bridge. Was that your way of thinking about it?

AJP: Yes, but there was also something else. When I read the book, I was swept away by it, and I thought it was really cinematic. I had in my mind all those MGM colors of the 1940s. And then I realized what a gift the novel was. When I started working on the script, it became clear that the story was all about memories, the memories of a middle-aged man looking back to the time when he was twenty-two years old. It's full of the nostalgia of memory because, for all the tragedy that happened, he misses those people.

That summer was the most important summer of his life. That was the summer when he discovered the intensity of life. It seemed more passionate to him than it ever did again. The sunlight was more mellow; the colors were more beautiful, you know, richer, more sensual, more filling. That thing that memory can do, and also what those characters represented to him. Those characters become mythic in his mind. I wanted the warmth of all that and the color palette that went with it, and that worked wonderfully for me.

Then we got to *her* memories, and we have a total reversal. We're now seeing it all through her eyes. At first, we thought we'd do it in black and white—it was Nestor Almendros I was working with this time—but it just seemed too damn obvious. Then we thought of desaturating the color, which we did. So there's just a little color left, more faded and strangely death-like in a way, you know, and just the opposite of what we've seen before. But there's still a sense of color being there.

We had terrible trouble technically with all of this. They said they knew how to do it in the processing, but two weeks before the film was due to open in New York, they still had not perfected how to do it. They'd been able to do it in test reels, but they couldn't do it consistently, and I was going out of my mind. They said, "You can always go back to full color." But I'd designed the whole sequence anticipating that the color would be desaturated: we sometimes used very exaggerated colors for the sets and costumes, knowing that it was all eventually going to be desaturated. If wasn't, it would all end up looking like a circus.

I was absolutely horrified, and the week before we were due, they tried something else. They thought it would work, and it did. I don't understand how it did—what process they came up with—just that it did. But they never told me they really didn't know how to do it until the time pressure had become so enormous.

The American Film Institute's Dialogue on Film #2: Alan J. Pakula

American Film / 1985

From *American Film*, November 1985. Copyright © American Film Institute.¹ Reprinted by permission.

Question: You've had a very long career in filmmaking. Do you see any progression or pattern to it?

Alan J. Pakula: The first film I ever produced—and I was a producer for a long time before I was a director—was *Fear Strikes Out*, with Tony Perkins. It was a work of personal passion on my part: the true story of Jim Piersall, a baseball player who had a mental breakdown. He recovered and came back. It interested me on several levels. There was the theme of a boy trying to find his own identity—his own life. A young man finds himself possessed, almost literally possessed, by his father, and finds that two lives are being led through his life—his father's and his own. The breakaway into his own identity—the breaking out of that chrysalis—is the major part of the story and of that character's return to health.

Now, I don't know how many pictures later, my most recent film, *Dream Lover*, a psychological thriller with Kristy McNichol, is the story of a girl dominated by her father who attempts to break away and lead her own life, with rather disturbing and perhaps shocking results. That's not all that it's about by any means, but the fact that, after all these years, those same things still haunt me means that you never get away from being who you are.

Q: Did you feel as a producer that you had enough creative input?

AJP: No producer ever feels he has enough creative input! A producer has an invaluable function: to be a good producer. And there are all kinds of producers. Look at what Bob Redford did on *All the President's Men*. That is a film that was only made because he said, "I know nobody wants to make political pictures because they're box-office poison, but I don't care. I'm going to get it made." He got it made, and he never forgot why he was getting it made. And he not only made great contributions in the development of the film but also helped create an environment in which we could all do our best work. That to me is a first-rate producer.

I have a rule for producers: there can only be one person in control on that set, only one authority figure, one father figure, one psychoanalyst, and that's the director. And if the producer comes on there and starts talking to those actors and starts trying to be creative on that set, watch out. You're going to have a castrated director.

Q: How would you define the role of the director, then?

AJP: Part of the job is being an artist, part of it is being a general—organizing the troops—and part of it is being a communicator, so that the other creative people can do their best work within your concept. And the other part is being a psychiatrist. In particular, working with the actors. And that is not said in a facetious way, because acting is an emotional tool, and you have to have some sense of the person who's doing it and what they have to contribute to their character in order to get the performance you want out of them.

Ingmar Bergman once said, "If you don't have something to say, don't make a film." And, of course, he's correct. A director has to have a concept, some driving passion. Once you have that concept, you must communicate that concept to other people. And you communicate about a film whatever will help the people you're working with. I don't discuss everything with the actors that I discuss with the cinematographer.

On *All the President's Men,* I said to Gordon Willis, when we discussed photographing the newsroom, "I want a world without shadows. I want a world which is a world of truth, somewhere where nothing gets away, where everything is examined under this merciless glare." I worked that out with the art director and with Gordon Willis. I didn't sit down and say to the actors, "Now I want this to be a hard, sharp-focus picture. . . ." They can't act sharp focus.

So you talk to the actors about their characters and what happened. Why were you obsessed with going after that story? Who were you? What were your fears? What were your motivations? Those are things they can act. What you do is choose what you say to each person. Your job as a director is to keep the whole thing in your mind. On good days you can, and on bad days you'll go crazy.

Q: Do you have any philosophy about how you interact with all the different personnel while on location?

AJP: If you are working with people you don't have a rapport with—who don't relate to you—you're already in trouble. I would say for that reason that the importance of casting holds not just for the actors but for all the key people—your cinematographer, your production designer, your costume designer.

Let me give an example of a production designer, George Jenkins. On my latest film, *Dream Lover*, I had one of those pivotal scenes in which the girl is alone in an apartment and is attacked by a strange man. In working out the set with the art director, I thought, "He'll hide in the bathroom," or, "He'll come out of the bathroom." But then, when I staged the scene, I thought, "It's absolutely wrong to play it there. It should be in the living room or the kitchen." Then I realized, "There's no place for him to hide and, if he can't hide, the whole scene's down the drain." It was a terror moment. I was rehearsing and walking around the set thinking, "Where the hell do I hide this man?" And I opened the front door, and there was a little alcove on either side, which I hadn't asked George Jenkins to supply. So you can go right to the door, and you don't see that man hiding until you're right at the door. I had never asked for it—it was wonderful. But George gives you little surprises like that and eccentricities beyond what you've worked out on the floor plan. We have that kind of rapport, and it's essential.

One thing you'll find is that once you've set your locations and you've had your sets designed, the look of the picture is locked in. I don't care what your cinematographer does. If it's a tiny room, you're photographing tiny spaces. If it's a colorful room, you're making a statement about bright color. And to suddenly say, "I'm starting to shoot this film, so now I'll create my visual style," is nonsense. The visual look is total ensemble work, and it is very important that it be set very early on.

Q: Do you get as involved with the camera as you do with the production design?

AJP: The camera and camera movement are part of the vocabulary you use to make your statement. If you overuse camera movement, it's like screaming, "Help, help, help," all the time, or having twenty-five exclamation points. If you're looking at the eyes and face of a character, and they're revealing emotions, why the hell move the camera, unless that movement makes a statement? On the other hand, if I have a woman laughing on the phone, and she gives this huge speech that's wildly funny, and I pan down to her hands, and her fingernails are digging holes into her palms, and they're bleeding, there's a reason for that camera movement.

There is one move in *All the President's Men* which takes place in the Library of Congress. The camera starts on reference cards, library cards, the files. These two men, Dustin Hoffman and Bob Redford, are on the trail of something—you can see dozens of these little cards. Then the camera pulls up, and it pulls up to the top of the library. They are in this huge, dome-like building, and they are dwarfed. It was a tour de force camera move, but it was making a point: "My God, how tiny these people are, and how endless the search!"

Q: What is your approach toward the use of music in your films?

AJP: In general, music and sound effects are dangerous weapons because they are overused so much. *Klute* and *The Parallax View* were films where the use of music was absolutely essential. Michael Small did an extraordinary thing for *Parallax View*. I said to him, "Some way you have to characterize a group of people, the heavies, the Parallax People, who are never shown in this film. We don't know who they are." Essentially, I was saying they represent the danger of domestic fascism hiding behind symbols of patriotism. And he created this cheerful, Sousa-like score. But there's an edge to it. There's something under that cheerful martial thing that becomes threatening after a while.

In *Klute*, there was another major problem for music to solve. It was the story of a girl who's obsessed with seducing. She's a girl who feels impotent herself; the only time she feels any sense of power is when she's sexually in control and knows a man wants her in a way she doesn't want him. It's this need to seduce that almost kills her.

So I said to Michael, "How can we express this in the score? I want her pulled in—as though she is pulling herself toward her own destruction." We're talking about a siren song. He said, "Then we should use a woman's voice." There's a sick voice—like her own voice—pulling her forward, and it's threatening. It's endangering.

In *Sophie's Choice*, I ran the film for Marvin Hamlisch. And I said to him, "The film is so emotional. It's about such horror that it runs the great danger of becoming emotional pornography. I would like something that gives a kind of dignity and—I'll use a strange expression—a sense of occasion about these people." Marvin wrote baroque music, which had that dignity, and a kind of romantic quality, but controlled, and with a sense of occasion and an almost processional quality about it.

Q: Does your rehearsal pattern vary with every film, and do you have general rules before you start shooting?

AJP: I rehearse differently for each film, and a lot depends on the actors. There are some actors who benefit from rehearsal and some who are frightened of it. The most important thing about rehearsals for me, if nothing else, is that everybody gets to know each other. Hopefully, by the end of the rehearsal time, they get to trust each other. And that is terribly important to me because I ask actors to go up there and take risks and not play it safe. If they feel I'm going to jump on them if they do something wrong, then they're going to do very safe work, and it's going to be dull work.

The other thing that's terribly important for me is to see what those actors have to give the parts—to see where their instincts take them, to see what they have to contribute that I never would have thought of. And to see the dangers of those actors in those parts—to see where they're going to go wrong, wrong for the film.

On some films, I will do a lot of blocking in rehearsal. On *The Sterile Cuckoo*, we rehearsed for four weeks, and I blocked it like a play. On *Sophie's Choice*, we rehearsed for about three and a half weeks, and I would say that, most of that time, much to my surprise, we sat around a table and just kept reading through the script. That worked for Meryl in particular. I don't think that Kevin Kline was as crazy about working that way at that point, because he is a man who works through his muscles and his nerve endings. He starts to feel the character when he moves. Meryl was just the opposite. Of course, she'd been studying Polish for all those months, and she had already gone through a certain period of discovery when she said to me one day, "I was making a sound this morning, a Polish sound. And I suddenly felt the character." This mystical thing of acting!

Part of the thrill of working with new people all the time is that you find out what's right for them. I'd never worked with Kristy McNichol before *Dream Lover*. I think she's one of the most gifted actresses I've ever worked with. Her questions were all character questions, all about the girl, and would the girl behave this way and that way. She had a sense of that character.

While we rehearse, I throw everyone else off the set. Once I've locked the scene in with the actors, I run it for the cameramen and for the technical people. I talk about coverage. Then I work with the technical people only. The stand-ins come on, and I tell the actors to get off the set and do whatever they have to do, prepare make-up or whatever. When the technical people are ready, and we've lit the whole scene, we do the final rehearsals, and we shoot. That's essentially how I work.

When actually shooting, I will very often change one actor's performance by talking to the other actor, asking for a change. Because if you're working with a good actor, that actor will respond to the change. There's a scene in *All the President's Men* in which Dustin Hoffman is interviewing this little bookkeeper, Jane Alexander. He is trying to get her to talk. He is hanging on every word, just so afraid that if he ever breaks the spell, she'll stop talking, stop revealing everything he wants to know. I wanted that kind of concentration, and all I said to Jane was, "Whisper; make it hard for him to hear you. Every take you do, lower your voice one more notch." And Dustin was absolutely focused. He could not break into it and say "louder" because he knew as the character she would withdraw.

Q: How would you assess your work—what are your strengths and weaknesses?

AJP: What are my strengths and weaknesses? I'd have to lie down on a couch to answer that one! I think if I'm passionate about something, and there's a specific concept in what I do, I'll get it done. And if I fail, I fail in a specific way. I think that sometimes I become so intensely involved with the material and certain things have such a specific meaning for me that I may be surprised if they don't have that same meaning to the audience. And maybe I become too oblique, although I try to go for very simple narrative pull in my films.

My films are very much narrative films. They reflect my childhood. They reflect going to films in the 1940s and loving a story. They're far from avant-garde, although I experiment with techniques. I'd say I'm from a kind of Charles Dickens school of filmmaking. Somewhere we go back to the fact that we all have obsessions. If we're creative, if we're lucky, we have things that drive us, mysteries that we have to live and relive and act out and re-enact. And each time, if you're creative and you're lucky, you get a picture or a book or a story out of it.

Note

1. An inquiry into the arts and crafts of filmmaking through interview seminars between fellows and prominent filmmakers held at Greystone, under the auspices of the American Film Institute's Center for Advanced Film Studies. This educational series was directed by James Powers.

Family Ties Bind Pakula to His *Morning*

Bruce Weber / 1989

Some years ago, producer-director Alan J. Pakula sat down to talk with his wife, Hannah, about a movie he had in mind to write based on circumstances parallel to their own meeting and marrying. "It was a piece I couldn't write if I hadn't had a comparable experience," he recalls. "And I said to my wife, 'If I do this film, everybody's going to think it's us. They're all going to think they're looking inside our bedroom.' And my wife said, 'If you worry about that, you're not going to write anything.' And I said, 'I'm going to remind you that you said that.'"

The film, *See You in the Morning*, a romantic comedy or domestic drama, depending on how you look at it, opens at neighborhood theaters on Friday. "It's not true confessions," Pakula says, "but it's a personal film." And indeed, for Pakula, who turned sixty-one on April 7, it is a personal project in more ways than one.

In a career spanning more than three decades and a remarkable variety of movies, his credits are formidable. Since 1957, he has served as producer, director, or both on eighteen previous films—including *To Kill a Mockingbird*, *Klute*, *All the President's Men*, for which he garnered an Academy Award nomination for best director, and *Sophie's Choice*, which he not only coproduced and directed, but whose screenplay he adapted from the William Styron novel, an effort that won him a second nomination for an Oscar. For his next project, he will direct Harrison Ford in *Presumed Innocent*, an adaptation, by Frank Pierson, of Scott Turow's best-selling novel about a prosecuting attorney accused of murdering his beautiful colleague, with whom he's had an affair. But *See You in the Morning* is the only film Pakula has produced and directed from his own original screenplay.

It's a professional scenario that suggests control, which is, apparently, a subject that Pakula thinks a lot about. He has realized, he says, that at the heart of many of the films he has directed—from *The Sterile Cuckoo* in 1969 to *Klute* in 1971 to the impending *Presumed Innocent*—is a male character who confronts the consequences of his comfort and/or authority and the personal terror of having to yield them.

"I made a note for a film long ago," he says, by way of illustration, "an opening scene of a dream. In it, there's this frightened person, terrified, impotent in terms of his fate, running from things, being pursued, bewildered, insecure, just a dream of all kinds of infantile terror. And in the dream, suddenly you hear this"—he bangs several times on his desk—"and you cut. And there is this middle-aged man lying in bed. And you hear a voice: 'It's seven o'clock. Time to wake up, Mr. President.' A man who is in control, and inside there's a frightened child. That interests me. Why? You can draw your own conclusions."

A dapper man, chatty, soft-spoken but insistently self-scrutinizing, Pakula is an animated pop psychologist, interested in and amused by the way his mind works and occasionally seeming chagrined by the fact that he thinks about it so much. In his Manhattan office, with photos of possible Midwestern locations for *Presumed Innocent* posted on bulletin boards and a thoroughly annotated copy of the novel on his desk ("Ask Scott how he came to make Sandy an Argentinian Jew"), he admits to the inherent conflicts of conducting a lengthy evening interview with his tie tied and his blazer buttoned but his shoes off.

"There's a whole area of me that's very buttoned up," he says. "I'm a man who really doesn't like to be embarrassed. But somewhere or other, you say, 'This means enough that I'll risk making a fool of myself.' Making films means enough to me to expose myself to public judgment."

In *See You in the Morning*, a dignified New York psychiatrist, played by Jeff Bridges, fearful of losing the woman he loves precisely because he hasn't shown, to her satisfaction, that she means enough to him, proposes to her dressed up as Cupid, powdered with talc, carrying a bow and arrow, and wearing only a diaper. The ruse, initially unwritten by Pakula, arose out of Bridges's clowning on the set. "Jeff was stunned when I said, 'What about using it?'" Pakula says. He was prepared to reshoot it, but audiences in early screenings responded "with a huge roar, a roar of delight." Delighted himself, he left it in.

"In my own life, I've been my own cautions," Pakula says. "Once or twice, I've thrown them to the wind. And I've ended up very happy because I've managed to do that." In the sense that it, too, ends happily, *See You in the Morning* is sort of a romantic comedy, though it isn't entirely funny. A baldly emotional film, with characters who are at their wits' end much of time, it has a bravely complex chronology, full of flashbacks that suggest people who are haunted by the past. In a word, it is about remarriage, telling the story of the courtship and early wedded life of the psychiatrist, Larry Livingston, and a photographer, Beth Goodwin, played by Alice Krige. Larry's first marriage, to a fashion model (Farrah Fawcett), dissolves suddenly in the movie's opening sequence.

And in its second sequence, Beth is left widowed by the suicide of her husband (David Dukes), a concert pianist whose career has been destroyed by a mysterious paralysis of his right hand. Beth and Larry are subsequently introduced by an appealingly meddlesome mutual friend (Linda Lavin), and three years later, after much self-protective agonizing on both their parts, they marry, which is when the problems start.

Larry moves in with Beth and her two children in their brownstone in Chelsea, in the meantime trying to maintain father status with his own two kids, who live with their mother and a man named Morty in an unspecified place, though they fly in for the wedding from Paris and spend some time at the home of their grandmother, known as Neenie (Frances Sternhagen), in Maine.

If it sounds complicated (there are a lot of other characters), it's meant to be. "I'll tell you exactly how it came about," says Pakula, whose own first marriage, to the actress Hope Lange, ended twenty years ago. His current wife, a biographer, the former Hannah Cohn Boorstin, was a widow when they met; they married in 1973. He has five stepchildren, though none of his own, a situation somewhat reflected by Linda Lavin's family (the kids are adopted) in his movie.

"There are two seminal stories," he says. "The first happened a couple of years before I married Hannah. I was living in New York, and my stepdaughter from my first marriage was graduating from grade school. I went out to Los Angeles for her graduation. And I bought her a horse. She loves horses. One day, on the way to the stable, where she was, I stopped by her father's wife's house—her father was separated from her stepmother then; they got back together and lived happily ever after—and her stepmother said, 'Leave your car, I'll drive you to the stable.'

"We took her youngest child, her child by my stepchild's father, and we're going down a canyon road, and she runs out of gas. We get out, and there I am with this little boy and this attractive woman, and I start hitching. And a car stops, and in the car is a very nice man, with his own son, and I said, 'Really, boy, thanks for picking us up.' And he said, 'Oh, it's a delight to do something for such an attractive, all-American family.'

"And I wanted to say, 'No, no, no, you don't understand. This is not my wife. This is not my child. This is actually the first wife of my wife's first husband, and the child of the first husband of my wife. And we're going down to see the daughter of her first husband and my wife.' But then I thought, 'This man does not need this.' And at that moment I realized my life has gotten more complicated than I thought about in my visions of myself."

Pakula laughs. Who wouldn't? Then he tells the second story, which involves him and his present wife, shortly after their marriage, on a cruise with his five stepchildren. "We're all quite close," he says. "We were on this ship, and there had been a young woman with a child of about seven or eight sitting at the dinner table with us. And the last night, she came over to my wife, and she said, 'I just want you to know how terrific it has been for me to sit next to a family that has such a good time together.'

"As we're going back to our cabin, my wife said, 'I feel really bad about that. She's going through a rough time in her life, and she's looking at us and thinking we've had all the luck. And I know what that feels like.' So the next morning, my wife explained it to her: 'None of these kids has my husband's name. A lot of tragedy happened before we found each other. So hang in there. It can happen.'

"When I heard that, I thought someday I'd like to write a story about that theme, that people have baggage. I thought, 'That's a theme I know something about.' I also wanted the film to be some kind of celebration of the power of human beings to start over again, to love and commit again. And not just adults, but kids."

Though the facts of *See You in the Morning* don't quite conform to Pakula's own biography, he admits to borrowing some specifics from himself. In a shtick that runs throughout, for example, Larry makes up fantastic tales for his children, featuring characters known as Yllib and Nibor, the kids' names, spelled backwards. "That's something I did with a stepdaughter from my first marriage," Pakula says.

Still, he adds, as he was writing, the characters didn't come alive until he could separate their experiences from his own. And he is quick to point out the differences. For one thing, Larry and Beth are in their midthirties, younger than he was while he endured his own tough times. Also, he says, "During the comparable time in my own life—the separation, the divorce, the remarriage—I was mainly in California. These people live in a very different way, in a brownstone in New York. I deliberately did not place them in a setting that would be literally familiar to me. I had to get away from the literal."

In any case, Pakula prefers to talk about the film thematically, which is understandably, if paradoxically, when the talk becomes most personal. He interchanges pronouns tellingly. "Coming out of a bad experience, a relationship that failed, there's a part of you that matures underneath that," he says. "But there's a part of you that goes back to younger kinds of insecurities and vulnerabilities. Rejection can do that to you.

"To go back, after a committed relationship, to the superficialities of dating, the uncommitted quality of dating, is bizarre and unnerving. It seems as if you're going back to some adolescent conduct. The very idea of making a pass, or accepting a pass, and how far do we go and how deeply do we get involved; all of those things can be very insecure-making.

"Also, there's something else. If you've been married and divorced, once you fall in love with someone else, commit yourself to someone else, that's the final death of the marriage. That's the final killing it off. Divorce isn't as final as falling in love again, especially since this is the mother of his children for this guy.

"This is a way I'm not like him. I can relate to him, but it's not exactly like me. But somewhere, it means closing the door on ever living with his children on an ordinary daily basis as a father. And being there is finally a major, major definition of parenting. So this man is very attracted to this woman, and they are people who take love seriously. But I think once things have not worked out the way you've expected them to, to trust that again is very tough. So that at the end, he has to come out and say to her, the toughest thing for a man to say to any woman: 'I'm scared.'"

It's a long speech, abridged here, but ultimately it brings Mr. Pakula back to the notion of airing the things most important to him in public. And he ends, more or less, where he began. When he first finished the script, he says, he sent it out to two studios. One of them was Lorimar Pictures, since swallowed up by Warner Bros., which financed the film.

"That was on a Thursday," he says. "And by Monday night we had a deal. And going to bed that night, I said to my wife, 'You know, I feel kind of lost. That was my secret project, and now it's not a secret anymore.' And there was a long beat of silence in the darkness. And from the other side of the bed came a voice: 'And how do you think you'd be feeling if you hadn't sold it?'"

Renowned for his work in the fields of advertising, fashion, and fine art, acclaimed photographer **Bruce Weber** is also a filmmaker of note as well as an occasional contributor to the *New York Times*. There have been numerous published collections of his photography, which has also been exhibited at museums around the world.

A Walk with Good and Evil: Alan J. Pakula Interviewed

Ana Maria Bahiana / 1990

From *Cinema Papers*, no. 81, December 1990. Reprinted by permission.

During the last months of 1986, Hollywood was ablaze with a fierce bidding war. It seemed that every single producer and director wanted to turn Scott Turow's yet-to-be-published novel, *Presumed Innocent*, into a film. Alan J. Pakula, a writer and director with an intense interest in the same battles of good and evil that form the core of Turow's novel, was one of the most industrious contenders in that war, albeit a behind-the-scenes one. "I more or less talked [producer] Sydney [Pollack] into buying it for me," Pakula says. "I was fascinated by the book, by its wonderful exploration of our system of justice. It also was a crackling good suspense yarn."

A New York native with a bachelor's degree in drama studies and a longstanding interest in psychology, Pakula has an extensive and brilliant filmography to his credit, including an essential trio of thrillers that dissect some of America's most sensitive nerves: sex, power, and rage in *Klute*; politics, power, and mischief in *The Parallax View*; politics, power, mischief, and the media in *All the President's Men*. He received a New York Film Critics' Award and an Oscar nomination for the last, a London Film Critics' Award for *Klute*, and an Academy Award screenplay nomination for *Sophie's Choice*, his painful 1980s masterpiece.

With his new film, Pakula makes his mark in 1990, a year that may come down in American film history as part of an era of excesses, self-indulgence, and outrageously expensive and silly movies. *Presumed Innocent* is none of these, and it shines brightly as a mature, almost serene meditation on the tangled worlds of crime and punishment, sin and guilt, repentance and atonement.

Extremely faithful to Turow's novel, Pakula's film chronicles the dizzying descent of a rational, decent, perfectly normal man, district prosecutor Rusty Sabich (Harrison Ford), into the hellish judicial maze he is supposed to manage after his colleague and ex-lover Carolyn Polhemus (Greta Scacchi) is brutally murdered and probably raped. He quickly becomes the prime suspect and, finally, the accused. As Pakula says, "It's a story of power and how it affects men and women. It's a story that asks what is justice, and if it is attainable."

Ana Maria Bahiana: Was your intention, in bringing *Presumed Innocent* to the screen, to be truthful to the original novel?

Alan J. Pakula: Yes. Given that millions of people bought and read the book, I felt it would have been arrogant of me to violate what it was about. Also, I wanted to be truthful to an experience that I had been thrilled by. That was enough of a challenge without rewriting the book. Anyway, Scott is a genius when it comes to plot, so I wasn't about to try to top him on that.

Bahiana: Did you have any specific problems in the adaptation?

Pakula: Nothing but. There had to be grounding and some kind of reality at the beginning. That's why I set it in a small town, so you could relate to these people on a simple level. The telling of this complicated story depends on the audience understanding a lot of complicated things, and you have to clear up that information. I had the same problem with *All the President's Men*.

Harrison [Ford] was very helpful on this one. He kept asking me questions like, "Do you understand this?" I remember the second time I met Harrison, I went to Wyoming and read the script. He said to me, "Explain the B file." I then spent three hours explaining it. I then realized that if it took me that long to explain it, something was wrong with the script. So, we kept working on it and trying to simplify it.

What we found when we previewed the picture is that when you get 450 people into a theater, as opposed to a few people in a projection room, there is a wave of understanding that happens. I don't know if they hypnotize each other or how they communicate. But somehow, we just felt the audience getting things faster.

Bahiana: It is interesting that you mentioned *All the President's Men* because both films have an ending that's well-known to a lot of people. How do you handle a problem like this?

Pakula: By being true to the story. The story is my discipline, and I have to tell it as if it is being told for the first time. I have to be careful to maintain the integrity of anything that's written in the screenplay and of all the actors who play the parts. It's not just a trick at the end. In this case, I wanted people to be fascinated by the story even if they knew the ending. At the same time, if you don't know it, that is another thrill.

Bahiana: Turow has recently published another book, *The Burden of Proof*, exploring the character of Sandy Stern, the Jewish Argentine lawyer played by Raul Julia in your film. Would you be interested in turning that novel into a film as well?

Pakula: At this point, I'm working on a script of my own, but who knows what could happen in a few years. I liked working on Scott's material a great deal; he's a wonderful storyteller and has this fascination with the interplay between good and evil in seemingly ordinary people and in the system itself. So, would I be attracted? Yes, I would.

Bahiana: Besides being thrilled by the book in general, what else attracted you to this project? Was it that interplay between good and evil, which you have also dealt with in other films?

Pakula: I have explored American journalism and how it works. I have also been interested in the particulars of the American justice system and how it works. I don't think it is that different from one society to another, and it sometimes works in spite of itself. The notion of justice is such a glorious idea, and yet it also deals with criminal behavior. It represents the best in man, and the worst. That fascinates me.

There was also the fact that the book was written by someone who knew the environment well. It is a tale of reality, which I loved. More important is the character of Rusty Sabich. I am fascinated by rational people who find themselves doing irrational things; people who think they are civilized and in total control of themselves and their lives but wind up not in control; people who are reminded of the fact that they can be better and start having compassion for themselves and other people and are not so arrogant in their judgments. Those complexities fascinated me.

There is also the erotic obsession of this character, which is full of pleasure but gives him no happiness. It is a disturbing kind of pleasure, a pleasure without fulfillment. It is compulsive and obsessive, and that kind of thing also fascinates me.

Bahiana: You have approached this theme before, in *Klute*.

Pakula: Yes, where a character uses sex for other reasons than itself. For whatever reasons, such things interest me. I can't tell you why. I don't know what it tells about me, and I'm not sure I want to know.

Bahiana: *Presumed Innocent* has in fact two outstanding female characters involved in this strange battle for power who both, at some point, can be taken for villainesses. Was that what interested you in the shaping of these characters?

Pakula: Well, yes, they are two wonderful parts for women. But I was worried, after reading the book, that audiences would not understand. I did not want them to come out looking like simply bad people: they are fascinating, complicated women. That's why it was so important to cast Greta Scacchi as the great seducer, Carolyn.

You're dealing with a story of a man who is sexually obsessed by a woman who tears his whole life apart. You have a very short time in which to establish this sexual obsession because she's dead at the beginning of the picture. Greta has this bigger-than-life desirability that reminds me of the sexual icons of the screen in the 1940s, when I was young. Her character is so complex: she's a seducer; she's incredibly intelligent and a wonderful lawyer; she has compassion. That interests me more than somebody who is just bad. Yes, she uses seduction to get her ways, but how many men wouldn't use it, if anybody wanted them? George Bush tried everything else . . .

Bahiana: Considering the climate in Hollywood these days, when only mega-budget productions with lots of special effects and huge body counts are made, your film is almost a daring enterprise.

Pakula: Well, Warners didn't think it was. The fact that this book is one of the biggest sellers in the history of America had a lot to do with their willingness to take a chance. Also, it's not just a character study: it's an exciting suspense story, with a fascinating plot. I love that kind of storytelling. It's like the pictures of the 1940s that I grew up with.

Bahiana: What's your opinion about what is going on in the industry right now, especially this summer, with all the juvenile action/sci-fi films?

Pakula: I think it goes in waves. The head of the studio said to me, "A lot of us and a lot of filmmakers have been having fun with all the special effects and violent toys, but the next thing you know, there'll be another wave and another kind of film." Hollywood has traditionally gone through different waves, although this one has lasted a very long time.

You see, I find there is room for all kinds of films. Certainly, *Dick Tracy* and *Die Hard 2* [both 1990] should be made. They are wonderful, child-like, thrilling experiences. It's just that we should be making other kinds of movies as well. If you look back to the 1940s, all different kinds of films were made: women's pictures, adventure movies, big Westerns, science fiction, and so on.

So my only frustration is not that Hollywood makes what it does, because childhood fantasies and childhood adventure are some of the wonderful things film can do, but that there should be all kinds of things for audiences. Who wants to eat nothing but popsicles?

Bahiana: Given that, how would you describe *Presumed Innocent*?

Pakula: It's a classic, commercial, Hollywood film. That's really what I wanted to make, with that kind of excitement and character. It is not just out of a physical amusement park.

Bahiana: You have done different kinds of films, but you seem to come back, always, to thrillers. Is there any particular reason?

Pakula: I sure like doing thrillers. For one thing, they allow me to use a very specific style, a kind of hypnotic style. You can't do that in comedy. I like that style and relate to it. Maybe there's a part of me that loves going, "What's going to happen next?" and is thrilled by suspense. Ultimately, you make a film for yourself because you want to see that kind of film.

Bahiana: Do any of your films stay with you for some time after you have finished them?

Pakula: This one. I am haunted by it and the people in its story. It stays with me. *Klute*, too: I couldn't get out of that.

On *See You in the Morning*, I had the whole experience—I also wrote the script. I then wished it well and went on to the next. I felt that way with *Starting Over* and with a lot of my films. It's not a question of liking one more. But there is something unconscious that keeps pulling me into this one. It's like Harrison's character's obsession with Greta's. You kind of just want to get away but can't.

Bahiana: Rusty Sabich's sexual obsession is, as you said, painful and joyless and gets extraordinary punishment at the end. The same thing happens with Donald Sutherland's character in *Klute*. Would you make a film where sex is joyful and goes unpunished?

Pakula: I'm trying. I like it a lot. When I read the book *Presumed Innocent*, I said that I think what Rusty did was unfortunate, but the punishment really seemed rather extraordinary to me. When I was working on it, I called it "Sex and Punishment"—I always have subtitles dealing with what a film's about. When you're dealing with this kind of obsession, there is something of the sense of the forbidden. It's not just simple, healthy sexuality. There is the sense of violating your own code, the excitement of doing that, of the malevolent person who gets eroticized by way of doing the forbidden.

I am currently working on this new script, which is an outrageous comedy caper. Nobody's punished for the sex. The sex is really going to be outrageously cheerful. They might be punished for other things. They have to be punished for something.

Bahiana: Are you obsessed with the forbidden, with guilt and punishment?

Pakula: Maybe you can say come from a generation where sex was a lot less complicated than it is now. There is no word in the English language that's more of a turn on than "don't." It eroticizes.

In this script, there is an adulterous affair, and I think that adds to a certain kind of eroticizing, a certain sense of danger, and a certain kind of chilling quality. That lasts a lot longer and has a lot more to do with punishment than cheerfully jumping into the sack with two or three people by dawn's early light.

Brazilian-born **Ana Maria Bahiana** is the author of eight books on film, music, and pop culture and a contributor to several anthologies. She has also written for a wide range of international publishers.

Disaster? Was There a Disaster?

Ian Fisher / 1997

Even Alan J. Pakula, the veteran director who has seen his share of hard times on movie sets, does not shy away from the word "disaster" to describe some aspects of filming *The Devil's Own* last year. Brad Pitt, one of the two stars, threatened to quit early in the shoot, complaining that the script was incomplete and incoherent. He later denounced the movie as "the most irresponsible bit of filmmaking—if you can even call it that—that I've ever seen." The costar, Harrison Ford, kept his mouth shut at the time but said recently that there was little that he would disagree with in Pitt's criticisms. Ego clashes, budget overruns, and long delays plagued the project.

Every few years, Hollywood produces a movie that, months before its release, is labeled the next *Ishtar* [1987], *Bonfire of the Vanities* [1990], or *Heaven's Gate* [1980]. Usually, the same factors are present—big stars, a big-name director, big money, and big, last-minute rewrites, all colliding like cars in a freeway pileup.

The Devil's Own had all those elements. And yet, judging from the reviews, it has avoided joining Hollywood's pantheon of debacles. Even *Weekly Variety* said that the movie, "a well-crafted suspenser, bears no signs of the much-reported on-set difficulties." The film tells the story of a New York City police officer (Ford) who takes into his family's home a young man (Pitt) who turns out to be a fugitive Irish Republican Army soldier.

Hollywood has a long tradition of being able to redeem the most troubled shoots with good, and occasionally great, movies. *Casablanca* [1942] and *The Godfather* [1972] are two prominent examples. Still, Pakula does not seem eager to repeat the experience of *The Devil's Own*. "I can't imagine what it would have been like if it had been my first film," he said in his Manhattan office, recounting the stream of negative stories that appeared last year in both the Hollywood trade papers and the mainstream press during the shoot's six long months.

All the same, for Pakula, the generally positive reviews offer some vindication, suggesting that perhaps things were not as bad as they seemed. He was quick to point out that other films he had made had not exactly gone smoothly either: Jane Fonda tried to quit his second movie, the 1971 film *Klute*, and, in *All the President's Men* (1976), Robert Redford and Dustin Hoffman would often, separately, call their real-life reporter counterparts, Bob Woodward and Carl Bernstein, to decide how a certain scene should be played.

"There's rewriting, and there's rewriting," said Pakula, who will be sixty-nine next month and who, with his white beard and conservative blazers, looks and speaks like an English professor who happens to have a connection to Hollywood. "There's rewriting when you start to make one kind of movie, and then everybody panics, or the studio panics, and you wind up making another. That was never the case here. How to tell the story might have changed; individual plot things might have changed. It was always telling the same story."

The ripest bit of gossip from the set—personal animosity between the stars over whether this would be a Brad Pitt film or a Harrison Ford film—was not true, Pakula said, despite many press reports that the two actors were not on speaking terms for months.

In recent interviews, both Pitt, who at thirty-three has become a big box-office draw, and Ford, at fifty-four an aging star who is nonetheless at the top of his game, said there had been no personal conflicts between them. ("It wasn't the clash of the Titans the press made it out to be," said a crew member, who spoke on the condition of anonymity. "After all, you were dealing with two guys who probably wouldn't have had much in common under ordinary circumstances.")

No one griped about the size of trailers or the number of close-ups, Pakula said; rather, the conflicts were artistic. Because Pitt and Ford are both stars, the original script had to be rewritten to create a more complicated relationship between the two men, and specifically to create a fuller role for Ford's character, a good-hearted Irish American street sergeant named Tom O'Meara.

Pakula said there was also a secondary problem, derived from the fact that the film's plot did not fall along conventionally simple Hollywood lines. The characters played by Ford and Pitt are both "good guys," according to their own distinct moral codes: Ford as the upright American cop who deplores violence and Pitt as an IRA gunman for whom violence is a reasonable solution to his people's three hundred years of troubles.

But the story requires a conflict between the two men, and one of them has to die, even though there are few film stars in leading roles who relish being rubbed out. "In American film, there is a good guy and a bad guy," Pakula said. "It's the first thing my grandson always asks: 'Who's the good guy and who's the bad guy?' When I say, 'Harrison Ford and Brad Pitt are both good guys,' that throws him."

"What's interesting to me is what happens when people with two different senses of what is right and what is wrong meet," he added. "What's interesting is the fact that these two men can love and respect each other. It makes it more complicated—much more interesting and much more human."

But Pitt worried that his role might devolve into that of a traditional bad guy pursued by Ford, à la *The Fugitive* [1993]. Pakula said this was never his intention. To find an analogy, he went back to the 1948 Western, *Red River*, in which a weathered rancher, John Wayne, is defied by his young protégé, Montgomery Clift, on an epic cattle drive from Texas to Missouri.

In *Red River*, all turns out well when the tart-talking woman (Joanne Dru) separating the men reminds them that they really love each other. "The whole picture was leading up to something very different," Pakula said. But the studio executives "just felt it was too unconventional, too dangerous, to have one great star kill another star."

The final showdown of *The Devil's Own* was a central part of the original script by Kevin Jarre, who wrote *Tombstone* [1993] and *Glory* [1989]. About five years ago, the producer Lawrence Gordon, whose earlier projects include *48 Hours* [1988], *Field of Dreams* [1989], and *Waterworld* [1995], the Kevin Costner film memorable largely for having been wildly over budget, took the script to Pitt, who was not yet a household name.

The project languished until 1995, when Pitt suggested taking the script to Ford. To many people's surprise, Ford accepted, even though O'Meara was originally conceived more as a character role, an emotional backstop to Pitt. Ford suggested Pakula—the two had worked together on *Presumed Innocent* in 1990—and filming started last February, in the midst of an unusually harsh winter in New York.

Trouble began immediately because the script was still in flux. This is what prompted Pitt's comment to *Newsweek* about how "irresponsible" it was to be going ahead with the movie at that point. The comment was considered a major blow to the picture's potential for success, but no one has really disagreed with him. "We were all a bit unhinged by the failure to come up with more of a script," Ford said in a recent telephone interview. "So I didn't have any dispute with him over the accuracy of the comments."

Ford acknowledged, however, that the comments put a certain spin on the publicity: "At least you know what the first few questions will be," he said. And while he said he was satisfied by the final product, he did not give it an unqualified endorsement. "I make them; you decide if you like them," he said. "I'm pleased with a great deal of work in this film, but I'm not ever really, really happy. I'm a perfectionist, I suppose. So I am denied the pleasure."

At a recent press conference for the movie, Pitt made it clear that he had made his comments at the very outset of the filming, long before any part of the production was finished. "I have to be honest about what I said, even though it didn't do anyone any good," he said. He added, "How can we start a film when we don't have it all lined up?"

Several script doctors were brought in to address the problems, which delayed the picture, pushed up the budget, and only added to tensions on the set. Gordon, the producer, would not say what the film finally cost, but he disputed numbers widely reported in Hollywood trade papers. He said the original budget was "much higher" than the reported $50 million and that the final cost was lower than $90 million. "I won't say much lower, but lower."

"There is no secret that we were writing and shooting" at the same time, Gordon said. "That's a very unpleasant approach to filmmaking. You just slog through it. It's like being in the infantry and fighting in the rain and snow."

He added, however, that things could have been much worse. "I'm coming off *Waterworld*," he said. "For me, you know, it was not that tough."

Still not finished two months before it opened, *The Devil's Own* required unusual last-minute tweaking. Pakula had been unhappy with the final scene, a showdown on a boat with a cargo of Stinger missiles that Pitt's character is trying to sail back to Ireland. According to the director, the original scene, shot in Greenport, Long Island, felt truncated, so it was rewritten and reshot over two days in a studio in California early last month.

The aim was largely to complete the relationship between the two men, which again reinforced the idea, Pakula said, that "these two men still respect and care about each other and recognize that they are basically two good men." Pakula added a line of dialogue for Pitt, echoing a line from earlier in the film, to explain his path of destruction in New York: "It's not an American story. It's an Irish one."

"That is what the film was," the director said. "Sometimes it takes longer to get there, and sometimes you get there in a shorter time."

Ian Fisher worked at the *New York Times* for twenty-seven years, moving from clerk to foreign correspondent to head of digital operations for the entire newsroom. He's currently employed by Bloomberg, where his recent writing includes extensive coverage of the COVID pandemic.

Additional Resources

The following are useful reading sources about Alan J. Pakula and his collaboration with Robert Mulligan, including further interviews.

Appelo, Tim. "*Presumed Innocent*'s Alan Pakula." *EW*, August 10, 1990.

Belton, John, *Cinema Stylists*. Metuchen, NJ, and London: Scarecrow, 1983.

Biskind, Peter. *Star—The Life & Wild Times of Warren Beatty*. London: Simon & Schuster, 2010.

Boorstin, Jon. *Making Movies Work: Thinking Like a Filmmaker*. Los Angeles: Silman-James, 1995.

Brown, Jared. *Alan J. Pakula—His Films and His Life*. New York: Back Stage Books, 2005.

Cavett, Dick. "An Interview with Alan J. Pakula." *Cinemonkey* 5, no. 1 (Winter 1979): 25–29 (transcript of interview from *The Dick Cavett Show*, https://archive.org/details/Cinemonkey_016_1979-Winter).

Coursodon, Jean-Pierre, and Bertrand Tavernier. *50 ans de cinema americain*, 742–48.

Hebert, Hugh. "Front Office, Back Street, High Rise." *The Guardian*, January 21, 1972.

Hirshberg, Jack. *Redford/Hoffman: A Portrait of* All the President's Men. New York: Warner Books, 1976.

Holmes, Nathan. "Deep Backgrounds: Landscapes of Labor in *All the President's Men*." *Imaginations: Journal of Cross-Cultural Image Studies* 9, no. 1 (2018): 87–107.

Kaplan, Alexander. "*The Parallax View*." https://www.filmscoremonthly.com/notes/parallax_view.html.

Keathley Christian, and Robert B. Ray. *All the President's Men*. London: Bloomsbury, 2023.

Kiselyak, Charles. *Fearful Symmetry (The Making of* To Kill a Mockingbird*)*. Written and directed by Kiselyak, available with the DVD of *To Kill a Mockingbird*, 1998.

Koppl, Rudy. "Michael Small: Scoring the Director's Vision." *Music from the Movies*, no. 21, Autumn 1998, 46–53.

Kraft, Elizabeth. "*All the President's Men* as a Woman's Film." *Journal of Popular Film and Television* 36, no. 1: 30–37.

Martin, Adrian. *The Sterile Cuckoo*. https://filmcritic.com.au/reviews/s/sterile_cuckoo.html.

Ryan, Tom. "The World of Alan J. Pakula." *Lumiere*, January–February 1973, 13–16.

Sinyard, Neil. "Pakula's Choice: Some Thoughts on Alan J. Pakula." *Cinema Papers*, July 1984.

Tonguette, Peter, ed. *The Film Journal* 11 (January 2005). https://web.archive.org/web/20150429135751/http://www.thefilmjournal.com/issue11/issue11current.html.

Wood, Robin. "Alan J. Pakula and Robert Mulligan." In *Cinema: A Critical Dictionary—The Major Film-Makers*, edited by Richard Roud, 763–64. London: Secker & Warburg, 1980.

Index

Aimée, Anouk, 19

Alexander, Jane, 71, 77, 115

Almendros, Nestor, xxv, 109

An Amazing Time (2012), xxxiii–xxxiv

Anderson, Kevin, viii

Anouilh, Jean, 5, 51, 81

Antigone (1944), 5, 51, 81

Arthur, Robert, xiii

Bacall, Lauren, 13

Beatty, Warren, xxxi, 31, 33, 35, 42, 43, 44, 45, 48, 49, 60, 77, 89, 90, 95, 100, 105

Belasco, David, 59

Belton, John, xvi–xvii, xviii

Beresford, Bruce, xxxviin20

Bergen, Candice, xxxii

Bergman, Ingmar, 92, 112

Bernstein, Carl, 53, 54, 55, 64, 69, 70, 71, 74, 87, 88, 89, 96, 102, 105, 128

Big Heat, The (1953), xiii

Blackboard Jungle (1955), xxxi

Bobrow, Andy, xxviii, xxxii, xxxv

Bogart, Humphrey, 13, 57

Bonfire of the Vanities, The (1990), 127

Boorstin, Jon, 41–42, 64

Bottoms, Timothy, 105

Bradlee, Ben, 58–60, 65, 66, 71, 90

Bridges, Jeff, xxxiii, 118

Brooks, James L., xxx, 90, 108

Bulworth (1998), 43

Burden of Proof, The (1990), 123–24

Burton, Wendell, 8, 83, 105

Bush, George, 125

Caan, James, xxxiii, 88

Cagney, James, 32

Calamity Jane, 80

Caligula (1945), 81–82

Camus, Albert, 81–82

Candidate, The (1972), 52

Capra, Frank, 56, 89

Casablanca (1942), 127

Cassavetes, John, 41

Catcher in the Rye, The (1951), 72

Chaplin, Charlie, 81–82

Chaplin, Sydney, 81–82

Chekhov, Anton, 15, 81, 92, 101–2

Chinatown (1974), xxviii, 49

Citizen Kane (1941), 92

Claire's Knee (1970), 53

Clayburgh, Jill, 90, 108

Clift, Montgomery, 129

Climax! (1954–58), xii

Colorado Film Commission, 81

Committee to Reelect the President (CREEP), 60, 72

Confessions of Nat Turner, The (1967), 97, 98

Conrad, Joseph, xv

Conversation, The (1974), xxviii

Coppola, Francis Ford, 71

Costner, Kevin, 129

Coursodon, Jean-Pierre, xxxi
Cronyn, Hume, 42, 45, 48–49, 107
Curtis, Tony, xiii–xiv, xxii

Daniels, William, 48
Day, Doris, xiv
Deep Throat, 54, 67–68, 74
Dick Cavett Show, The (1968–86), xxxiv
Dickens, Charles, 116
Dick Tracy (1990), 125
Die Hard 2 (1990), 125
Dietrich, Marlene, 22
Downhill Racer (1969), 52
Dreiser, Theodore, 84
Duvall, Robert, xxxviin20

Eagleton, Thomas, 72
Eames, Charles, 61
8½ (1963), 92
Eisenhower, Dwight D., 47
Engels, Russ, viii
Ephron, Nora, 56
Evans, Robert, 49

Fear Strikes Out (1955), xii
Felker, Clay, 58
Fellini, Federico, 92
Field of Dreams (1989), 129
Final Days, The (1976), 60, 69, 89
Finney, Albert, viii, xxxv
Flynn, Errol, 87
Fonda, Jane, xi, xxvi, xxx, xxxi, xxxii, 8, 14, 17, 20, 21, 22, 25–26, 34, 35, 51, 79, 80, 84–85, 88, 89, 90, 92, 94, 95, 105, 107, 128
Foote, Horton, xvi, xix, xxii, xxxiii, xxxiiin20
Ford, Harrison, xi, xxxi, xxxii, 117, 123, 126, 127, 128–30
Ford, John, xvii, 16, 42
48 Hours (1988), 129

Friendly Persuasion (1956), 5
Fugitive, The (1993), 129

Gabbard, Glen, xii
Gabbard, Krin, xii
Garbo, Greta, 22, 28
Gilbert, John, 28
Giler, David, 34
Glory (1989), 129
Godard, Jean-Luc, 12
Godfather, The (1972), 71, 127
Godfather II, The (1974), 71
Goldblatt, Stephen, xxv, xxix
Goldman, William, 51, 68, 86, 102
Gordon, Lawrence, 129–30

Haldeman, John, 68, 75
Hamlisch, Marvin, 114
Harper (1966), 12
Hartman, Don, xi, 5, 51, 82
Haynes, Todd, xxiv
Heart of Darkness (1899), xv
Heaven's Gate (1980), 127
Hepburn, Audrey, 82
Hirshberg, Al, xii
Hitchcock, Alfred, xxiii, xxxv, 7, 8, 17, 41, 42, 57, 72–73, 82, 88, 90, 92
Hoffman, Dustin, xi, xxxiii, 51, 52–55, 58, 70–71, 74–75, 77, 79, 86–88, 90–91, 113, 115, 128
Hudson, Rock, xiv, xvi, xxii
Hunt, Howard, 75
Hunter, Ross, xxiv
Hunter, Tab, xii

Iceman Cometh, The (1956), 59, 104
Ishtar (1987), 127

Jameson, Richard T., xxxi, 51
Jarre, Kevin, 129

Jenkins, George, vii, 20–21, 32–33, 41, 45–46, 113

Jeremiah Johnson (1972), 52

Jones, Kent, xxiii–xxiv

Katzka, Gabriel, 33

Kaufman, Bel, xxi

Kazan, Elia, 19

Kessler, Lyle, vii, xxxv

Kline, Kevin, xxxiii, 98, 115

Koppl, Rudy, xxxiv

Krasner, Milton, xxv, 106

Krige, Alice, 119

Kristofferson, Kris, 94, 95

Ku Klux Klan, 45

Lang, Charles, 106

Lange, Hope, xxx, 45, 119, 120–21

Lavin, Linda, 119

Lee, Harper, xvi, 6

Lee, Phillip, xii

Leigh, Janet, 9

Lelouch, Claude, 19

Le petit soldat (1963), 12

Lerner, Dan, viii

Lewis, Andy, 21, 27, 84–85

Lewis, David, 21, 27, 84–85

Lewton, Val, xxiv

Lie Down in Darkness (1951), 97

Lorimar Pictures, 121

Lubitsch, Ernst, 90

MacNicol, Peter, 98

Malden, Karl, xxiv, 4

Markle, Fletcher, xix

Martin, Adrian, xxxi

Mary Tyler Moore Show, The (1970–77), 90, 108

Matthau, Walter, 89

Mayes, Wendell, xxii

Mazursky, Paul, vii

McAlpine, Don, vii–ix, xxv, xxix

McGinn, Walter, 44–45

McGovern, George, 72

McNichol, Kristy, xxxi, xxxv, 111, 115

McQueen, Steve, xix, 7, 8, 35

Minnelli, Liza, xi, 8, 34, 35–36, 79, 83, 90, 106

Moby-Dick (1851), 98

Modine, Matthew, viii

Moon for the Misbegotten, A (1973), 59

Mosel, Tad, xxi

Mr. Smith Goes to Washington (1939), 56–57

Mulligan, Robert: *Ah, Wilderness!* (1959), xvi; *The Alcoa Hour* (1955–56), xvi; *Baby the Rain Must Fall* (1964), xix, xx, xxiv–xxv, 8, 15, 51; *Blood and Thunder* (1962), 5; *Comes a Day* (1958), 5; *Come September* (1961), xiii, xiv, xvi, xix, xxii; *Fear Strikes Out* (1956), xii–xiii, xvi, xix, xx, xxiv, xxxi, 3, 4, 15, 51, 111; *The Great Impostor* (1960), xiii–xiv, xxii; *Inside Daisy Clover* (1965), xx–xxi, xxv, 8, 15; *Judgment at Nuremberg* (1957–60), xvi; *Laurette* (1960), 5; *Little Women* (1957), xix, xxi; *Love with the Proper Stranger* (1963), xviii–xix, xxi, xxiii, 7, 8, 15, 51; *The Pursuit of Happiness* (1971), xxvi; *The Rat Race* (1960), xiii, xviii, xix, xxii, xxxviin6; relationship with Alan J. Pakula, xi–xxvii, xxx, xxxi, xxxiii, xxxv, xxxvi, 3–8, 15, 42, 51, 105–6; *The Spiral Road* (1962), xiii, xv, xvi; *The Stalking Moon* (1968), xxii–xxiv, 8, 15, 51, 106; *Studio One* (1956–57), xvi; *Summer of '42* (1971), xxvi–xxvii; *There Must Be a Pony* (1962), 5; *To*

Kill a Mockingbird (1962), xi, xiii, xiv, xv–xvii, xxi, xxiii, xxxi, 3, 6, 15, 22, 42, 51, 117; *Up the Down Staircase* (1967), xxi–xxii, xxiii, 8, 15, 51

Murphy, Bridey, 18

Murray, Betty, 45

Murray, Don, 45

Nathan, Vivian, 25–26

Nichols, John, xxiv, 19, 24–25

Night of the Hunter, The (1955), 13–14

Nixon, Richard, 56, 60, 63, 64, 69, 78, 89

Notorious (1946), 7

Nykvist, Sven, xxv

Olivier, Laurence, 48, 70

Olsen, Theodore V., xxii

O'Neill, Eugene, 103

Oswald, Lee Harvey, 44

Pakula, Alan J.: as a collaborator and in interviews, xxx, xxxii–xxxv; relationship with Robert Mulligan, xi–xiii, xv–xxiv

Works by: *All the President's Men* (1975), xi, xxvi, xxvii, xxix, xxxi, xxxii, 42–43, 47, 51–80, 83–84, 85–91, 96, 102–3, 107–8, 111–12, 115, 117, 122, 123, 128; *Baby the Rain Must Fall* (1964), xix, xx, xxiv–xxv, 8, 15, 51; *Blood and Thunder* (1962), 5; *Comes a Day* (1958), 5; *Comes a Horseman* (1977), xxvii, xxix, xxxiii, 51, 79–81, 84, 87–88, 90, 92, 100, 105, 106, 108–9; *Consenting Adults* (1982), xxvii, xxviii, xxix, xxxi, xxxiii, xxxv; *The Devil's Own* (1997), xi, xxvii, xxviii, xxx, xxxi, xxxii, 127–30; *Dream Lover* (1984), xxvii, xxxi, xxxv, xxxvi, 111, 113, 115; *Fear Strikes Out* (1956),

xii–xiii, xvi, xix, xx, xxiv, xxxi, 3, 4, 15, 51, 111; *Inside Daisy Clover* (1965), xx–xxi, xxv, 8, 15; *Klute* (1971), xi, xxv, xxvi, xxvii, xxviii, xxix, xxx, xxxi, xxxii, xxxiii, xxxiv, 3, 7–10, 11–27, 33, 35, 45, 51, 53, 57–58, 59–60, 62–63, 67, 71, 79, 80, 83, 84–85, 87, 88, 89, 90–91, 95, 99, 100, 102, 106, 107, 114, 117–18, 122, 124, 126, 128; *Laurette* (1960), 5; *Love and Pain and the Whole Damn Thing* (1972), xxv, xxvi, xxvii, xxx, xxxv–xxxvi, 3, 7, 10, 16, 27–28, 51, 105; *Love with the Proper Stranger* (1963), xviii–xix, xxi, xxiii, 7, 8, 15, 51; *Orphans* (1987), vii–viii, xxv, xxvii, xxix, xxxi, xxxv, xxxvi; *The Parallax View* (1974), xi, xxvi, xxvii–xix, xxx, xxxi, xxxii, xxxv, 29–50, 51, 52, 53, 57, 59–60, 62, 66, 71, 76–78, 84–86, 95–96, 108, 114, 122; *The Pelican Brief* (1983), xi, xxvii, xxviii, xxix, xxxi, xxxvi; *Presumed Innocent* (1989), xi, xxvii, xxviii, xxix, xxxi, xxxii–xxxiii, 117, 118, 122–26, 129; *Rollover* (1981), xxix, xxxi, xxxii, 94–96, 100–102; *See You in the Morning*, vii–ix, xi, xxvii, xxviii, xxx, xxxi, 117–21, 126; *Sophie's Choice* (1982), xi, xx, xxv–xxvii, xxviii, xxx, xxxi, xxxii, xxxiii, xxxiv, xxxvi, 42, 97–99, 100, 103–5, 109–10, 114, 115, 117, 122; *The Stalking Moon* (1968), xxii–xxiv, 8, 15, 51, 106; *Starting Over* (1979), xi, xxvi, xxvii, xxx, xxxi, xxxii, xxxvi, 79, 90, 108, 126; *The Sterile Cuckoo/Pookie* (1969), xi, xxiv–xxv, xxvi, xxvii, 3, 8, 15, 17, 18–20, 24–25, 27, 35–36, 51, 79, 83–84, 99, 36, 106, 107, 115, 117–18; *There Must Be a Pony* (1962), 5; *To Kill a Mockingbird*

(1962), xi, xiii, xiv, xv–xvii, xxi, xxiii, xxxi, 3, 6, 15, 22, 42, 51, 117; *Up the Down Staircase* (1967), xxi–xxii, xxiii, 8, 15, 51; *The Widower* (see *Love and Pain and the Whole Damn Thing*)

Pakula, Hannah, 50, 117, 119–21

Parallax View, The (1970), 33–34, 42–43

Paramount, xi–xiv, 4, 6, 15, 42, 43, 49, 51, 82

Patsos, George, viii

Peck, Gregory, xvi, xxii, 6, 106

Perkins, Anthony, xii, 4–5, 111

Piersall, Jimmy, xii, 111

Pierson, Frank, 119

Pitt, Brad, 127, 128–30

Pollack, Sydney, 122

Powers of Ten (1977), 61

Prentiss, Paula, 35

Presumed Innocent (1987), 117, 118, 122–24, 125, 126

Psychiatry and the Cinema (1987), xii

Psycho (1960), 9

Rear Window (1954), 82

Rebecca (1940), 8

Redford, Robert, xi, xx, xxi, 51–53, 55, 58, 60, 69–72, 74–75, 79, 86–88, 89, 90, 91, 111–12, 113, 128

Red River (1948), 129

Remick, Lee, xix

Renoir, Jean, 92

Reynolds, Burt, 90, 108

Richlin, Maurice, xiv

Robards, Jason, 58–59, 71, 74, 79, 88

Roman Holiday (1953), 82

Rotunno, Giuseppe, xxv, xxix

Ruby, Jack, 44

Russell, Rosalind, 90

Safire, Bill, 60

Saint, Eva Marie, 106

Sargent, Alvin, xxii, xxv, 19, 27, 83

Scacchi, Greta, 124–25, 126

Schary, Dory, 82

Schulman, Arnold, xviii

Semple, Lorenzo, Jr., 33

Set This House on Fire (1960), 97

sex, lies, and videotape (1989), 50

Sex and the Movies (1968), xiv

Shadow of a Doubt (1943), 57

Shakespeare, William, 92

Shampoo (1975), 49

Shapiro, Stanley, xiv

Sherman, Stanford, 36

Sirk, Douglas, xiii, xv, xxiv

Sloan, Hugh, 54–55, 58, 108

Small, Michael, xxxiv, 22, 41, 42, 46, 47, 114

Smith, Maggie, 34

Sophie's Choice (1979), 97–99, 103, 105, 109, 119

Sousa, John Philip, 70, 114

Spellbound (1945), 8

Spider's Strategy, The (1970), 12

Stanley, Kim, xix, 5

Starting Over (1973), 90

Sterile Cuckoo, The (1965), xxiv, 19, 83

Sternberg, Josef von, 22

Stevens, George, xxii

Stewart, James, xvi

Sting, The (1973), 52

Stone, Judy, xxxiv

Strangers on a Train (1951), 7–8

Streep, Meryl, xi, xxxii, 98, 115

Stroheim, Erich von, 79

Stuart, Gilbert, 54

Studio One (1948–58), xix, xxi

Styron, William, 97–98, 117

Sutherland, Donald, xxvi, xxx, 24, 126

Tavernier, Bertrand, xxxi

Tempest (1982), vii

Tender Mercies (1983), xxxviin20

Terms of Endearment (1983), 108

Terms of Endearment (1975 novel), 108

Thalberg, Irving, 82

Time to Love and a Time to Die, A (1958), xiii

Tombstone (1993), 129

To Sir with Love (1967), xxi

Tourneur, Jacques, xxiv

Tracy, Spencer, xvi

Traveling Lady, The (1954), xix

Trintignant, Jean-Louis, 19

True Grit (1969), xxxviin23

Truffaut-Hitchcock (1967), 7

Turow, Scott, 119, 122–24

Uncle Vanya (1898), 101–2

Unmarried Woman, An (1978), 90

Unsworth, Geoffrey, xxv

Vachon, Christine, xxiv

Vertigo (1958), xxxv

Wakefield, Dan, 90

Walker, Alexander, xiv

Warner Bros., 5, 15, 24, 60, 87, 89, 121, 125

Washington Post, 55, 58–60, 65–66, 69–72, 79, 88–90, 107–8

Watergate, 47, 65, 69, 76, 86

Waterworld (1995), 129, 130

Wayne, John, 129

White, William Allen, 32, 48

Wild Bunch, The (1969), xxxviin23

Willis, Gordon, xi, xxv, xxix, xxxiii, 20, 22, 30, 38, 41, 45–46, 54, 62, 65–66, 71–72, 77, 81, 88, 92, 106, 112

Will Penny (1967), xxiii

Wolfe, Thomas, 81

Wood, Natalie, xx

Woodward, Bob, 52–53, 54, 55, 58, 64, 67–68, 69, 70, 74, 75, 86–88, 96, 102, 105, 128

Writers Guild strike, 43, 46

Wuthering Heights (1847), 81

Wyler, William, 5

Young Mr. Lincoln (1939), xvii

Ziegler, Ron, 69

About the Editor

Photo courtesy of Simon Schluter

Melbourne-based critic **Tom Ryan** has been a regular contributor to film magazines and the arts pages of newspapers for more than forty years. He has also contributed numerous chapters to anthologies about film and sport, is the author of *The Films of Douglas Sirk: Exquisite Ironies and Magnificent Obsessions* for the University Press of Mississippi, and has previously edited volumes on Baz Luhrmann and Fred Schepisi for UPM's Conversations with Filmmakers Series.